Behaviour Managem and the Role of the Teaching Assistant

Behaviour Management and the Role of the Teaching Assistant draws on the latest research as well as teaching assistants' own views to enable readers to reconsider TA deployment and to maximise the benefits TAs have to offer in supporting children's behaviour. It considers the difficulties facing TAs, summarises the key stages in the evolution of their role in the classroom and highlights the significant challenges of TAs' role definition.

Using current research findings, this book provides guidance and practical activities to support schools in empowering TAs to work with children whose behaviour challenges. Each chapter considers a range of strategies for working with TAs, as well as the strengths and limitations of these approaches. There are also a range of self-/school-auditing and self-evaluation tasks with key points to consider and practical in-school suggestions at the end of each chapter.

This is essential reading for professionals at all levels working in schools wanting to understand how teaching assistants can best be supported to successfully manage behaviour in schools.

Emma Clarke leads on a primary PGCE course after teaching in mainstream schools for almost eighteen years. Her interests include approaches to managing behaviour, challenging behaviour in primary schools and TAs' role in supporting children in this regard. She has presented her research both nationally and internationally, as well as publishing in books and peer-reviewed journals.

Behaviour Management and the Role of the Teaching Assistant

A Guide for Schools

Emma Clarke

Routledge
Taylor & Francis Group

LONDON AND NEW YORK

First published 2021
by Routledge
2 Park Square, Milton Park, Abingdon, Oxon OX14 4RN

and by Routledge
52 Vanderbilt Avenue, New York, NY 10017

Routledge is an imprint of the Taylor & Francis Group, an informa business

British Library Cataloguing-in-Publication Data
A catalogue record for this book is available from the British Library

Library of Congress Cataloging-in-Publication Data
Names: Clarke, Emma, (Writer on education), author.
Title: Behaviour management and the role of the teaching assistant : a
  guide for schools / Emma Clarke.
Description: 1. | New York, NY : Routledge, 2020. | Includes
  bibliographical references and index. |
Identifiers: LCCN 2020018251 | ISBN 9780367175603 (hardback) | ISBN
  9780367175610 (paperback) | ISBN 9780429057434 (ebook)
Subjects: LCSH: Teachers' assistants–Education (Elementary) | Classroom
  management. | Behavior disorders in children. | Behavior modification.
Classification: LCC LB2844.1.A8 C53 2020 | DDC 371.14/124–dc23
LC record available at https://lccn.loc.gov/2020018251

ISBN: 978-0-367-17560-3 (hbk)
ISBN: 978-0-367-17561-0 (pbk)
ISBN: 978-0-429-05743-4 (ebk)

Typeset in Melior
by River Editorial Ltd Devon, UK

MIX
Paper from
responsible sources
FSC™ C013985
Printed in the United Kingdom
by Henry Ling Limited

To the Stevens that started this and JV and PG who inspired it.

Contents

Introduction   1

Part 1   7

1 Who are TAs and what do they do?   9

2 Behaviour in primary schools   17

3 Perspectives on behaviour   25

4 Approaches to managing behaviour   35

5 How and why is the TA role changing and what does that
   mean for schools today?   51

6 TAs supporting children's behaviour – advantages
   and limitations   64

7 TAs, teachers and school behaviour policies   75

   Part 1 conclusion   88

Part 2   93

8 Clearly defined TA role and its impact on managing behaviour   95

9 Others' views of the TA role and their impact on TAs   107

   Part 2 conclusion   118

Part 3   **121**

10 Training and the TA   123

11 Power and the TA   142

12 Whole-school approaches and the TA   158

13 Deployment and the TA   172

    Part 3 conclusion   188

Part 4   **191**

14 Empowering TAs to work with children   193

    Part 4 conclusion   217

    Index   218

Introduction

What to expect from this book and ideas on using it

How you might engage with the book and how it is structured to help you do this

In this section I will share some ideas about how you might engage with this book, who it might be useful for and what you might reasonably expect to do as a result of reading it. I am loathed to tell you what you should and should not do as a busy professional and the choice of how much or how little you engage with the suggested activities in the book is, of course, entirely down to you. When reading the book there are several ways to engage with it. You may choose to read it from cover to cover, or to select a range of chapters that interest you the most, or that are the most pressing or important to address in your setting. You may also dip in and out of the book depending on how priorities or circumstances change within your school or setting, or depending on what information you need to develop.

The book is structured in four sections and within these sections are a range of chapters that delve deeper into the content and context of the areas addressed. Part 1 provides an overview of national and international issues that influence both behaviour and TAs. Part 2 examines the issues TAs face as a result of role definition, role-creep and their boundary crossing work as well as considering the influence of other's perspectives on the work TAs do. Part 3 narrows down to look at specific institutional, or in-school factors that influence how TAs manage behaviour whilst in Part 4 the book will support you in examining your own context and how it supports, or can be developed to support TAs to manage behaviour effectively.

Part 1 includes chapters focusing on the issues that underpin this book:

- Who are TAs and what do they do?

- Behaviour in primary schools

- Perspectives on behaviour

- Approaches to managing behaviour

- How and why the TA role is changing and what this might mean for schools today

- TAs supporting children's behaviour – advantages and limitations

- TAs, teachers and school behaviour policies

Part 2 focuses on understandings of the TA role including:

- Clearly defined TA role and its impact on managing behaviour

- Others' views of the TA role and their impact on TAs

Part 3 looks at specific in-school factors that influence TAs' work and their management of behaviour:

- Training and the TA

- Power and the TA

- Whole-school approaches and the TA

- Deployment and the TA

The final section of the book, Part 4 suggests practical, context relevant strategies that schools and settings could use:

- Empowering TAs to work with children

The book then concludes with a summary of the key tensions and opportunities for TAs, children and schools, as well as a final audit task.

Each chapter within these sections follows a similar structure to help you navigate the book. Each chapter begins with a bullet point list of the key points the chapter will cover. The chapter will then look at what we know about the issues from research, focusing on published research and empirical studies. This then leads into a consideration of what the impact of the research might be in school. This section is more practically focused considering what difference the research findings may (or may not) have in schools and key points that would need consideration in any school or setting. The final section of the chapters provides a brief summary and bullet points detailing what has been considered in the chapter.

Throughout each of the chapters there are a range of activities. You might find it useful to glance at the activities and reflections even if you chose not to complete them at this stage as they may be useful later on, for example if you have been asked to prepare a staff meeting, some training or need to consolidate your thoughts to write an essay. If you do aim to complete the activities and reflections, my hope is that these can be used to make some concrete changes to your thinking, practice or whole-school ways of working. You might also be surprised by how much you already know!

The 'Pause Points' are intended to be relatively short activities to either give you time and space to clarify your thoughts before or after reading a section. Some will ask you to build on and develop your thinking from other sections, whilst others are stand-alone activities. The 'Reflection Activities' usually come at the end of chapters and take a little more time. These usually ask (but not expect!) you to complete some form of task in as much or as little depth as if helpful for you. These tasks often consider some of the main aspects that have been covered in the chapter and often have a practical, school-based focus. The aim is that they will help you to develop a global audit of the way TAs are used in your setting, or help you gain a more holistic idea of the ways in which TAs could be used to support behaviour.

Each chapter rounds off with 'Recommended Reading'; while this might largely be research reports and books it will also include a range of other media where possible. I would also suggest having a look at the reference list for each chapter if you are interested in furthering your knowledge about a specific aspect.

Who the book is for

The book aims to support professionals at all levels working in schools, as well as those with an interest in education to understand how teaching assistants can successfully support behaviour. It is intended to be a practical and useful guide for members of the school community; teaching assistants, teachers, senior leaders and governors, as well as those with an interest in TAs' work in schools. It is not intended as a 'you must' tome, but hopefully one that will help you to identify all of the good practice your school or setting already has, and possibly help you to offer some suggestions to improve it even further. The ideas this book puts forward are based on existing research as well as my own findings when I was a teacher-researcher in school. However – and it is a big however – it is important to always consider that your own context – funding, staff, children's needs, management style and so on – will all influence what you can, what you are able to, and what you want to change.

It will not be news to any of the readers of this book that behaviour is a pervasive issue in education, this can be seen in both the number of government publications about behaviour in England, as well as teachers' concerns. Teaching assistant (TA) numbers have continued to increase and have more than doubled from 53,400 in 2000, to 176,200 employed in primary schools across England alone in 2017 (DfE, 2017). As will be discussed throughout this book, this growing group of adults has been suggested to be in a key position to work with children who have behaviour difficulties. Although research and guidance about using TAs generally in schools has increased in recent years, the research this book is based upon is the first study of its kind to specifically consider how TAs can support the management of behaviour.

As we have noted, throughout the book you will find a range of activities and reflection points. It might be helpful to pause here before we have really begun and draw together some of your initial thoughts.

🫖 **Pause point**

■ What common features do the TAs you have encountered have?

■ What do you know about what is and what is not part of their role?

■ What do you need to (or want to) know about TAs managing behaviour?

The term teaching assistant (TA) is used throughout this book but is also intended to include any adult who works in a similar role with children and those who are known under allied titles such as leaning support assistants, nursery nurses and so on. This book focuses on the way TAs are currently used in the context of English mainstream primary schools, but is also be useful for alternative provision, international schools and those who work in similar context outside England. The broad body of research on TAs highlights counties such as Canada, Australia, Cyprus, Finland, Germany, Iceland, Malta, Northern Ireland, Scotland and Hong Kong all of which experience similar tensions and issues with the equivalent of TAs in their country. As a result, if you are reading this sitting in the sunshine in Australia or in the snow in Finland you may recognise many of the issues discussed.

Although this book draws on reading and research on the work of TAs in primary schools you may well see a range of parallels between the issues and themes discussed if you work in secondary education, alternative provision (for example pupil referral units) or special schools.

The content of this book comes from a range of sources. I taught in a number of primary schools for just over seventeen years. I taught in schools where there we no TAs at all, and some where there were more TAs than teachers, as well as some schools in-between. Because of this, some of the themes this book raises come from my personal experience working in schools where children display a range of behaviours, but often those that would be considered as challenging. Some of it also comes from years working with a range of TAs, sometimes with just one TA over a long period and sometimes with a large number of TAs who worked with specific children at specific times. This practical experience is supported with a prolonged engagement with research on behaviour and working with TAs; this formed the basis of my PhD which investigated how TAs manage behaviour. This gives me – I hope – a sound basis of experience as well as theory to draw on. Some of the themes in this book might reflect your own experiences or those of colleagues and some might be new to you but I hope that the combination of experience and research supports you in reflecting on your own and others' practice in a positive and purposeful way.

Reference

Department for Education. (2017). *School Workforce in England November 2017*. London: DfE. Retrieved from https://www.gov.uk/government/statistics/school-workforce-in-england-november-2017

Part I

Who are TAs and what do they do?

Part 1 of this book will move on to consider who TAs are and what work they routinely undertake. The aim of this part of the book is to provide some general background information to develop the subsequent chapters. It might be useful to all readers to review some of the basic facts about who TAs are and who they work with. There may be some surprises here for readers as the research that has been conducted suggests that in recent years moves towards more direct teaching roles for TAs is largely under-researched and not clearly understood. Indeed, that is just the tip of the iceberg as research shows a general lack of clarity about what TAs' roles could, should or might encompass and how their work relates to that of teachers.

As part of the consideration of who TAs are in this chapter, we will also consider the population of TAs and look at how some of the tensions this group experiences might be as a result of the feminised workforce.

The chapter also introduces the research base on TAs and discusses its strengths and limitations. The research covered in this section might be new to many readers but will hopefully begin to make clear how the multiple perspectives on who TAs are and what their role(s) might be in school affects the subsequent discussions about their role in managing behaviour.

This section of the book will also introduce the chapter layout that will become familiar to you over the subsequent chapters and sections. It begins with the aims of the chapter, followed by a consideration of the key research findings. It then moves on to look at what this might mean practically in school and a summary of key findings follows this. The chapter ends with recommended reading.

This chapter considers who TAs are and how we know what we know about the work they do. Its aim is to provide context for the subsequent chapters. This chapter will:

■ Consider what characteristics TAs have

■ Detail the experiences TAs have in school

■ Investigate what research can tell us about TAs' work

■ Look at the limitations of current and extant research on TAs

■ Discuss some of the issues TAs face which have made them marginalised in policy and practice

 ## What does the research tell us?

Who are TAs and what do they do?

Although it is not possible to categorically state what an 'average' TA is like, drawing on what research tells us, the workforce of TAs has been reported as almost all female (92 per cent in 2014 rising to 95 per cent three years later [DfE, 2014, 2017]). The average TA is suggested to be aged between forty-one and fifty, have a lower level of formal education than teachers (the typical school leaving age of the TA population is sixteen) and with family responsibilities (Bach, Kessler and Heron, 2006; Blatchford, Russell, Bassett, Brown and Martin, 2007; DfE, 2011; HMI, 2002; Quicke, 2003). Blatchford et al. (2007) found from their large-scale survey that 43 per cent of TAs had nine or more years' experience, and 63 per cent had been in the same school for at least five years, with half of these having more than ten years' experience in the same school.

As noted earlier, the number of TAs employed in English schools continues to rise significantly, with around 178,000 (DfE, 2017) TAs employed in state primary and nursery schools. To put this into some context, the number of full-time equivalent primary and nursery school teachers stood at almost 215,000 in 2016. This means the ratio of teachers to TAs in primary schools is around 11:9, not quite 1:1 but not a million miles away either. Working with other adults, TAs in particular, is a fact of life for most teachers now with the Education Endowment Foundation research (Sharples, Webster and Blatchford, 2015) stating TAs accounted for over a quarter of the workforce in mainstream schools in England and 35 per cent of the total workforce in primary schools. Looking purely numerically at the statistics this suggests that there are currently more TAs in English nursery and primary schools than teachers. This information might be surprising but it highlights the importance and possibly challenge for schools and teachers of meeting Standard 8 of the Teachers' Standards (DfE, 2011) which relates to fulfilling the wider responsibilities as a teacher, specifically the importance of deploying support staff effectively.

The book will consider in detail, in Part 2, and in Chapter 13 specifically, the range of different methods of deploying TAs and the advantages and disadvantages of each. As a result, we will just touch on some of the aspects of TA deployment here to provide an overview. Although TAs can be deployed in a number of different roles, they mostly continue to work supporting children with special educational needs and disabilities (SEND) including those with behavioural difficulties (Blatchford, Russell, Bassett, Brown and Martin, 2004; Groom and Rose, 2005; Ofsted, 2008; Sharples et al., 2015; UNISON, 2013; Webster and Blatchford,

2013; Webster, Blatchford and Russell, 2012). Blatchford et al.'s research (2007) – which developed into the largest piece of research worldwide into the work TAs do – showed that of the 658 TAs they sampled working in Key Stage two (KS2 7–11 year olds) in England and Wales – on average they spent 60 per cent of their time working to provide support for specific groups, or individual children who had some form of additional need, either educational or behavioural.

This shows that many TAs (and in Blatchford et al.'s [2007] study most TAs in KS2) work with children who have some form of SEND, which may well include behavioural difficulties. The Department for Education (DfE, 2012) highlighted the link between pupils identified as having SEND with what they suggested were higher levels of self-reported or observed misbehaviour and significantly higher rates of both fixed term (nine times more likely) and permanent (eight times more likely) exclusions. As a result, this means many TAs are regularly, if not exclusively, working with children who have problems with behaviour. Although this in itself may not necessarily be a specific issue, it is the often-unplanned nature of this deployment that is problematic. Often TAs are expected to support children who have some forms of SEND academically and the behavioural support they provide is either a secondary consideration, or more often, not an explicit consideration at all.

As we progress through this book, a range of other issues which impact on TAs will be considered that highlight why this unplanned work with children who may be showing challenging behaviours is difficult for TAs. The key message in this book, therefore, is that if TAs are deployed to work with children with behavioural difficulties this is a clearly planned strategy and that the necessary support (for the child, TA and teacher) is put into place. The book also aims to reinforce how this way of working with TAs needs to be clearly considered in a range of whole-school documentation and policies to support TAs in fulfilling this role.

 Pause point

This chapter so far has considered some of the key information research shows us about TAs and their role in schools. Think about:

- How closely do the research findings tally with your own setting and experiences of TAs?

- What differences (if any) have you identified between your own experience and setting and these?

What do we know about TAs?

Although the amount of research on TAs' work has increased in recent years, almost all of it has investigated how they support children's academic outcomes rather than the support TAs offer children in other ways, and these 'soft skills' have largely remained unexplored. The largest study of TAs' work was conducted by Blatchford, Russell and Webster (2012) and much of what has been used in schools, for example 'Making the Best Use of Teaching Assistance' guidance by the Education Endowment Foundation (EEF) (Sharples et al., 2015) had been drawn from this. Although this research is unrivalled in terms of the range of data collected, the number of participants and scope, there are aspects which are challenging. The key aspect that makes the study problematic is that the research team did not actively speak to any TAs during the study or gather any of their perceptions or perspectives on the roles they undertake. TAs have, by and large, had very little opportunity to inform research from their perspective and this may, in part, be due to the roots of the TA role which has been considered from the deprecating view of them as a 'mum's army' of 'paint pot washers' (Bach et al., 2006). Despite a significant shift in attitudes, it has been argued by many that TAs are still marginalised in wider educational discourses and policies and that a 'feminised' perspective persists in research on TAs. This 'feminised' view can be argued to be a result of the TA role being almost exclusively female and this in itself has been suggested to be the cause of a range of persisting difficulties for TAs, including their status and power in schools. These will be explored and discussed in detail as we move through the chapters and the book.

Parallels can be drawn between the research that exists on TAs and that on children with social, emotional and behavioural difficulties (SEBD). Armstrong (2014) noted in his analysis of research into SEBD that work in what he described as a small field of study was similar to research on TAs, which is often practice-based and small-scale. Giangreco, Suter and Doyle (2010) also suggested that the studies on TAs at that time did little to help answer questions specifically related to the appropriateness or effectiveness of TAs' deployment and the work they undertook.

 Pause point

■ Have you seen any marginalisation of TAs in any of the schools or settings you have experienced?

■ What impact might the lack of wider research on TAs supporting children outside their academic work have?

 What this might mean in school

As we have discussed, much of what we know about TAs and their work in school focuses on their impact on children's academic progress. Much of this research, aside from the Deployment and Impact of Support Staff (DISS) report is relatively small-scale and has focused on describing the work TAs do at the classroom level

(Cremin, Thomas and Vincett, 2003; Devecchi, 2005). This means that actually, as has been argued, few answers exist 'related to questions about the effectiveness' of TAs' work due to the 'limited available research base' (Giangreco and Broer, 2005; Giangreco et al., 2010; Giangreco, 2013).

1. **Although studies into TAs' work are growing, they are not always enough to base sound evidence-based decisions on. Existing research might be best used as a suggested guide rather than a prescription.**

The lack of available research on TAs' work outside of academic support is very limited indeed, despite repeated calls by researchers for this to be addressed. This means it is easy for schools not to consider as deeply as is needed, how the way they use TAs might either support or limit the impact TAs can have on the development of children's non-academic, or 'soft', skills. In their updated guidance on 'Making the Best Use of Teaching Assistants' (Sharples, Webster and Blatchford, 2018, p.7) the EEF noted that this aspect of the research 'needs more attention'. The areas that need more attention included developing social and emotional skills as well as those related to support for behaviour.

2. **When deploying TAs, explicit thought needs to be given to the way in which they are supported to develop children's 'soft skills'.**

Allied to the fact that explicit thought needs to be given to how TAs are deployed in schools, and because there is so much pressure on schools in England to produce academic results, TA support is often still given to those children who are struggling academically. Schools face the pressure of Ofsted and test results published nationally in league tables. This may well mean that many schools use TAs to support children academically without thinking about the additional support these children may need socially and behaviourally. Rather than behavioural support being an unintended consequence of TAs working with specific children or specific groups, it needs to be part of whole-school planning considerations.

3. **Whole-school planning must consider the needs of the groups or individuals TAs may be deployed to work with, as they may need more than simply academic support.**

Research shows us that most TAs are women and that the percentage of female TAs is growing. This has meant that the TA role is often unconsciously (and sometimes overly) associated with maternal and female traits. This means that much of the work TAs do, as well as TAs themselves, have been marginalised from educational policy, wider discourse and sometimes even within schools.

4. **Attention needs to be given to ensuring TAs are not marginalised from the life of the school and have opportunities to be included in the school culture.**

Finally, we have noted that the number of TAs is growing and particularly in primary schools there may well me more TAs than teachers. Working with other adults and deploying them effectively is part of the Teacher Standards by which all qualified teachers are judged.

5. **Working with TAs and deploying them in a way that effectively supports their work with children, teachers and develops their own professionalism, is essential.**

 ## Reflection activity

This chapter has provided some overarching, general information about who TAs are and what they do. Can you begin to consider how TAs are used in your setting or experience, which groups they work with and whether any of their work includes developing children's 'soft-skills'? Using what we have discussed, can you also begin to reflect on what challenges and opportunities there might be in TAs' work for the TAs themselves, the teachers and the children in the table (see Figure 1.1)?

 ## Summary

This introductory chapter has begun to introduce some of the wider context around who TAs are, what we know about them and the ways in which they work. In this chapter, we have looked at the general characteristics of the population of people working as TAs in England as drawn out from research. We have seen that almost all TAs are women and have begun to consider a little about what issues might stem from this. The types of research available to inform practice have been reviewed and the gap in studies on how TAs support children in non-academic ways has

Who do TAs work with?	Which skills do they focus on developing		What opportunities might there be for:			What challenges might there be for:		
	Academic	Soft	TAs	Teachers	Children	TAs	Teachers	Children

Figure 1.1 Challenges and opportunities in TAs' work with others

been reflected on. In addition, the ways TAs work in school and the children they often work with have been considered. The often-unplanned ways in which TAs might work with children who exhibit challenging behaviour have been discussed and the problems stemming from this have begun to be considered.

Key points

This chapter has:

■ Defined what is meant by the term TA in this book, which includes all adults who support children socially and/or academically in school. They may be called by a range of titles but essentially fulfil similar roles to that of a TA.

■ Given an overview of TAs' characteristics, noting that the role is predominantly and increasingly fulfilled by women who have additional family or caring responsibilities. TAs are likely to have been employed in the same school for at least five years.

■ Introduced some of the problems that exist on research into TAs, specifically that it has focused on how they support children academically. Research has also in the main not included TAs' perspectives or views, or looked specifically at the other forms of support they provide in schools.

Further reading

■ Blatchford, P., Russell, A. and Webster, R. (2012). *Reassessing the Impact of Teaching Assistants*. London and Oxon: Routledge.

■ Maximising the Impact of Teaching Assistants. (2018). https://educationendowmentfoundation.org.uk/projects-and-evaluation/projects/maximising-the-impact-of-teaching-assistants/

References

Armstrong, D. (2014). Educator Perceptions of Children Who Present with Social, Emotional and Behavioural Difficulties: A Literature Review with Implications for Recent Educational Policy in England and Internationally. *International Journal of Inclusive Education, 18*(7), 731–745.

Bach, I., Kessler, S. and Heron, P. (2006). Changing Job Boundaries and Workforce Reform: The Case of Teaching Assistants. *Industrial Relations Journal, 37*(1), 2–21.

Blatchford, P., Russell, A., Bassett, P., Brown, P. and Martin, C. (2004). *The Role and Effects of Teaching Assistants in English Primary Schools (Years 4 to 6) 2000 – 2003: Results from the Class Size and Pupil Adult Ratios (CSPAR) Project. Final Report. (Research Report 605)*. London: DfES.

Blatchford, P., Russell, A., Bassett, P., Brown, P. and Martin, C. (2007). The Role and Effects of Teaching Assistants in English Primary Schools (Years 4 to 6) 2000–2003. Results from the Class Size and Pupil–Adult Ratios (CSPAR) KS2 Project. *British Educational Research Journal*, *33*(1), 5–26.

Blatchford, P., Russell, A. and Webster, R. (2012). *Reassessing the Impact of Teaching Assistants*. London and Oxon: Routledge.

Cremin, H., Thomas, G. and Vincett, K. (2003). Learning Zones: An Evaluation of Three Models for Improving Learning through Teacher/Teaching Assistant Teamwork. *Support for Learning*, *18*(4), 154–161.

Department for Education. (2011). *Teachers' Standards: Guidnce for School Leaders, School Staff and Governing Bodies* (Vol. 2011). London: DfE.

Department for Education. (2012). *Pupil Behaviour in Schools in England*. In *Research Report DFE-RR218*. London: DfE.

Department for Education. (2014). *Statistical First Release School Workforce in England: November 2014*. London: DfE.

Department for Education. (2017). *School Workforce in England: November 2017*. London: DfE.

Devecchi, C. (2005). *Teacher and TAs Working Together in a Secondary School: Should We Be Critical?* Retrieved from www.leeds.ac.uk/educol/documents/170933.doc

Giangreco, M. (2013). Teacher Assistant Supports in Inclusive Schools: Research, Practices and Alternatives. *Australasian Journal of Special Education*, *37*(02), 93–106.

Giangreco, M. and Broer, S. (2005). Questionable Utilization of Paraprofessionals in Inclusive Schools. *Focus on Autism and Other Developmental Disabilities*, *20*(1), 10–26.

Giangreco, M., Suter, J. and Doyle, M. (2010). Paraprofessionals in Inclusive Schools: A Review of Recent Research. *Journal of Educational and Psychological Consultation*, *20*(1), 41–57.

Groom, B. and Rose, R. (2005). Supporting the Inclusion of Pupils with Social, Emotional and Behavioural Difficulties in the Primary School: The Role of Teaching Assistants. *Journal of Research in Special Educational Needs*, *5*(1), 20–30.

HMI. (2002). *Teaching Assistants in Primary Schools an Evaluation of the Quality and Impact of Their Work*. London: HMI.

Ofsted. (2008). *The Deployment, Training and Development of the Wider School Workforce*. London: Ofsted.

Quicke, J. (2003). Teaching Assistants: Students or Servants? *FORUM*, *45*(2), 71–74.

Sharples, J., Webster, R. and Blatchford, P. (2015). *Making Best Use of Teaching Assistants: Guidance Report*. London: Education Endowmnet Foundation.

Sharples, J., Webster, R. and Blatchford, P. (2018) *Making Best Use of Teaching Assistants: Guidance Report*. London: Education Endowment Foundation.

UNISON. (2013). *The Evident Value of Teaching Assistants: Report of a UNISON Survey*. Retrieved from www.unison.org.uk/content/uploads/2013/06/Briefings-and-Circular-sEVIDENT-VALUE-OF-TEACHING-ASSISTANTS-Autosaved3.pdf

Webster, R. and Blatchford, P. (2013). *The Making a Statement Project Final Report. A Study of the Teaching and Support Experienced by Pupils with a Statement of Special Educational Needs in Mainstream Primary Schools*. London: Institute of Education.

Webster, R., Blatchford, P. and Russell, A. (2012). Challenging and Changing How Schools Use Teaching Assistants: Findings from the Effective Deployment of Teaching Assistants Project. *School Leadership & Management*, *33*(1), 78–96.

2 Behaviour in primary schools

Now you have some ideas on what is included in this book and some ways in which you might want to engage with it, this next section moves on to lay the foundations for the subsequent chapters.

Chapter 2 of this book begins with an overview on behaviour in English primary schools, considering the impact of policy on the way behaviour is currently, and has historically, been managed. In England behaviourism has been the prevalent model advocated (strongly) by a range of successive governments and this has narrowed the behaviour management strategies that are commonplace in primary classrooms. Chapter 3 compares and contrasts behaviourism and its central tenets of rewards and sanctions, which make up the backbone of almost all school behaviour policies in England, with a number of other approaches. Chapter 4 then moves on to consider whether behaviour in English schools is improving or worsening and looks at a range of evidence to support and challenge these views.

Chapter 5 investigates how TAs' role has evolved and changed in line with some of the policies discussed in Chapter 1. It looks at the change in TAs' roles from a 'mum's army' to 'para-professionals' and how the expectations of them in schools have changed in relation to this. Chapter 6 weaves these two themes together by investigating the advantages and disadvantages of TAs managing behaviour, reflecting in the disparate range of expectations of them in relation to managing behaviour set out in government policy. This section of the book ends with a consideration of behaviour polices, and their impact on teachers and TAs.

Throughout each chapter in this section there are Pause Points and Reflection activities to support you in engaging with the research and in considering how this might influence the way TAs work in your setting or school.

This chapter discusses the current state of behaviour in English primary schools. It looks at some of the research around whether behaviour in schools is improving or worsening and investigates the sources these views are drawn from. It also looks at government guidance in relation to how behaviour should be managed.

This chapter will:

- Consider current perceptions of behaviour in mainstream English primary schools

- Look at the range of arguments on whether behaviour in schools is improving or getting worse

Before this chapter begins in earnest, it might be helpful to stop and think about your own views in relation to children's behaviour.

 Pause point

- Do you think behaviour is improving or worsening in schools?

- What are you basing your judgement on?

- What steps do you think can be taken to improve behaviour?

- How much do you know about different perspectives on managing behaviour?

Education Support published its most recent Teacher Wellbeing Index (Education Support Partnership, 2019) which suggested from its YouGov survey of just over 3,000 education professionals that 51 per cent of those who took part suggested children's behaviour has a negative impact on their physical and mental health. There have also been a number of shocking headlines about standards of behaviour in schools worldwide and incidents of violent attacks on teachers have featured in the British media. This can lead to those both outside and inside our education system worrying. Despite this, there is actually no agreement in research, from the Department for Education (DfE) or the body that inspects English schools (Ofsted), about behaviour in schools worsening.

 ## What does the research tell us?

Concerns over standards of behaviour in English schools have been a pervasive long-term political issue for British governments. Reports about behaviour in schools can be found in documents as early as 1927, with the Hadow Report (Gray, Miller and Noakes, 1994) which raised concern over what was perceived as the worsening of standards of behaviour in schools over ninety years ago!

One reason it is difficult to categorically state whether children's behaviour is getting better or worse is because attitudes towards behaviour can be argued to exist along what has been described as a 'continuum of tolerance' (McCall, 2004). What are seen as acceptable standards of behaviour move up and down along this continuum, with changes in political attitudes and social pressures. This means that it is very difficult to categorically state whether it is children's behaviour that is improving or worsening or whether changes are due to a shift along the continuum in relation to what is and what is not seen as acceptable behaviour. As a result, any agreement across published literature as to whether standards of behaviour are improving or worsening is difficult to find.

A survey from the Teacher Support Network and Parentline Plus in 2010 (House of Commons Education Committee, 2011) showed that 92 per cent of respondents thought that behaviour standards had declined during their career and that this had caused 70 per cent to consider an alternative profession. This was supported by claims from the DfE (2011) that three quarters of the teachers they surveyed stated that standards of behaviour were 'driving professionals out of the classroom'. More recent data suggests teachers' concerns over pupils' behaviour continue, with Education Support Partnership (2019) reporting in their Teacher Wellbeing Index that their respondents' concerns over behaviour had increased, with 33 per cent suggesting it was a factor for leaving the profession in 2017 to 40 per cent in 2018 and 42 per cent in 2019.

On the other hand, Rigoni and Walford (1998) argued that there was no objective data to support a golden age of teacher respect by pupils, and that respect had always been individual, as opposed to profession wide. Findings from Ofsted reports, typically held as an indicator of standards, only showed a slight variation in standards of children's behaviour, with 93 per cent of primary schools achieving good or outstanding grades for behaviour in 2012, compared to 89 per cent in 2009/2010 (DfE, 2012; House of Commons Education Committee, 2011). This shows an upwards trend of behaviour improving rather than worsening. Nevertheless, concerns have been raised by teachers about how reflective and objective Ofsted judgements were, with apprehension about how some schools were able to 'fool' inspectors by providing a false picture of the reality of their school (Bennett, 2015). The reliance on Ofsted inspections as an objective indicator of standards of behaviour were further called into question with a large number of inspectors deemed 'not good enough' (Richardson, 2015).

This suggests that actually gaining an accurate picture of trends in children's behaviour is not a simple process. Many factors need to be taken into account, including the teacher's experience, training, relationships within the school as well as the wider context of education. For example, there are now growing concerns (although it could be argued this is not wholly new – at least not from within the teaching profession) about teachers' workload and well-being (DfE, 2019). Perhaps with increased workload and pressure from externally published league tables and school inspections amongst other things, some teachers find children's behaviour more challenging in these high-stakes and high-pressure environments.

School budgets have also been even more stretched in recent years, which has meant reduced access to external training courses and consultancy services for many schools which may also impact on how confident teachers feel managing children's behaviour.

One of the key political message to English schools, in relation to behaviour from the British government, along with increased control, was what was observed as an inescapable link between fixing behaviour and fixing learning (Maguire, Ball and Braun, 2010). Here, as noted, TAs were expected to play a key role in fixing both (DfES, 2001, 2003a, 2003b, 2006, HMI, 2002; Morris, 2002).

 Pause point

Before we move on, read a behaviour policy from an English primary school (these are all published on school websites) or the one from your setting:

■ What does it say about the way behaviour should be managed?

■ What roles does it set out for senior managers and for teachers?

■ Does it make any links between behaviour and learning?

Children's behaviour in English schools has been addressed by a focus on control – a recurrent and sustained theme in government publications (Bennett, 2017; DfE, 2013, 2016). Armstrong (2014) argued that this demonstrated government policies on behaviour, rather than being progressive, were actually retrogressive and 'against and away' from modernising discussions around behaviour. He stated this was evident in English policy's focus on 'discipline, authority and respect', rather than on any consideration of what might be causing issues of misbehaviour (Armstrong, 2014). The new Code of Practice for SEND revised the terminology used in reference to behaviour difficulties, from Behavioural, Social and Emotional Difficulties to Social, Emotional and Mental Health Needs (DfE and DoH, 2015). However, changing the terminology associated with behaviour did not change the British government's focus on teacher control, despite implicit suggestions in the new terminology that mental health issues might drive some behaviours. Indeed, it has been proposed that:

> Schools have become skilled at meeting government targets, but too often have had their ability to do what they think is right for their pupils constrained by government directions or improvement initiatives.
>
> (DfE, 2010, p.8)

What this might mean in school

As we have discussed, coming to any definitive conclusions on children's behaviour either improving or worsening is difficult and context always needs to be taken into account. What we do know is that the pressures on teachers in relation to their workload and well-being are very high and it is reasonable to suggest that this will impact on how they cope with children's behaviour.

1. **Teachers' workload and well-being are causes for concern in England and many other countries. Whole-school planning needs to reduce unnecessary workload for those employed in schools.**

We have also discussed how figures related to perceptions of children's behaviour as either worsening or improving are at times contradictory. For example, figures form the English school inspection body (Ofsted) contradict those from other surveys. It is key to remember that context is important in these judgements and that what an experienced and happy teacher can comfortably manage in relation to behaviour may be incredibly or impossibly challenging to a new and/or unhappy or unsupported teacher.

2. **When putting in place plans to support teachers in relation to well-being or managing behaviour, these need to be highly individualised and depend on the context that individual is in.**

The government has suggested that there are clear links between improving behaviour and improving learning. It could also be possibly argued that the inverse of this relationship exists: that when children are able to learn well, they also behave well.

3. **Are references made to teaching and learning or the learning environment in the behaviour policy? Have clear links between the two been established?**

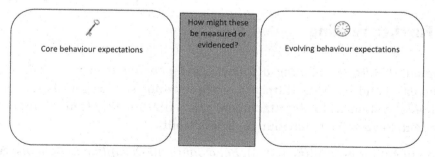

Figure 2.1 Core and evolving behaviour expectations

Reflection activity

We have discussed here how perspectives on what is, and what is not, appropriate behaviour in schools has changed and evolved. Behaviour expectations also differ in different countries and contexts. Using the diagram in Figure 2.1, can you begin to think about which expectations of behaviour you would consider might be core and not context or culture dependent, and which you think might be fluid, or evolving? It might also be interesting to see of you can consider how these behaviours might be measured or understood and reported to categorically state whether behaviour is improving in schools or not.

 Summary

This chapter has reflected on whether behaviour in schools is getting better or worse. It has argued that this might be considered as reflecting wider social and political views, and existing on a continuum, rather than a definitive, black and white measure. It also needs to be acknowledged that behaviour is context and content dependent rather than a static state. Rigoni and Walford (1998) have argued that there is no objective data to support a golden age of teacher respect by pupils argued by some to have existed, and that children's respect and, as a result, some of their behaviour, has always been individual, as opposed to profession wide.

 Key points

This chapter has:

- Reviewed current perceptions of behaviour in English primary schools

- Investigated arguments that behaviour is worsening (or improving)

- Reflected on the issues in measuring changes in behaviour

 Further reading

- Bennett, T. (2017). *Creating a Culture: Independent Review of Behaviour in Schools*. London: DfE. https://assets.publishing.service.gov.uk/government/uploads/system/uploads/attachment_data/file/602487/Tom_Bennett_Independent_Review_of_Behaviour_in_Schools.pdf

- Department for Education. (2016). *Behaviour and Discipline in Schools: Advice for Headteachers and School Staff*. London: DfE.

■ Education Endowment Foundation. (2019). *Improving Behaviour in Schools*. London: EEF. https://educationendowmentfoundation.org.uk/news/new-eef-report-6-recommendations-for-improving-behaviour-in-schools/

References

Armstrong, D. (2014). Educator Perceptions of Children Who Present with Social, Emotional and Behavioural Difficulties: A Literature Review with Implications for Recent Educational Policy in England and Internationally. *International Journal of Inclusive Education, 18*(7), 731–745.

Bennett, T. (2015, June). Schools "Ignore Bad Behaviour" to Fool Ofsted Inspectors, Says Classroom Tsar. *The Guardian.* Retrieved from www.theguardian.com/education/2015/jun/16/schools-ignore-bad-behaviour-fool-ofsted-tom-bennett

Bennett, T. (2017). *Creating a Culture: Independent Review of Behaviour in Schools.* London: DfE.

Department for Education. (2010). *The Importance of Teaching: The School's White Paper 2010.* London: DfE.

Department for Education. (2011). *Ensuring Good Behaviour in Schools.* London: DfE.

Department for Education. (2012). *Pupil Behaviour in Schools in England Research Report (DFE-RR218).* London: DfE.

Department for Education. (2013). *Behaviour and Discipline in Schools: Guidance for Governing Bodies.* London: DfE.

Department for Education. (2016). *Behaviour and Discipline in Schools: Advice for Headteachers and School Staff.* London: DfE.

Department for Education. (2019). *Reducing Teacher Workload.* London: DfE.

Department for Education and Skills. (2001). *Schools Achieving Success.* London: DfES.

Department for Education and Skills. (2003a). *Raising Standards and Tackling Workload: A National Agreement.* London: DfES.

Department for Education and Skills. (2003b). *Developing the Role of Support Staff – What the National Agreement Means for You.* London: DfES.

Department for Education and Skills. (2006). *Raising Standards and Tackling Workload Implementing the National Agreement. Note 17. (Effective Deployment of HLTAs to Help Raise Standards).* London: DfES.

Department of Health and the Department for Education. (2015). *Special Educational Needs and Disability Code of Practice: 0 to 25 Years Statutory Guidance for Organisations Which Work with and Support Children and Oung People Who Have Special Educational Needs or Disabilities.* London: DoH and DfE.

Education Support Partnership. (2019). *Teacher Wellbeing Index 2018. CEO Education Support Partnership.* 1–60.

Gray, P., Miller, A. and Noakes, J. (1994). Challenging Behaviour in Schools: An Introduction. In Gray, P., Miller, A. and Noakes, J. (Eds.), *Challenging Behaviour in Schools* (pp. 1–4). London: Routledge.

HMI. (2002). *Teaching Assistants in Primary Schools an Evaluation of the Quality and Impact of Their Work.* London: HMI.

House of Commons Education Committee. (2011). *Behaviour and Discipline in Schools.* (February), 83. London: DfE.

Maguire, M., Ball, S. and Braun, A. (2010). Behaviour, Classroom Management and Student 'Control': Enacting Policy in the English Secondary School. *International Studies in Sociology of Education, 20*(2), 153–170.

McCall, C. (2004). Perspectives on Behaviour. In Wearmouth, J., Richmond, R., Glynn, T. and Berryman, M. (Eds.), *Understanding Pupil Behaviour in Schools: A Diversity of Approaches* (pp. 16–24). London: David Fulton Publishers.

Morris, E. (2002, July 26). *Professionalism and Trust – The Future of Teachers and Teaching.* London: DfES.

Richardson, H. (2015, June 19). Ofsted Purges 1,200 "Not Good Enough" Inspectors. *BBC News.* Retrieved from www.bbc.co.uk/news/education-33198707

Rigoni, D. and Walford, G. (1998). Questioning the Quick Fix: Assertive Discipline and the 1991 Education White Paper. *Journal of Education Policy, 13*(3), 443–452.

3 Perspectives on behaviour

Chapter 1 aimed to set the scene and illustrate how difficult it is to make any clear judgements about children's behaviour. This is because these judgements are often embedded in social and cultural perspectives at the time, as well as in government policy and discourses. This chapter looks at some approaches to managing behaviour and those that have been promoted by the British government. It looks at the strengths and limitations of a range of approaches and considers what the impact of these might be in schools. It begins with a brief chronological overview of how approaches to behaviour have (or have not) changed.

This chapter will:

- Reflect on the behaviour management strategies recommended by the British government

- Consider how attitudes and policy associated with managing behaviour in England has evolved

- Discuss the 'marketisation' of schools and how this has influenced attitudes towards behaviour

- Examine how themes of inclusion, well-being and mental health for children have evolved and how external policy has impacted on these

 ## What does the research tell us?

Reports about behaviour in schools can be found in government documents as early as 1927, with the Hadow Report (Gray, Miller and Noakes, 1994) noting concern about what was perceived as a reduction of standards of behaviour in schools. This was a theme that continued and still continues to be evident in many British government publications.

A brief overview of some of the key developments in perspectives on behaviour in England, and how they have influenced current practice in schools, will now follow. This will provide some context for the discussions that will follow in this chapter.

1980–2000

In 1989 the influential government report 'Discipline in Schools', also known less formally as the Elton Report (DfES, 1989), was published. This encouraged whole-school approaches, recommended removing power from individual teachers and advocated partnership and consistency (Rowe, 2006) in relation to behaviour management. Nevertheless, there was criticism of the report for its emphasis on the external manifestations of behaviour – what could be seen in the classroom – rather than on the causes of behaviour. It was suggested that the report's tone was influenced by educational psychology, which was the dominant discourse at that time (Didaskalou and Millward, 2004). In 1994, the publication of the seminal 9/94 circular supported the Elton report's previous endorsements of behaviourism, rewards and sanctions, bringing with it what was perceived by some as an overemphasis on control and management of behaviour (Didaskalou and Millward, 2004). This continued to be reinforced in 1997 with the publication of 'Excellence for All Children: Meeting Special Educational Needs' (DfEE, 1997) which, despite highlighting the need for increased inclusion, again focused primarily on behaviourism (a detailed discussion on behaviourism will follow in Chapter 4) and control in the classroom (Didaskalou and Millward, 2004). In the same year, the publication of the White Paper 'Excellence in Schools' (DfEE, 1997), dealing with English schools, gave what was suggested to be a 'glowing endorsement' of Assertive Discipline strategies, strictly rooted in behaviourist principles, whose benefits were seen as incontrovertible (Rigoni and Walford, 1998).

2000–2008

In 2001 the White Paper 'Schools Achieving Success' (DfES, 2001), dealing with English schools, set out the government's plans for what it described as a systematic drive for higher national standards. The proposal suggested that the poor behaviour of a few children was a growing problem for teachers. It argued for greater parental accountability and, hand-in-hand with this, the expansion of Pupil Referral Units (PRUs) and Learning Support Units (LSUs). The paper also highlighted the need for training to ensure teachers remained what it described as 'confident and committed' to managing behaviour. In November of that year a speech by Estelle Morris, the Secretary of State for Education and Skills (2001), introduced the concept of greater choice for the consumer. This put behaviour in schools firmly in the spotlight. Spratt, Shucksmith, Philip and Watson (2006) argued that this increased academic pressures on teachers and schools, and the results of greater parental choice led to a decrease in behaviour standards. This can be seen currently with arguments about what has been termed 'off-rolling' where schools remove pupils whose behaviour (or academic progress) causes concerns and might negatively affect their consumer image.

Pause point

Greater parental choice in which schools their children attend is now part and parcel of the English education system. Think about:

- How might this consumerism improve behaviour in schools?

- Aside from the extreme actions of 'off-rolling', are there other ways in which this consumer pressure may have a negative impact on children's behaviour?

- In your school/setting/experience have you witnessed any of either these positive or negative effects?

- What could be done to improve the positive and limit the negative impact?

In 2005, 'Managing Challenging Behaviour' (Ofsted, 2005) and 'Learning Behaviour: The Report of the Practitioners' Group on School Behaviour and Discipline' chaired by Sir Alan Steer (Department of Education and Skills and Steer, 2005) were published. The Steer Report, as it was often called, which was revised in 2009 (DfES, 2009), highlighted low-level disruption as the main issue teachers faced in the classroom. This supported previous findings from Ofsted (2005), with both of these noting the lack of clarity about overall standards of behaviour. In 2008, the Derrington Report (Derrington, 2008) was published and was the largest review of teachers' perceptions of behaviour. Again, low-level disruption was similarly highlighted as the biggest problem teachers encountered. Interestingly, the report also acknowledged that many of the teachers they surveyed did not recognise the effect of their own behaviour on their pupils.

2009 onwards

In 2009 'Delivering the Behaviour Challenge' (DCSF, 2009) took an even more strongly worded stance, stating, 'there will be good behaviour, strong discipline and order'. This was followed by the White Paper 'The Importance of Teaching' (DfE, 2010) and was supported by the Education Bill of 2011 (Education Act, 2011). These focused on the need for head teachers to maintain a culture of discipline and respect and set out a range of ways to help to increase the authority of teachers to discipline pupils. These publications were followed in the September of 2011 with three pilot programmes which considered using what was described as a 'military ethos' to manage behaviour (Clay and Thomas, 2014). Although there was anecdotal evidence from some providers, teachers and children that there were improvements in behaviour under this regime, a review of the project raised concerns over a wide range of methodological, sampling and reporting issues (Clay and Thomas, 2014), suggesting that the reported improvements were problematic at the very least.

Following this, the Rt. Hon Michael Gove MP (Department for Education and The Rt Hon Michael Gove MP, 2014), who was at the time Secretary of State for Education in England, suggested that tens of thousands of teachers did not feel confident enough to discipline pupils. In the same year Ofsted (2014) announced no-notice inspections of schools; these had a specific focus on behaviour in order to address what the Chief Inspector claimed was a 'culture of casual acceptance of low-level disruption and poor attitudes to learning'. The report (Ofsted, 2014) was based on the results of three-thousand inspections asserting that up to an hour of learning a day was lost due to issues with low-level disruption. At the same time, the government claimed that exclusions were at an all-time low (DfE and Nick Gibb MP, 2014), which they offered as proof that their tough reforms were a success. Despite this, recurring problems with low-level disruption continued to be highlighted by the government (DfE and Rt Hon Nicky Morgan, 2015) and they introduced the behaviour adviser, or 'czar', Tom Bennet to support teachers (Bennett, 2015, 2017).

Government policy has continued along these lines more recently with a renewed focus within Ofsted inspections on the quality of behaviour in schools, where behaviour and attitudes and personal development will form separate components of the report (Ofsted, 2019). A review was commissioned (Bennett, 2017) which supported the government's aims in:

> strengthening teachers' powers to tackle disruptive behaviour, making clear teachers can use reasonable force to maintain behaviour and extending their searching powers.
>
> (Secretary of State for Education, 2017, p.1)

This continued focus on 'tough' behaviour reforms and control and discipline in the classroom could be suggested to be at odds with developing well-being for children which has been a major policy drive in England and more widely (Bonell, Humphrey, Fletcher, Moore, Anderson and Campbell, 2014; DfE, 2014, 2016; DfE and DHSC, 2018; Ofsted, 2019). The Department for Education (DfE, 2018) highlighted their focus on ensuring schools promote pupils' mental health and well-being which includes, from 2020, teaching children to look after their well-being as mandatory (DfE and the Rt. Hon. Damien Hinds MP, 2019). This requirement follows a growing acknowledgement by government policymakers in England that a range of unmet needs might drive behaviour and that these should be addressed by schools (DfE, 2014). This focus on unmet needs, and mental health more broadly, was highlighted in research, with the House of Commons Health and Education Committees (2017) noting the growing prevalence of 'behavioural and emotional conditions such as anxiety, depression and conduct disorders'. However, they also argued that the expectation for schools to concurrently 'focus on achievement and on well-being' was 'a false dichotomy' (House of Commons Health and Education Committees, 2017).

 Pause point

The chronology shared here has considered the development of, and tensions existing within, our current views of behaviour in schools. Think about:

- What tensions have you seen, experienced or read about in relation to behaviour in school?

- How do any tensions or contradictions affect children?

- How might they also influence teachers?

- Would there be any impact on TAs? If so, what might these be and how might they be different to teachers' experiences?

As considered, schools currently face a range of tensions: increased academic pressures, a competitive climate resulting from greater parental choice and a growing number of children with unmet social, emotional and mental health needs. It has been suggested that these have led to a reassurance in 'zero-tolerance' policies and increased exclusion rates, or 'off-rolling', as schools attempt to maintain their competitive image (Bradbury, 2018; Parliamentary Select Committee for Education, 2018; Watkins and Wagner, 2000). It was argued that these often clinical and child-centred attributions of behaviour in government policy effectively deflected attention away from schools' shortcomings and stopped any consideration of the development of them as 'more humane, more inclusive places' (Armstrong, 2014; Maguire, Ball and Braun, 2010; Thomas and Loxley, 2001).

What this might mean in school

In this chapter, we have seen in the chronology that there has actually been little shift in strategies the British government has recommended schools in England utilise to manage behaviour and that words such as 'discipline', 'control' and 'respect' have been used when talking about expectations of children's behaviour for at least the last thirty years, despite developments in research in this area and the recent expectations for schools to simultaneously address children's well-being.

1. **Schools need to balance a range of competing polices. Care needs to be given to supporting children's well-being in areas such as the school's behaviour policy.**

We have seen from research that the government-advocated behaviourist strategy focusing on control and discipline, as well as increasing pressure on schools, has led to a range of responses which have effectively pushed those with behaviour problems either out of the education system entirely or, at the least, out of mainstream provision.

2. **Zero-tolerance policies on behaviour are increasing again in many schools. Great consideration needs to be given to who these policies support and what might happen to those who are excluded in some way from the daily life of the school.**

There are suggestions that more children are developing mental health issues (or that at the very least we are becoming more aware of them). Arguments have been put forward that, at times, schools are neither the most 'humane' or 'heathy' environments for children or teachers. Thought needs to be given to how to work within the competing policies of control and care and which of these are prioritised.

3. **Schools need to balance the dichotomous governmental focus on discipline and expectations to develop well-being. Careful whole-school planning is needed to balance these opposing expectations.**

These diverse expectations are usually met within the school's behaviour policy. Finding a way to support children's behaviour and well-being that are complementary and not conflicting might require, at least in part moving away from or broadening the government's narrow view on the importance of rewards and sanctions in a whole school behaviour policy.

4. **It is important that the behaviour policy considers the impact of how behaviour is managed on children's mental health and well-being.**

 Reflection activity

We have seen how the British government's views on behaviour management in English schools have remained stable and yet additional, and at times conflicting, polices have emerged. These include the drive for greater inclusion, supporting mental health and well-being, as well as the increasing needs for schools to 'compete' for enrolments. Making notes on the Venn diagram in Figure 3.1, can you begin to think about what are the school's and the children's requirements at the intersecting parts of the diagram, how are they fulfilled and by whom? What needs are there that might lay beyond the Venn and who might be responsible for these?

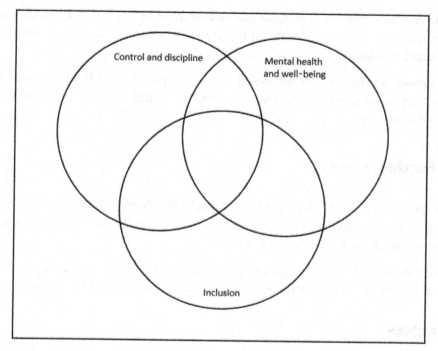

Figure 3.1 Requirements of the school and the child for wider support

 Summary

In this chapter, we have looked at a chronology of almost the last forty years of policy related to behaviour in schools in England. We have seen that there has been little modernisation of ideas on how behaviour should be managed. This makes more recent expectations on schools to support and develop children's mental health and well-being challenging. We have also considered how the marketisation of schools and increased parental choice has been suggested by some to have made schools less tolerant of children's behaviour and increased practices such as 'off-rolling' and zero-tolerance policies in an aim to maintain a competitive image in the 'market'.

 Key points

This chapter has:

■ Investigated policy on behaviour and the stagnation on ideas related to managing behaviour

■ Considered how current polices are difficult to align cohesively and the tensions between control and disciple and well-being

- Shared views that when schools compete against each other for enrolment that they may become less tolerant of behaviour to maintain their popularity with prospective parents

- Discussed arguments that increased choice for parents has led to some schools adopting zero-tolerance policies and even 'off-rolling' pupils to deal with children's behaviour.

 ## Further reading

- Department for Education. (2014). *Mental Health and Behaviour in Schools: Departmental Advice*. London: DfE. www.gov.uk/government/publications/mental-health-and-behaviour-in-schools–2

- Department for Education. (2019). *Off-rolling: Exploring the Issue*. London: DfE. www.gov.uk/government/publications/off-rolling-exploring-the-issue

References

Armstrong, D. (2014). Educator Perceptions of Children Who Present with Social, Emotional and Behavioural Difficulties: A Literature Review with Implications for Recent Educational Policy in England and Internationally. *International Journal of Inclusive Education, 18*(7), 731–745.

Bennett, T. (2015, June). Schools "Ignore Bad Behaviour" to Fool Ofsted Inspectors, Says Classroom Tsar. *The Guardian*. Retrieved from www.theguardian.com/education/2015/jun/16/schools-ignore-bad-behaviour-fool-ofsted-tom-bennett

Bennett, T. (2017). *Creating a Culture: Independent Review of Behaviour in Schools*. London: DfE.

Bonell, C., Humphrey, N., Fletcher, A., Moore, L., Anderson, R. and Campbell, R. (2014). Why Schools Should Promote Students' Health and Wellbeing. *BMJ (Online), 348*, 348–349.

Bradbury, J. (2018). Off-rolling: Using Data to See a Fuller Picture. *Ofsted Blog: Schools, Early Years, Further Education and Skills*. Retrieved from https://educationinspection.blog.gov.uk/2018/06/26/off-rolling-using-data-to-see-a-fuller-picture/

Clay, D. and Thomas, A. (2014). *Review of Military Ethos Alternative Provision Projects*. (December). London: DfE.

Department for Children, Schools and Families. (2009). *Delivering the Behaviour Challenge : OurCommitment to Good Behaviour*. London: DCSF.

Department for Education. (2010). *The Importance of Teaching: The School's White Paper 2010*. London: DfE.

Department for Education. (2014). *Mental Health and Behaviour in Schools: Departmental Advice*. London: DfE.

Department for Education. (2016). *Behaviour and Discipline in Schools: Advice for Headteachers and School Staff*. London: DfE.

Department for Education. (2018). *Workload Reduction Toolkit*. London: DfE.

Department for Education & Rt Hon Damien Hinds. (2019). *All Pupils Will Be Taught about Mental and Physical Wellbeing*. Retrieved from www.gov.uk/government/news/all-pupils-will-be-taught-about-mental-and-physical-wellbeing

Department for Education & Rt Hon Nicky Morgan. (2015). *New Reforms to Raise Standards and Improve Behaviour.* London: DfE.

Department for Education and Department for Health and Social Care. (2018). *Government Response to the Consultation on Transforming Children and Young People 'S Mental Health Provision : A Green Paper and Next Steps.* London: DfE & DfHSC.

Department for Education and Employment. (1997). *Excellence in Schools. White Paper. 3681.* London: DfEE.

Department for Education and Nick Gibb MP. (2014). *Thousands Fewer Pupils Excluded from School since 2010.* London: DfE.

Department for Education and Skills. (2001). *Schools Achieving Success.* London: DfES.

Department for Education and Skills. (2009). *Learning Behaviour: The Report of the Practitioners Group on School Behaviour and Discipline. (Chairman: Sir Alan Steer.).* London: DfES.

Department for Education and Skills and Steer, A. (2005). *Learning Behaviour: The Report of the Practitioners' Group on School Behaviour and Discipline.* London: DfES.

Department for Education and The Rt Hon Michael Gove MP. (2014). *Gove Gives Green Light to Teachers to Use Tough Sanctions to Tackle Bad Behaviour.* London: DfE.

Department of Education and Science. (1989). *Discipline in Schools. Report of the Committee of Enquiry. (Chairman: Lord Elton.).* London: DfES.

Derrington, C. (2008). *Behaviour in Primary Schools Final Report.* London: True Vision Productions.

Didaskalou, E. and Millward, A. (2004). Breaking the Policy Log Jam: Comparative Perspectives on Policy Formulation and Development for Pupils with Emotional and Behavioural Difficulties. In Wearmouth, J., Glynn, T., Richmond, R. and Berryman, M. (Eds.), *Inclusion and Behaviour Management in Schools: Issues And Challenges* (pp. 52–67). London: David Fulton Publishers.

Department for Education and The Rt. Hon. Michael Gove MP. (2014) *Gove Gives Green Light to Teachers to Use Tough Sanctions to Tackle Bad Behaviour.* London: DfE. Retrieved from https://www.gov.uk/government/news/gove-gives-green-light-to-teachers-to-use-tough-sanctions-to-tackle-bad-behaviour

Education Act 2011. (2011). London: DfE. Retrieved from http://www.legislation.gov.uk/ukpga/2011/21/contents/enacted

Gray, P., Miller, A. and Noakes, J. (Eds.) (1994). *Challenging Behaviour in Schools.* London: Routledge.

Health and Education Committees. (2017). *Children and Young People's Mental Health-the Role of Education.* Retrieved from https://publications.parliament.uk/pa/cm201617/cm-select/cmhealth/849/849.pdf

Maguire, M., Ball, S. and Braun, A. (2010). Behaviour, Classroom Management and Student 'Control': Enacting Policy in the English Secondary School. *International Studies in Sociology of Education, 20*(2), 153–170.

Ofsted. (2005). *Managing Challenging Behaviour.* London: Ofsted.

Ofsted. (2014). *Below the Radar: Low-level Disruption in the Country's Classrooms.* London: Ofsted.

Ofsted. (2019). *Summary and Recommendations: Teacher Well-being Research Report.* London: Ofsted.

Parliamentary Select Committee for Education. (2018). *Forgotten Children: Alternative Provision and the Scandal of Ever Increasing Exclusions.* Retrieved from https://publications.parliament.uk/pa/cm201719/cmselect/cmeduc/342/34203.htm#_idTextAnchor000

Rigoni, D. and Walford, G. (1998). Questioning the Quick Fix: Assertive Discipline and the 1991 Education White Paper. *Journal of Education Policy, 13*(3), 443–452.

Rowe, D. (2006). Taking Responsibility: School Behaviour Policies in England, Moral Development and Implications for Citizenship Education. *Journal of Moral Education, 35*(4), 519–531.

Secretary of State for Education. (2017). *Government Response Letter to Tom Bennett's Behaviour in Schools Review.* London: DfE.

Spratt, J., Shucksmith, J., Philip, K. and Watson, C. (2006). "Part of Who We Are as a School Should Include Responsibility for Well-Being": Links between the School Environment, Mental Health and Behaviour. *Pastoral Care in Education, 24*(3), 14–21.

Thomas, G. and Loxley, A. (2001). *Deconstructing Special Education And Constructing Inclusion.* Buckingham: Open University Press.

Watkins, C. and Wagner, P. (2000). *Improving School Behaviour.* London: Paul Chapman Publishing Ltd.

4 Approaches to managing behaviour

In the previous chapter, we noted that the British government's position on how English schools should manage behaviour has actually changed very little over the years. It might be easy to assume from the keywords in British government publications, that managing behaviour through rewards, sanctions, control and discipline was indeed the only way to approach things – however, of course, it is not! This chapter dips (necessarily briefly) into a number of other views and perspectives, recommends sources of further reading on managing behaviour and considers what these different strategies might look like in the classroom. It also compares and contrasts these approaches with those encouraged by the British government.

This chapter will:

■ Share a range of perspectives on managing behaviour and investigate how they are similar and different

■ Consider how strategies associated with the range of approaches discussed would be used in the classroom

■ Evaluate the strengths and limitations of a range of approaches to managing behaviour

 ## What does the research tell us?

In this section we will investigate a range of different perspectives on understanding – and as a result managing – children's behaviour in school. For brevity and ease, this will be a very simplified and artificially separated view of behaviour. In reality, our approaches are almost always a pragmatic blend of a number of strategies, not based on one single view or approach, but an amalgam of what we know works in that context, at that time, for that child or group of children. Nevertheless, it is important to gain an understanding of the underlying theories of behaviour that guide the strategies we use; as the beliefs of staff, schools and even governments influence how behaviour is managed, either tacitly or implicitly (Gray and Noakes,

1994; Johnson, Whitington and Oswald, 1994). Johnson and Sullivan (2016) suggested that managing behaviour 'is messy, complex and influenced by ideological differences about the status children and the ways to "discipline" them'. These 'ideological differences' and our views about the nature of children can have a big impact on the way we chose, either consciously or not, to manage their behaviour. Kohn (1996) argued that the way we run our classrooms is based on our underlying assumptions about human nature and urged teachers to always ask 'cui bono?', or who benefits from the strategies used – the staff, the children or both?

Ball, Hoskins, Maguire and Braun (2011, p.4) suggested that;

> there is currently in play in English education a seething and surging of behaviour discourse – a cacophonous flood of concepts, possibilities, excitements, requirements and practice, sometimes conflicting and contradictory ...

In order to navigate these possibilities and contradictions it can be helpful to have an understanding of some of the key aspects of conceptualising behaviour. For simplicity the approaches and research-based evidence we will discuss here fall under three very broad and artificially discrete groupings; psychological, sociological and medical models. In reality, as noted previously, there is much blurring and crossover between these models and the delineations drawn here between them are rarely seen in the real world of the classroom or in professional practice. It does, however, make it easier to see the differences and similarities between the approaches.

Psychological models

The first model we will consider is the one that underpins the most well-known and commonly used approaches – the psychological model. Psychological understandings of behaviour see the behaviour or issue being within the child, in what is known as a child-deficit model and they focus on external factors to manage behaviour as opposed to internal processes (Cooper and Jacobs, 2011). From this view, there is no specific expectation that relationships with the child are considered as a site of difficulty, or that perhaps the physical classroom environment is contributing to issues in behaviour. Rather, it is seen that there is some issue or problem *within the child* that is causing their behaviour.

One of the most well-known approaches under the psychological umbrella is the behaviourist approach. The behaviourist, or traditional view of school discipline (Johnson, Whitington and Oswald, 1994), has received both rave reviews and dire criticism over the years. It has been, and remains the dominant worldwide perspective on behaviour in schools (Cooper and Jacobs, 2011) and its roots can be found in Skinner's ideas and operant conditioning. Behaviourism is broadly founded on the premise that as a teacher you have both a right and a responsibility to establish order and that by definition the classroom belongs to you as the teacher (Porter, 2000). From this perspective, children operate in a simplified environment of cause and effect (Wearmouth and Connors, 2004) where both positive and negative reinforcements are believed to shape and control behaviour. These negative and positive reinforcements most commonly take the form of some sort of tangible reward or sanction. It can be seen in the classroom through the use of rewards, such as stickers, golden time or moving up on a chart as well as sanctions such as missing break time, moving down on a chart, being sent to another classroom and so on.

The behaviourist idea of 'teaching them [pupils] to behave' might be best known through what is possibly the most contentious manifestation of it – Assertive Discipline, originally developed by American duo Canter and Canter (Canter, 2010). In this approach Canter (2010) suggests teachers should expect '100% compliance, 100% of the time' and that this 'embodies responsiveness to teacher direction, co-operation and self-control'. This has also been developed by some schools to support a return to 'zero-tolerance' policies on behaviour. These policies, instigated by New labour in the mid-nineties were seen as a panacea to raise standards in all schools, but specifically those in disadvantaged areas (Sammons, 2008). These approaches take a hard line against any infringement of rules and have been advocated by the DfE's behaviour 'czar' Tom Bennett; nevertheless, some research has shown they can be both ineffective and counterproductive. It has been suggested that they can do more harm than good by actually increasing incidents of poor behaviour, as well as decreases in academic achievement and positive behaviours (Sugai and Horner, 2008). The EEF (2019) have noted that in the UK there is a lack of research-based evidence on the efficacy of these approaches, despite the strong and emotive views presented by both sides of the argument.

The behaviourist model for managing behaviour, along with other ways to support children's behaviour, has a number of advantages and disadvantages. It has been suggested that behaviourism is able to make quick changes (Canter, 2010) and to support schools in developing a consistent approach to managing behaviour, something highlighted as important by a range of research (Bennett, 2017; DfE, 2014; EEF, 2019; Ofsted, 2014). There have also been assertions that behaviourist approaches are easy for staff, including TAs, to learn, and require limited training. The framework of rules, rewards and sanctions has been argued to support staff as it was seen as 'emotionally safe' whereas less structured policies, which required teachers and TAs to consider their own views and feelings about behaviour, were seen as 'emotionally loaded' (Radford, 2000). The lack of emotional engagement can be viewed as both a key strength and a limitation of behaviourist approaches.

Managing behaviour from the behaviourist stance can be impersonal as it does not take into account the influence of emotions on children's behaviour and does not have any focus on responding to an individual's needs. The lack of emphasis on the emotional causes of behaviour has been reflected in various government documentation in England. The Elton report's (DfES, 1989) focus was that emotions were less important than the behaviour they generated (Didaskalou and Millward, 2004), following the view of Educational Psychology which was the dominant discourse when the report was released (Didaskalou and Millward, 2004). This is one of the main criticisms of the approach, where the lack of acknowledgement of the influence of social and emotional factors can result in a great degree of teacher power and resulting ethical issues (Wright, Weekes and McGlaughlin, 2004). The lack of emotional engagement is also at odds with much research that highlights the importance of relationships with children as effective in managing behaviour (EEF, 2019).

A key behaviourist strategy to manage behaviour – the use of rewards and sanctions – has received criticism. It has been suggested that the use of rewards and sanctions to manage behaviour should be scrutinised and that there are rarely clear links made between rewards (or sanctions) for learning and those for behaviour (Payne, 2015). This can cause confusion for children and make it difficult for them to understand why they have been either rewarded or sanctioned. Payne (2015) also pointed out that schools' systems of rewards and sanctions are at odds with the current approaches to learning in schools, which often focus on child-led enquiry, and accepts the importance of learning by trial and error – yet this is not seen in the behaviourist system. Hastings and Brown (2002) believe that, 'school behaviour policies in England under-theorize what it means to become fully morally responsible'. From a behaviourist perspective where children's behaviours must meet unbending acceptable criteria, it is difficult to see how the child is helped to understand for themselves what is acceptable and understand these 'moral' and ethical dimensions to behaviour and relating with others. Kohn (1996) also argued that the more we, as teachers, 'manage' children's behaviour and take away their responsibility for developing their own behaviour, 'the more difficult it is for them to become morally sophisticated people who think for themselves and care about others'.

The use of rewards (either formal or informal) to reinforce positive behaviours and sanctions to limit unwanted behaviours has also been suggested to oversimplify the complex motivations for behaviour. Although this might be of use when writing behaviour polices, it has been argued that it is naive to assume 'managing behaviour can be as simple as drawing up such a list (usually depressingly overlong) whereby misdemeanour x irrevocably equals consequence y' (Galvin and Costa, 1995). Nevertheless, for many years successive British governments have enforced the use of rewards and sanctions in English schools to manage children's behaviour. This has been seen in publications requiring schools to detail their use of rewards and sanctions in their whole-school behaviour policy (Bennett, 2017; DfE, 2013, 2016). The British government's continued promotion of the values of discipline, authority and respect in their publications (Bennett, 2017; DfE, 2013, 2016) resulted in schools' all but compulsory adoption of a whole-school behaviour policy that centred on rewards and sanctions, despite arguments that this focus was 'all but lost' in wider aspects of education (Payne, 2015). Indeed, Payne (2015) proposed that the behaviourist ideas that formed the foundation of most schools' polices represented 'a potentially confused set of aims and theoretical principles'.

Pause point

The discussion up to this point has focused on behaviourism, the most common model school apply to managing behaviour. Think about:

◼ How closely does this match what your school or setting uses?

◼ Do you recognise any of the strengths noted?

◼ Have you experienced, or can you think of any other advantages to this approach?

◼ Do you recognise any of the limitations of the approach?

◼ Have you experienced any others?

◼ Who gains most from this approach – children or teachers?

We have considered the dominant psychological model, the one most schools and teachers will be most familiar with. However, there are a number of other models within this paradigm, and the cognitive-behavioural model is one that might have some aspects that are common practice in schools too. This view does take account of emotions, although it is still a child-deficit model – the problem behaviour comes from the child. Unlike the purely behaviourist view, it has some emphasis on feelings and problem-solving and this meta-cognitive awareness can help to develop children's self-management skills. This aspect is very much lacking in the purely behaviourist model, which has no emphasis on self-management of behaviour, only external management by teacher or other powerful adult (such as a TA). In the classroom, cognitive-behavioural strategies are sometimes seen through self-management logs and challenging and discussing any negative attitudes or behaviours children display. The cognitive-behavioural perspective also encompasses theories of motivation as drivers of children's behaviour and an awareness that more than simple external or extrinsic rewards are beneficial. Nevertheless, it is, at its core, still closely linked to behaviourism with a clear model of consequences, sanctions and rewards. These features are contrasted with the behaviourist approach as shown in the table in Figure 4.1.

Moving in from this whistle-stop tour of psychological approaches to behaviour, we will now look at sociological models. The differences between the two are quite striking.

Sociological models

The sociological perspective differs from the behaviourist perspective as it tries to consider what might cause issues in behaviour. Unlike the psychological perspective, this understanding often sees the causes of behaviour not as existing within the child, but in the relationships, or in the environment, the child is in. There are

What these might look like in the classroom	
COGNITIVE BEHAVIOURAL	BEHAVIOURISM
✓ Use of self-monitoring logs ✓ Understand behaviour from pupils' point of view ✓ Clarify misperceptions and challenge negative attitudes ✓ Consequences, rewards and sanctions ✓ Impersonal processes	✓ Rewards and sanctions ✓ 'Golden time' ✓ Class rules written by the teacher ✓ Consistency from staff ✓ 'Traditional' view of discipline ✓ Teacher/TA in 'control' ✓ Impersonal process

Figure 4.1 Some of the key differences between behaviourist strategies and cognitive behavioural strategies in the classroom

a range of approaches within this sociological umbrella, but for the sake of time and simplicity we will group them into three wide classes. Humanism broadly considers whether problems in behaviour are the cause of unmet needs in the child, while from a systems theory view (sometimes also known as an ecosystemic perspective) behaviour issues arise from problems in the child's environment – including their relationships with peers and teachers. A psychodynamic perspective looks at how behaviour problems might be caused by aspects of the child's formative experiences and their relationships with others.

In the sociological models the teacher does not try to enforce control, but rather work with and alongside the child. Whereas behaviourism can see quick changes in behaviour but long-term issues with intrinsic motivations to behave in sanctioned ways, sociological models try to support the child in making long-term changes to their behaviour. These models flip behaviourism's focus on aspects including order, compliance and obedience and instead try to support children in developing autonomous ethics, emotional regulation, cooperation and integrity. It can be seen, just by looking at the key words used to sum up these approaches, how they lie at very ends of a continuum and as a result, need very different whole-school approaches and underlying practices.

We noted that some form of token economy, or visible rewards and sanctions, underpin what might be seen in the classroom from a behaviourist model. These are absent under the sociological models which use relational and empathetic approaches to support children instead. Although it is more challenging to demonstrate what these might look like in practice, we will now consider two different approaches that you might have seen used in some schools or settings.

Restorative approaches (RA or Restorative Justice as it is sometimes known) are used by the police, probation service and youth workers as well as by an increasing number of schools (for example those in Bristol, Barnet, Lewisham, Leeds and many others). Hansberry (2016) suggested that restorative approaches distinguished between ideas about managing *behaviour* and managing *relationships*.

At the core of RA, unlike behaviourism, is not the goal of changing children's behaviour, but changing the way children see and feel about each other, which in turn influences their behaviour. The focus of RA is through children putting things right, rather than simply being punished as might happen in a rewards-and-sanctions–based approach. However, using RA to manage behaviour is not something that can be done in isolation; it needs to be built into a whole school plan and ethos. Once it has been established it can be used with individuals, groups of children or even whole classes. Unlike behaviourist strategies, RA is not a quick fix and is a long-term programme to support children in managing their own behaviour. Here the focus is on repairing relationships rather than sanctioning, developing children's self-actualisation and skills for life, and is quite distinct from the focus on controlling children's behaviour in behaviourist approaches.

In practice these skills are nurtured, and accountability is provided through restorative conversations or restorative meetings, rather than rewards and sanctions. The meetings are based on a scripted series of questions, which provide support for both the teacher running the meeting and the children attending. The meetings (or conferences) or conversations can be large or small, formal or informal, but they rely on all staff using the process consistently. The same questions are asked to both the child who has caused the 'harm' and to the child who has been 'harmed'. These often include:

- Can you tell us about what happened and how you became involved?

- If necessary – What happened next and/or what else? (ask this until their story unfolds)

- What were you thinking at the time this happened?

- What have your thoughts been since?

- Who has been affected/upset by this and in what way?

- What has been the hardest thing for you?

(www.restorativejustice4schools.co.uk)

These conversations then form the basis of any next steps that need to take place. This approach exemplifies the emphasis on working with, rather than doing to, children in the sociological approaches and highlights their focus on the teachers' role as a facilitator, or sounding board, to help children develop and take ownership of their own behaviour (Cooper and Jacobs, 2011). A key shift between these two approaches is, from a behaviourist perspective accountability, often assumed through some form of sanction or punishment, whereas from a restorative perspective accountability means repairing any harm or damage done to relationships. These features are contrasted with the behaviourist approach as shown in the table in Figure 4.2.

What these might look like in the classroom	
RESTORATIVE APPROACHES	BEHAVIOURISM
✓ Focus on repairing harm done to individuals ✓ Responsibility and problem solving ✓ Dialogue and conversation (restorative conversations) ✓ Repair, apology and reparation ✓ Developing and maintaining relationships ✓ Interpersonal process	✓ Rewards and sanctions ✓ 'Golden time' ✓ Class rules written by the teacher ✓ Consistency from staff ✓ 'Traditional' view of discipline ✓ Teacher/TA in 'control' ✓ Impersonal process

Figure 4.2 Some of the key differences between behaviourist strategies and restorative approaches in the classroom

Another perspective within the sociological model is that of solution focused (SF) approaches. This is a therapeutic approach and is firmly embedded within the sociological family of perspectives. Although RA is very different to the behaviourist approach outlined earlier, SF is even more removed from behaviourist ideas. SF is based on the very simple premise of looking for strengths the child has, for things that are working well and building on them. It has been argued that problem-focused models, such as behaviourism, are too restrictive (Brown, Powell and Clark, 2012) whereas SF approaches allow for greater freedom as they actively focus on looking for solutions. One, if not the key, difference between SF and other approaches is the belief that the child is the expert and that teachers and TAs work alongside the child, supporting them rather than doing things to or for them. This is achieved through developing the child or children's 'inner resourcefulness' through asking the child, children or whole class to visualise their 'preferred future' or what it will look like when things are going the best they possibly could. From these detailed conversations children can then scale their progress towards these goals.

This sort of approach can work very well with individuals whose behaviour challenges adults, but also just as well with groups and whole classes. For example at the start of the year, topic, week and so on, children can be asked to describe what they will be doing (but not what they will not be doing) if they are at their very best. The TA or teacher can then look out for the features the child has described; other children too can look out for what their peers have described. This then begins a virtuous cycle where children and adults are looking for each other's strengths. This approach in particular also aligns with the DfE in England's guidance of meeting the social, emotional and mental health needs of children (DfE, 2014). In the guidance, the emphasis has moved from a focus on the externalised behaviour of children to a consideration that these

What these might look like in the classroom	
SOLUTION FOCUSED APPROACHES	BEHAVIOURISM
✓ Emphasises 'what works' rather than 'problems' ✓ Based on clear concepts, easy to learn ✓ Teacher/TA works alongside child ✓ Child is the expert ✓ Uses scaling to assess progress to goal ✓ Strength based, interpersonal approach	✓ Rewards and sanctions ✓ 'Golden time' ✓ Class rules written by the teacher ✓ Consistency from staff ✓ 'Traditional' view of discipline ✓ Teacher/TA in 'control' ✓ Impersonal process

Figure 4.3 Some of the key differences between behaviourist strategies and solution-focused approaches in the classroom

behaviours might be driven my unmet needs. These features are contrasted with the behaviourist approach as shown in the table in Figure 4.3.

Medical and biopsychosocial models

Understanding behaviour from a medical, or more recently a biopsychosocial, perspective is also a child-deficit model, where the 'problem' causing the behaviour is within the child and can be addressed, at least in part, by medical interventions, for example attention deficit hyperactivity disorder (ADHD). The medical model was at one time used to justify removal from mainstream schools (Wearmouth, 2004). Within this model the solutions to children's behavioural issues lie with other professionals, for example doctors, psychiatrists and so on; whereas in educational models power and action are within reach of the teachers (Didaskalou and Millward, 2004).

The more recent perspective of the biopsychosocial model considers how biological, psychological and social factors interact and influence behaviour (Visser, 2017). This forms a bridge between the three different perspectives. In this model a range of factors can fall under the 'biological' aspect. These can include early childhood experiences that affect the child's neurology, including diet and nutrition, how they were parented, the peer influences they were exposed to as well as the extent to which they were positively stimulated and interacted with through the early stages of their development. Within this is also the acknowledgement that any form of neglect, abuse or range of adverse childhood experiences (ACEs) can adversely affect children's social and cognitive functioning. It also considers neurological 'plasticity', the ability for the brain to change and develop new neural pathways, to essentially rewire itself depending on the environment it is in and the experiences it receives.

Under the psychological and sociological aspects of the model, a range of different approaches can be applied. These can range from behaviour plans to

What these might look like in the classroom	
BIOPSYCHOSOCIAL	BEHAVIOURISM
✓ Synthesises a range of approaches ✓ Considers the impact of early childhood and biology ✓ Includes environmental factors ✓ Psychological issues are considered ✓ Strategies used are holistic and take into account the complexity of the issue(s)	✓ Rewards and sanctions ✓ 'Golden time' ✓ Class rules written by the teacher ✓ Consistency from staff ✓ 'Traditional' view of discipline ✓ Teacher/TA in 'control' ✓ Impersonal process

Figure 4.4 Some of the key differences between behaviourist strategies and biopsychosocial approaches in the classroom

therapeutic interventions and anything between. What makes this approach different to the perspectives we have discussed is the idea that the strategies used are synthesised together and that there is a clear view on how the biological, the social and the psychological factors interlink and overlap. The approaches (plural is key here) used from this approach consider the impact of all three factors on the child's behaviour, rather than viewing them in isolation. Cooper and Jacobs (2011) suggest it is this consideration of a range of factors together that makes the biopsychosocial approach 'truly holistic', which helps to understand the 'complexities' both of a range of challenging behaviours, and of the associated interventions. These features are contrasted with the behaviourist approach as shown in the table in Figure 4.4.

 Pause point

■ How would the same behaviour issue be dealt with from these perspectives?

■ Which model might be the most supportive for children *and* staff?

■ Which model aligns most closely with your own personal values and beliefs?

What this might mean in school

This chapter has focused on the theoretical underpinnings of a range of strategies and perspectives for managing behaviour. From the discussion already, it can be seen that these different approaches will have different repercussions for schools, staff and children.

From the behaviourist standpoint, where extrinsic rewards and sanctions are used to control children's behaviour, writing a whole-school consistent approach to behaviour is easier than with some of the other approaches. One difficulty is actually ensuring this form of consistency especially (as noted in Chapter 10) between different groups of staff such as teachers and TAs.

1. **If using behaviourism to ensure consistency, care needs to be given to ensuring all staff have the opportunity to attend training and discussions so they all have the same understanding of the policy.**

There have been criticisms that behaviourism does not support children in developing the skills they need as adults, but rather focuses on compliance and obedience to a more powerful other, such as the teacher or TA. Separate work, for example in personal, social and health education (PSHE) or in activities such as Philosophy4Children (P4C) helps children make decisions and reflect on their own actions.

2. **Children may benefit from sessions to help them develop their own internal regulation, autonomy and ethical position if the school manages behaviour purely through rewards and sanctions.**

The British government included in some of its more recent publications the need for English schools to consider whether behaviour is the result of an unmet need (DfE, 2014). The behaviours children may display as a result of unmet needs cannot be addressed from a purely behaviourist perspective where the rewards and sanctions are applied consistently to all children. When some children are treated differently – perhaps to address a specific need they have – it quite rightly makes other children question how fair the system is.

3. **Thought needs to be given from a behaviourist perspective to how to address the diverse range of behavioural needs in a school or class in the same way a diverse range of learning needs is addressed and supported.**

The sociological perspectives we have discussed are not based on the use of rules and extrinsic sanctions and rewards in the same way that behaviourist systems are. This allows flexibility to meet and support a range of needs as flexibility and personalisation is facilitated by these models. This means that consistency is not valued as highly. While this may be good for supporting individuals, it makes writing a policy that all staff can apply simply, very challenging.

4. **When considering how to write a whole-school policy that moves away from rewards and sanctions much time will be needed with the whole staff to develop an understanding of the ethos and range of strategies that underpin it.**

As the approaches used in the sociological perspective are more wide-ranging and varied and not as simple as those of behaviourism, they are likely to have slower but more embedded results in children's behaviour. Regular opportunities for all staff to meet and discuss children, approaches and progress will be needed.

5. **Unlike behaviourist strategies, sociological ones will take longer to embed and it may take longer to see a change in children's behaviour. Training and opportunities for staff to engage in discussion will be needed to ensure commitment to these approaches.**

From behaviourist and medical models, staff agency and autonomy are constrained, whereas in sociological models, agency and autonomy is necessary and valued. This can lead to staff feeling either frustrated by the lack of ability to make individual professional decisions, or overwhelmed by the range of options open to them. Time for all staff to talk together about behaviour and how it is managed is important whichever perspective is adopted.The biopsychosocial perspective encourages a holistic understanding and approach to challenging behaviour from children. From this perspective, a range of strategies and professional services might be used in conjunction with one another. Although this personalised and individualised support may be highly beneficial, TAs' role may be one of just many and it is important they understand how their support fits within a wider range of strategies.

6. **An understanding of how and why certain approaches are used and how they fit together to support the child is needed when working in complex areas such as behaviour. Time needs to be provided for training, liaison and discussion. This is even more important if a range of professionals are working together to support a child.**

As with previous chapters, the importance of time to discuss and support understanding is important, regardless of which approach is taken by the school.

 ## Summary

In this chapter, we have introduced and thought about a range of perspectives on managing behaviour. These have been presented as discrete and separate; however, a professional working with a child they know will use their judgement as to which strategies will work best with that child in that context. There is usually much overlap in schools between these views, despite their incompatible theoretical groundings.

We have seen how practice in schools has remained static and how the British government's views have reinforced the dominance of behaviourist practices focused on rewards and sanctions in schools. In the chapter, the fragile balance between power and whole-school consistency from the behaviourist perspective was explored, as were ethical issues of teacher control.

Other perspectives that fall under the sociological approach were discussed and how these differed from the psychological views of behaviour being caused by a deficit within the child and looking at the environment and the systems the child was within for an explanation of the behaviour. We considered how the aims of this perspective were about *working with* the child rather than imposing or *doing to* the child.

Finally, we considered the medial and more recent perspective of the biopsychosocial model and how this can begin to address the complexity of behaviour in school due to its ability to consider the relationships and interaction between a range of social, biological and psychological factors. This model is also likely to include multidisciplinary teamwork such as teachers, TAs, educational psychologists as well as others such as child mental health workers (CAHMs), social workers, speech and language therapists and so on.

	Psychological	Sociological	Medical/ biopsychosocial
What I like about it			
How might it help teachers?			
What whole-school actions might need to be taken?			
How might it help TAs?			
What whole-school actions might need to be taken?			
How might it help children?			
What whole-school actions might need to be taken?			
What do I need to know more about?			

Figure 4.5 Your own views on the range of approaches discussed

Reflection activity

We have considered a wide range of different approaches to managing behaviour here in a slightly abstract and theoretical way. In this activity you might find it helpful to use the table in Figure 4.5 to think about what this might mean for you, staff, your setting and your children.

 Key points

This chapter has:

■ Highlighted three broad perspectives to understand the way in which behaviour can be managed – psychological, sociological and biopsychosocial

■ Noted that the prevalent model of managing behaviour in schools is behaviourism

■ Traced the government's historic and current push for schools to detail rewards and sanctions and therefore follow a behaviourist perspective to manage behaviour

■ Considered the sociological view of behaviour which understands behaviour problems to be caused by issues external to the child such as unmet needs or problems in relationships

■ Introduced the medical model of understanding behaviour in schools with a focus on seeing behaviour as a problem within the child that requires some form of external intervention (i.e. medication)

■ Discussed the key development of the biopsychosocial model which considers how a range of complex biological, social and psychological factors interlink

■ Noted that the biopsychosocial model might provide the most holistic way to understand and support children whose behaviour challenges.

Outlining some of the key issues in managing behaviour will provide you with some context for the discussions throughout the rest of the book. Although this book aims to support schools and those interested in education in (re)considering the role TAs can play in managing behaviour, it might also go hand in hand with a (re)consideration of a whole-school behaviour policy or approaches to managing behaviour more informally.

 Further reading

■ Canter, L. (2010). *Assertive Discipline* (4th ed.). Bloomington: Solution Tree Press.

▓ Cooper, P. and Jacobs, B. (2011). Evidence of Best Practice Models and Outcomes in the Education of Children with Emotional Disturbance/Behavioural Difficulties an International Review. https://ncse.ie/wp-content/uploads/2016/08/Research_Report_7_EBD.pdf

▓ Kohn, A. (1996). *Beyond Discipline: From Compliance to Community*. Alexandria: Association for Supervision & Curriculum Development.

▓ Milner, J. and Bateman, J. (2011). *Working with Children and Teenagers using Solution Focused Approaches*. London: Jessica Kingsley Publishers.

▓ Payne, R. (2015). Using Rewards and Sanctions in the Classroom: Pupils' Perceptions of Their Own Responses to Current Behaviour Management Strategies. *Educational Review, 67*(4), 483–504.

References

Ball, S., Hoskins, K., Maguire, M. and Braun, A. (2011). Disciplinary Texts: A Policy Analysis of National and Local Behaviour Policies. *Critical Studies in Education, 52*(1), 1–14.

Bennett, T. (2017). *Creating a Culture: Independent Review of Behaviour in Schools*. London: DfE.

Brown, E. L., Powell, E. and Clark, A. (2012). Working on What Works: Working with Teachers to Improve Classroom Behaviour and Relationships. *Educational Psychology in Practice, 28*(1), 19–30.

Canter, L. (2010). *Assertive Discipline* (4th ed.). Bloomington: Solution Tree Press.

Cooper, P. and Jacobs, B. (2011). *Evidence of Best Practice Models and Outcomes in the Education of Children with Emotional Disturbance/Behavioural Difficulties an International Review*. Retrieved from http://aboutones.com/wordpress/wp-content/uploads/2014/10/7_NCSE_EBD.pdf

Department for Education. (2013). *Behaviour and Discipline in Schools: Guidance for Governing Bodies*. London: DfE.

Department for Education. (2014). *Mental Health and Behaviour in Schools*. London: DfE.

Department for Education. (2016). *Behaviour and Discipline in Schools: Advice for Headteachers and School Staff*. London: DfE.

Department of Education and Science. (1989). *Discipline in Schools. Report of the Committee of Enquiry. (Chairman: Lord Elton.)*. London: DfES.

Didaskalou, E. and Millward, A. (2004). Breaking the Policy Log Jam: Comparative Perspectives on Policy Formulation and Development for Pupils with Emotional and Behavioural Difficulties. In Wearmouth, J., Glynn, T., Richmond, R. and Berryman, M. (Eds.), *Inclusion and Behaviour Management in Schools: Issues and Challenges* (pp. 52–67). London: David Fulton Publishers.

Education Endowment Foundation. (2019). *Guidance Report Improving Behaviour in Schools*. London: Education Endowment Foundation.

Galvin, P. and Costa, P. (1995). Building Better Behaved Schools: Effective Support at the Whole School Level. In Gray, P., Miller, A. and Noakes, J. (Eds.), *Challenging Behaviour in Schools* (pp. 145–163). London: Routledge.

Gray, P. and Noakes, J. (1994). Providing Efefctive Support to Mainstream Schools: Issues and Stragegies. In Gray, P., Miller, A. and Noakes, J. (Eds.), *Challenging Behaviour in Schools* (pp. 79–90). London: Routledge.

Hansberry, B. (2016). *A Practical Introduction to Restorative Practice in Schools*. London: Jessica Kingsley Publishers.

Hastings, R. and Brown, T. (2002). Behavioural Knowledge, Causal Beliefs and Self-efficacy as Predictors of Special Educators' Emotional Reactions to Challenging Behaviours. *Journal of Intellectual Disability Research*, *46*(2), 144–150.

Johnson, B. and Sullivan, A. (2016). Against the Tide: Enacting Respectful Student Behaviour Polices in 'Zero Tolerance' Times. In Sullivan A., Johnson B. and Lucas B. (Eds), *Challenging Dominant Views on Student Behaviour at School: Answering Back* (pp. 163–180). Singapore: Springer.

Johnson, B., Whitington, V. and Oswald, M. (1994). Teachers' Views on School Discipline: A Theoretical Framework. *Cambridge Journal of Education*, *24*(2), 261–276.

Kohn, A. (1996). *Beyond Discipline: From Compliance to Community*. Alexandria: Association for Supervision & Curriculum Development.

Ofsted. (2014). *Below the Radar: Low-level Disruption in the Country's Classrooms*. London: Ofsted.

Payne, R. (2015). Using Rewards and Sanctions in the Classroom: Pupils' Perceptions of Their Own Responses to Current Behaviour Management Strategies. *Educational Review*, *67*(4), 483–504.

Porter, L. (2000). *Behaviour in Schools: Theory and Practice for Teachers*. Buckingham: Open University Press.

Radford, J. (2000). Values into Practice: Developing Whole School Behaviour Policies. *Support for Learning*, *15*(2), 86–89.

Sammons, P. (2008). Zero Tolerance of Failure and New Labour Approaches to School Improvement in England. *Oxford Review of Education*, *34*(6), 651–664.

Sugai, G. and Horner, R. (2008). What We Know and Need to Know about Preventing Problem Behavior in Schools. *Exceptionality*, *16*(2), 67–77.

Visser, J. (2017). Classroom Behaviour: Finding What Works for You. In Colley, D. and Cooper, P. (Eds.), *Attachment and Emotional Development in the Classroom: Theory and Practice* (pp. 279–290). London: Jessica Kingsley Publishers.

Wearmouth, J. (2004). Engaging with the Views of Disaffected Students through "Talking Stones". In Wearmouth, J., Richmond, R., Glynn, T. and Berryman, M. (Eds.), *Understanding Pupil Behaviour in Schools: A Diversity of Approaches* (pp. 37–49). London: David Fulton Publishers.

Wearmouth, J. and Connors, B. (2004). Understanding Student Behaviour in Schools. In Wearmouth, J., Richmond, R., Glynn, T. and Berryman, M. (Eds.), *Understanding Pupil Behaviour in Schools: A Diversity of Approaches* (pp. 1–15). London: David Fulton Publishers.

Wright, C., Weekes, D. and McGlaughlin, A. (2004). Teachers and Pupils – Relationships of Power and Resistance. In Wearmouth, J., Richmond, R., Glynn, T. and Berryman, M. (Eds.), *Understanding Pupil Behaviour in Schools: A Diversity of Approaches* (pp. 67–88). London: David Fulton Publishers.

5 How and why is the TA role changing and what does that mean for schools today?

In the previous chapter some of the very broad conceptualisations of managing behaviour were considered. We looked at how they differed from each other and how they affected agency and autonomy for the adult that was working with the child or class. We also discussed the impact of government policy on the strategies used to manage behaviour in schools and the stagnation that has occurred. In this chapter we will again reflect on government policy in England and how it has affected the role of the TA. Although this is specific to England, many other countries, including Canada, Australia, Cyprus, Finland, Germany, Iceland, Malta, Northern Ireland, Scotland and Hong Kong, have followed a very similar path and, as a result, had similar experiences. This chapter will look at the continuing evolution of TAs' role in school and how the changes have intentionally and unintentionally influenced what they do and how they are able to do it.

This chapter will:

- Discuss how the role of the TA has evolved
- Consider how and why changes have affected schools and TAs
- Share tensions in definitions of TAs' role
- Investigate the impact of changes in TA's role on teacher and TA relationships

 ## What does the research tell us?

Research (Webster, Blatchford and Russell, 2013) described the expansion of TAs' role as a 'black box', suggesting that there are a range of hidden and problematic issues surrounding it and that there was (and still remains) limited research about the way in which TAs are used in schools, and the impacts this has. Nevertheless, the number of TAs employed by schools has continued to rise and this has resulted in what has been a professionalisation of their role, which has seen a rise in TAs' status and also in the jobs they are currently expected to undertake in schools. Historic (and very demeaning!) descriptions of the role as 'a bit of money for housewives' (Smith, Whitby and Sharp, 2004) are now largely unrecognisable, with TAs seen as professionals rather than 'second class citizens' (Barkham, 2008; Galton and MacBeath, 2008). Indeed, the evolving TA role has increasingly been described as 'interesting and professional', shifting away from the perception of the TA as someone who only 'staples something to a board for eight hours a day' (Cockroft and Atkinson, 2015), and TAs are currently defined in literature as both para-professionals and pedagogues.

The pragmatic rather than strategic increase in TAs' numbers and roles has resulted in a number of issues. The evolution of TAs' from a 'mum's army' to one where most time is spent engaged in direct pedagogical work with children has come with a lack of a shared, clear and cohesive understanding of the current role, either for TAs or others. Quicke (2003) suggested that rather than a clarification of the role, uncertainty had increased instead with TAs left in an ambiguous position with no clear boundaries. This was supported by later research suggesting a continued lack of clarity on roles, autonomy and professional identity (Blatchford, Bassett, Brown and Webster, 2009). Seventeen years after Quicke's research, the situation remains the same, if not worse. The uncertainty many TAs now feel about what their role includes and what it does not is particularly problematic when it comes to managing behaviour. The time line in the following section shares some of the key changes in TAs' roles and how these have influenced the work they undertake in schools now. This will be useful to provide a deeper understanding of how and why the roles have changed in the way they have and why TAs' work in the way they currently do in schools.

Changes in TAs' role

1960–2000

Concerns about TAs' roles is not a new thing by any means. The lack of clarity about the role TAs played in schools was being questioned by the government in reports going as far back as far as Plowden in 1967 (McVittie, 2005). The report argued that TAs should play a more supportive role to teachers than merely 'washing glue pots'. Further government reports (Bullock [1975], Warnock [1978] cited in McVittie, 2005) reinforced this view, with the 1981 Education Act arguing TAs should have a role in the increasingly integrated approach for children with Special Educational Needs and Disabilities (SEND) in mainstream schools. This shows that for almost thirty years TAs and inclusion have been linked, as well as there having been moves to support their pedagogical, rather than purely supportive role.

Research (Blatchford, Webster and Russell, 2012) suggested that TAs' role in schools became particularly influential with the introduction of the National Curriculum and the consequent league tables of national test results that followed in

1992. This pronounced 'increase in bureaucratic processes and performance culture' (Blatchford et al., 2012), as it was described, exponentially increased teachers' workload. TAs were seen as a way to reduce some of this new extra burden on teachers (DfES, 2001). TAs' previous role in working with children with SEND was further developed in many schools with the publication of the Code of Practice in 1994 (Blatchford et al., 2012).

In 1997 the 'Excellence in Schools' White Paper (DfEE, 1997) continued to promote the importance of TAs, claiming that innovative posts would be created and that TAs would be able to improve standards through working with children and, therefore, free up teacher time. The introduction of the National Literacy Strategy in 1998, and the National Numeracy Strategy in 1999 formalised TAs' role in providing additional academic support for children, specifically the one in four who were not meeting government prescribed standards (Blatchford et al., 2012). In 2000 the term teaching assistant was formalised (DfES, 2000) and was intended to define 'the essential "active ingredient" of their work' (Gerschel, 2005). This shows quite a shift where TAs' role became central to remedying a number of key issues at that time (and still currently); inclusion, academic standards and teacher workload.

2000–2002

In 2001, with concern from teachers growing over issues including workload, morale, recruitment and retention, the School Teacher's Review Body recommended a review of working conditions which was carried out in the same year by PriceWaterhouseCoopers (Blatchford et al., 2012). It was accompanied by a number of British government publications and statements (DfES, 2001; Morris, 2001) that championed the development and expansion of TAs' role, the growth of which was now deemed 'essential to tackle workload and pupil standards' (Blatchford et al., 2012; Trent, 2014). Estelle Morris, who was at the time the Secretary of State for Education and Skills in England, advocated support staff's new role as one which could remove burdens from teachers (Morris, 2001). This was accompanied by a £350 million budget to enable the recruitment of an additional 20,000 TAs by 2002, and the continued assertion that TAs were crucial in the drive to improve standards (DfES, 2001; Morris, 2001). This continued shift in expectations of TAs resulted in a fundamental and radical change, blurring boundaries between what had previously been considered teachers' work and TAs' work. These changes were supported by an HMI report (2002) highlighting the increased learning support TAs provided, as well as citing inspection evidence supporting the contention that TAs improved the quality of teaching. HMI (2002) also further distorted the distinction between the teacher and TA, suggesting that when TAs were successful it was as a result of using 'the skills characteristic of good teachers'. The publication cautioned, nevertheless, that 'no one should pretend that teaching assistants are teachers'.

2003 onwards

In January 2003, with the publication of 'Raising Standards and Tackling Workload: A National Agreement' (DfES, 2003), Higher Level TA (HLTA) positions were created. Suggested components of these new roles included peer mediation and acting as specialists in counselling and managing Emotional and Behavioural Difficulties (EBD) (DfES, 2006). The National Agreement (DfES, 2003) also consolidated earlier publications (DfES, 2001; HMI, 2002; Morris, 2001) which stressed TAs' fundamental role in redressing concerns about teacher workload and pupil standards. In September of that year, in a drive to improve teachers' work–life balance, TAs took over the role of routine administration and clerical jobs in order to free up more teacher time (Blatchford et al., 2012). This was accompanied by the guidance 'Developing the Role of Support Staff – What the National Agreement Means for You' (DfES, 2003) which unequivocally stated that 'support staff are at the heart of proposals for reform'.

In 2004, the Ofsted report 'Reading for Purpose and Pleasure' (Ofsted, 2004) raised the first note of caution about TAs' increasingly direct pedagogical role and suggested that it required investigation. Despite this, and as a direct consequence of the introduction of planning, preparation and assessment (PPA) time for teachers, many schools continued to extended their use of TAs – and particularly HLTAs – to cover classes and increase the time TAs spent 'teaching' (Blatchford et al., 2012). TAs' pedagogical roles have continued to increase, and for the last ten years at least have outweighed any other aspect of their deployment (Blatchford, Russell, Bassett, Brown and Martin, 2007; Trent, 2014).

This chronology shows how TAs roles have changed from largely offering support to the teacher to offering support to children. In many schools this evolution has happened slowly and sometimes without clear planning. In some schools, TAs have been used strategically and in others to fight fires and plug the gaps as and when they appear. However TAs have been deployed, many people argue that they 'could not run their schools without them' (UNISON, 2013).

😀 Pause point

- It has been suggested that TAs' role has changed from 'paint-pot washer' to 'pedagogue'. How much of that do you think is true?

- TAs now routinely undertake more 'teaching' than any other role. What are the advantages of this for TAs? For schools? For children?

- Are there any disadvantages of TAs' pedagogical role? For whom?

- Why might TAs have taken on more of a teaching role without explicit whole-school planning?

How these changes have affected schools

TAs have now spent more time working in a direct pedagogical role than in any other form for at least the last ten years. This is often something that has happened organically in a lot of schools and has not been part of a long-term development plan. One of the issues with this is the understanding of what TAs do – often their job descriptions and levels of training and support provided for them has not changed to reflect this. Some have also questioned the benefits of TAs' role expansion in these often unplanned ways (O'Brien and Garner, 2002). It has been suggested that the restructuring of TAs' role has been guided by considerations external to teaching and learning, with TAs essentially left to fill the gap formed by government drives, issues associated with behaviour, new curriculum initiatives and teachers' increasing workload (Blatchford et al., 2007). This situation is not unique to England but, as noted, has also resonated with research highlighting internationally similar issues in Canada, Australia, Cyprus, Finland, Germany, Iceland, Malta, Northern Ireland, Scotland and Hong Kong (Butt and Lowe, 2011; Cajkler and Tennant, 2009; Giangreco, 2013; Rose and Forlin, 2010; Trent, 2014).

As discussed, it is challenging to clearly define what TAs' role is and what marks it as different to a teacher's role. Despite these challenges, there is much agreement in research about the 'multifaceted' nature of TAs' role (Collins and Simco, 2006; Fraser and Meadows, 2008; Kerry, 2005; Mistry, Burton and Brundrett, 2004; Moran and Abbott, 2002). Smith et al. (2004) identified forty-eight different job titles under the umbrella term of 'TA' in their research and Kerry (2005) found eleven. The labels identified ranged from 'dogsbody' to 'mobile paraprofessional' (Kerry, 2005), each of which would have associated advantages or disadvantages when it comes to managing behaviour. One of the labels – 'factotum' – was revelatory in terms of the different characteristics that it suggested defined TAs, including;

> team player, ear lender, achiever, comforter, investigator, negotiator, supervisor, inspirer, story-teller, task setter, analyser, nurturer.
>
> (Kerry, 2005, p.378)

Defining what roles TAs undertake in schools should be a simple and straightforward task. Yet changes in the tasks they fulfil in schools has made this very challenging, and as a result left much confusion about what TAs actually do in schools – and specifically how their role differs from that of a teacher.

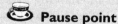 **Pause point**

- What do you think the key differences are between a teacher's and a TA's role?
- What are the advantages of TAs having a clearly defined role?
- Are there any disadvantages?

Research (Anderson and Finney, 2008; Cockroft and Atkinson, 2015) has found that despite being highly valued by schools, TAs faced large obstacles with regard to key factors such as role definition, pay and career structure. Although TAs in schools are provided with job descriptions and are employed within pay bands which should define the key tasks and roles they are expected to undertake, this clarity often does not translate into practice. To make things even more complex, it was argued (Radford, Bosanquet, Webster and Blatchford, 2015) that the British government had purposefully avoided providing explicit guidance in relation to TA and teacher roles in English schools (this will be discussed in more detail in Chapters 7, 8 and 9).

One of the reasons it is so difficult to define TAs' role is because they are so multifaceted. TAs have been described as a key link between different groups in school (parents, children and teachers) who function to 'glue the parts together' (Cajkler and Tennant, 2009). Rather than there being clarity, it has been suggested that TAs operate in a liminal zone with few clear boundaries, where their working identities and roles need to be negotiated, not only with teachers and senior leaders in schools, but also with parents and children. This often results in TAs straddling the boundary of being a teacher and not a teacher (Mansaray, 2006). This lack of clear distinction, it has been suggested, leads to 'role creep' (Blatchford et al., 2007) or a blurring between what is a TA's role and what is a teacher's. TAs' fulfil such diverse aspects of school life that this has resulted in what have been described as fuzzy (Mansaray, 2006) or fluid boundaries between the TA and teacher roles. Lehane (2016) reported that TAs in her study describe themselves as 'go-betweens', which supported Howes's (2003) assertion that TAs work was 'in between' and that this enabled them to do extremely important work between the 'structures and formalities of schooling' (p.150).

The TA' role as 'fluid'

Despite the difficulties in defining TAs' role, Devecchi, Dettori, Doveston, Sedgwick and Jament (2011) argued that rather than being wholly negative, this level of what she termed 'fluidity' in the definition of the TA role could be both a blessing and a curse. Mansaray (2006) maintained that the role was beneficial 'because of its liminality, not in spite of it', believing that imposing artificial divisions on what TAs could and could not do was actually part of the problem rather than part of the solution. He argued that pupils were comfortable with the fuzzy boundaries and lack of role clarity present; instead it was the imagined 'neat division of labour and social space' which were potentially problematic (Mansaray, 2006). Flexibility and fuzzy boundaries between teachers' and TAs' work are also important in enabling TAs to fulfil the broad range of tasks that were suggested to fall within their purview. These were suggested to include: providing pastoral, administrative and academic support; working in partnership with the teacher; and enhancing their subject knowledge in order to challenge and extend children's learning (HMI, 2002). It can also be argued that variability is necessary to work effectively in busy classroom environments, with different personalities and idiosyncrasies, when events often occur in an unplanned or unexpected ways. It was contended (Maguire, Ball and Braun, 2010) that it was often forgotten in research that schools are social settings, and that behaviour is a product of time and contexts, which requires a flexible approach (Calder and Grieve, 2004; Holland and Hammerton, 1994; Porter, 1989; Watkins and Wagner, 2000).

The suggested fluidity TAs experience in their role, as well as being a (possible) blessing also has associated disadvantages. Moran and Abbott (2002) stated that a crucial ingredient of team success in the working relationship between teacher and TA was a clear definition of the TA role. Groom and Rose (2005) also noted that the greater the uncertainty about the TA role, the less effective the TA was, whilst Trent (2014) later argued that comprehending what it meant to be a TA was a challenging task. This all signals issues with TAs' working and the support they are able to offer if there remains a lack of clear understanding of what their role is, and, importantly, is not.

Mackenzie (2011) also found a lack of congruence in teachers' and TAs' perceptions of classroom roles, which reflected Thomas' (1992) earlier view that the cultural norms of schools, particularly primary schools, did not actually support clear role definition. Mansaray (2006) agreed, suggesting:

> Current policy is an attempt to order the complexity of place and space within schools, controlling and maintaining the boundaries of 'teachers' and 'others' in the light of ambiguities in the educational process.
>
> (p.173)

This discussion shows that, despite a range of research on the TA role, we still seem no clearer to understanding fully what it is and how to define it. This may, in part be due to the organic and pragmatic, as opposed to strategic, way in which the TA role has evolved.

☕ Pause point

- Reflect on the suggested tasks that fall within TAs' remit from HMI:
  - Pastoral support
  - Administrative support
  - Academic support
  - Partnership with the teacher
  - Challenging and extending children's learning
- Can you think of any of any other duties TAs might be expected to fulfil that do not come under these headings?
- What additional disadvantages might there be to 'fuzzy' boundaries in TAs' work, particularly in relation to managing behaviour?
- What additional advantages might there be to 'fuzzy' boundaries in TAs' work, particularly in relation to managing behaviour?

Thomas (1992) suggested that when considering classroom teams, it could be 'downright impossible to discover how roles were formulated'. He argued that regardless of their vague definition, TA roles did exist but were often implicit and assumed rather than defined (Thomas, 1992). Tucker (2009) also suggested that TAs roles were self-determined, with a discernible tension felt in discussions to agree future developments of the role. Hancock, Hall, Cable and Eyres's (2010) research similarly found a lack of clear definition of TAs' roles, with their involvement in schools being 'personally and socially constructed'. Additionally, they noted TAs as 'boundary crossers' and stated that within a week or even a day they were repeatedly 'moving in and out of their own and teachers' roles' (Hancock et al., 2010). These views regarding the tensions in understanding and defining TAs' role in schools show there is little uniform understanding, or definition of teacher/TA role boundaries, despite their significance to the success of the relationship between the two. Sharples, Webster and Blatchford (2015) called for schools to 'rigorously define' the TA role, with Graves (2012) in England, and Giangreco (2010) in the US, asserting that a parallel redefinition of the teacher role was essential.

What this might mean in school

The research we have considered in this chapter seems to show some polarisation. There are arguments that TAs' roles should be clear to enable teachers, TAs and children to know what can be expected of each. There is also the counter-argument – that defining the roles is impossible because what TAs are expected to do is so varied and context-dependent that any clear definition is impossible. This makes the situation very tricky for individual TAs, teachers and schools, but does enable context to be considered. There has been a shift, as the chronology showed, from expectations of TAs providing support for the teacher to providing direct support for children. It is essential to consider whether TAs in your own school or setting are used to support teaching or learning, or both.

1. **It is key for schools and settings to know what they do and do not expect of TAs; even if this is varied or a relatively long list, it needs consideration.**

2. **It also needs to be clear to staff if TAs are used to support the teacher or the learner or if a combination of both, and how expectations of them differ between the two types of support.**

As we have seen, TAs' roles have changed, but sometimes schools' or staffs' perceptions have not always shifted so much. Indeed, sometimes in research TAs and their work is still marginalised. It is necessary for schools and settings to think about the way they frame TAs – are they paraprofessionals or a 'mum's army'?

3. **Policy documents, meetings, access to whole-school training and so on all send key messages to TAs about their role in school. Ensure implicit expectations of their work and role in school reflects their improving professional standing.**

Job descriptions should provide a formal record of expectations of TAs' roles, but, as we have discussed, making these very specific is challenging, impractical and may not actually be helpful. However, if TAs are not able to use their job descriptions as a detailed indicator of what is expected of them induction, training and support need to be provided and carefully planned to ensure TAs feel confident and prepared to tackle the range of roles asked of them.

4. **TAs need planned induction, training and development opportunities to ensure they are supported in meeting the varied range of tasks they might be asked to fulfil.**

5. **Time needs to be set aside to regularly meet with TAs to discuss their role and what they are and are not expected to do.**

In this chapter we also considered the concept of role creep – the blurring of the boundaries between teachers' work and TAs' work – and how this can affect TAs and teachers. Although it might be impossible (and possibly disadvantageous) to stop roll creep entirely, it can be mediated by opportunities for the teachers and TAs that work together to meet as regularly as is feasible and talk about their expectations of each other and the contexts the TA is working in.

6. **Teacher and TA teams need planned and regular opportunities to meet and discuss their roles in relation to each other.**

 ## Reflection activity

In this chapter we have discussed, a theme we will return to – the challenges in defining TAs' role and the reasons for this. We have also looked at why a degree of flexibility in TAs' roles is important. Can you begin to list all of the expectations schools and settings might have of the TAs they employ? As you look down your (ever-growing) list, reflect on how many of these roles might also be undertaken by other professionals either within, or associated with, the school or setting. What – in your view – makes a TA either particularly suited (or unsuited) to some of the tasks you have listed? How might this affect the way they work in your school, setting or experience?

 ## Summary

In this chapter we have looked at the ways in which TAs' roles in schools have shifted from supporting the teacher to supporting children and how in England the government anticipated the changing role could plug the gaps in the rather incompatible issues of teacher workload, academic standards and inclusion.

We have also considered one of the key tensions, which is a clear and unambiguous definition of TAs' role in schools. Mansaray (2006) described TAs' role as 'transitional, incomplete, ambiguous and incoherent', which shows why producing a clear definition is challenging. Graves (2013) supported this and suggested that TAs', and specifically HLTAs' roles, were 'chameleon like' which, she proposed, conspired against TAs developing a distinct professional identity of their own. Indeed, Graves (2013) suggested that TAs' role was defined only in the negative, that TAs were '*not* teachers' which, she argued, obscured what exactly 'their role *is*'.

Key points

This chapter has:

■ Shown how TAs' role has transformed from 'paint pot washers' to 'pedagogues'

■ Detailed through a chronology of changes how and why TAs role in schools have evolved and why TAs' role now includes direct pedagogical work as a key facet

■ Considered research suggesting that role boundaries between the teacher and the TA should be clear, but shown that this is not the case

■ Suggested that the flexibility and 'chameleon' qualities in TAs' role definition has advantages and disadvantages for schools, teachers, TAs and children

■ Argued that the lack of clarity or 'fluidity' that exists in TAs' boundaries enables them to fulfil a diverse range of tasks, which is important when managing behaviour

■ Discussed how a lack of shared or agreed understanding of TAs' assumed roles in school can constrain effective relationships with teachers as well as TAs' efficacy and status in the classroom

■ Considered how TAs' 'weaker' (Blatchford, Russell and Webster, 2013) position relative to teachers, and challenges in understanding what their 'self-determined' (Tucker, 2009) role is may constrain TAs' ability to manage behaviour.

Further reading

■ Anderson, V. and Finney, M. (2008). I'm a TA Not a PA! In Richards, G. and Armstrong, F. (Eds.), *Key Issues for Teaching Assistants: Working in Diverse Classrooms*. London: Routledge.

■ Blatchford, P., Webster, R. and Russell, A. (2012). *Reassessing the Impact of Teaching Assistants*. London and Oxon: Routledge.

▪ Sharples, J., Webster, R. and Blatchford, P. (2018). *Making Best Use of Teaching Assistants: Guidance Report*. London: Educational Endowment Foundation. https://educationendowmentfoundation.org.uk/tools/guidance-reports/making-best-use-of-teaching-assistants

References

Anderson, V. and Finney, M. (2008). I'm a TA Not a PA! In Richards, G. and Armstrong, F. (Eds.), *Key Issues for Teaching Assistants: Working in Diverse Classrooms* (pp. 73–83). London: Routledge.

Barkham, J. (2008). Suitable Work for Women? Roles, Relationships and Changing Identities of 'Other Adults' in the Early Years Classroom. *British Educational Research Journal, 34*(6), 839–853.

Blatchford, P., Bassett, P., Brown, P. and Webster, R. (2009). The Effect of Support Staff on Pupil Engagement and Individual Attention. *British Educational Research Journal, 35*(5), 661–686.

Blatchford, P., Russell, A., Bassett, P., Brown, P. and Martin, C. (2007). The Role and Effects of Teaching Assistants in English Primary Schools (Years 4 to 6) 2000–2003. Results from the Class Size and Pupil–Adult Ratios (CSPAR) KS2 Project. *British Educational Research Journal, 33*(1), 5–26.

Blatchford, P., Russell, A. and Webster, R. (2013). *Maximising the Impact of Teaching Assistants: Guidance for School Leaders and Teachers*. Oxon: Routledge.

Blatchford, P., Webster, R. and Russell, A. (2012). *Reassessing the Impact of Teaching Assistants*. London and Oxon: Routledge.

Butt, R. and Lowe, K. (2011). Teaching Assistants and Class Teachers: Differing Perceptions, Role Confusion and the Benefits of Skills-based Training. *International Journal of Inclusive Education, 16*(2), 207–219.

Cajkler, W. and Tennant, G. (2009). Teaching Assistants and Pupils' Academic and Social Engagement in Mainstream Schools: Insights from Systematic Literature Reviews. *International Journal of Emotional Education, 1*(2), 71–90.

Calder, I. and Grieve, A. (2004). Working with Other Adults: What Teachers Need to Know. *Educational Studies, 30*(2), 113–126.

Cockroft, C. and Atkinson, C. (2015). Using the Wider Pedagogical Role Model to Establish Learning Support Assistants' Views about Facilitators and Barriers to Effective Practice. *Support for Learning, 30*(2), 88–104.

Collins, J. and Simco, N. (2006). Teaching Assistants Reflect: The Way Forward? *Reflective Practice, 7*(2), 197–214.

Department for Education and Employment. (1997). *Excellence in Schools. White Paper. 3681*. London: DfEE.

Department for Education and Skills. (2000). *Working With Teaching Assistants : A Good Practice Guide*. London: DfES.

Department for Education and Skills. (2001). *Schools Achieving Success*. London: DfES.

Department for Education and Skills. (2003). *Developing the Role of Support Staff – What the National Agreement Means for You*. London: DfES.

Department for Education and Skills. (2006). *Raising Standards and Tackling Workload Implementing the National Agreement. Note 17*. London: DfES.

Devecchi, C., Dettori, F., Doveston, M., Sedgwick, P. and Jament, J. (2011). Inclusive Classrooms in Italy and England: The Role of Support Teachers and Teaching Assistants. *European Journal of Special Needs Education, 27*(2), 171–184.

Fraser, C. and Meadows, S. (2008). Children's Views of Teaching Assistants in Primary Schools. *Education 3–13*, *36*(4), 351–363.

Galton, M. and MacBeath, J. (2008). *Teachers under Pressure*. London: SAGE Publications Ltd.

Gerschel, L. (2005). The Special Educational Needs Coordinator's Role in Managing Teaching Assistants: The Greenwich Perspective. *Support for Learning*, *20*(2), 69–76.

Giangreco, M. (2010). Utilization of Teacher Assistants in Inclusive Schools: Is It the Kind of Help that Helping Is All about? *European Journal of Special Needs Education*, *25*(4), 341–345.

Giangreco, M. (2013). Teacher Assistant Supports in Inclusive Schools: Research, Practices and Alternatives. *Australasian Journal of Special Education*, *37*(02), 93–106.

Graves, S. (2012). Chameleon or Chimera? The Role of the Higher Level Teaching Assistant (HLTA) in a Remodelled Workforce in English Schools. *Educational Management Administration & Leadership*, *41*(1), 95–104.

Graves, S. (2013). New Roles, Old Stereotypes – Developing a School Workforce in English Schools. *School Leadership and Management*, *34*(3), 255–268.

Groom, B. and Rose, R. (2005). Supporting the Inclusion of Pupils with Social, Emotional and Behavioural Difficulties in the Primary School: The Role of Teaching Assistants. *Journal of Research in Special Educational Needs*, *5*(1), 20–30.

Hancock, R., Hall, T., Cable, C. and Eyres, I. (2010). 'They Call Me Wonder Woman': The Job Jurisdictions and Work-related Learning of Higher Level Teaching Assistants. *Cambridge Journal of Education*, *40*(2), 97–112.

HMI. (2002). *Teaching Assistants in Primary Schools an Evaluation of the Quality and Impact of Their Work*. London: HMI.

Holland, P. and Hammerton, P. (1994). Balancing School and Individual Approaches. In Gray, P., Miller, A. and Noakes, J. (Eds.), *Challenging Behaviour In Schools* (pp. 244–261). London: Routledge.

Howes, A. (2003). Teaching Reforms and the Impact of Paid Adult Support on Participation and Learning in Mainstream Schools. *Support for Learning*, *18*(4), 147–153.

Kerry, T. (2005). Towards a Typology for Conceptualizing the Roles of Teaching Assistants. *Educational Review*, *57*(3), 373–384.

Lehane, T. (2016). "Cooling the Mark Out": Experienced Teaching Assistants' Perceptions of Their Work in the Inclusion of Upils with Special Educational Needs in Mainstream Secondary Schools. *Educational Review*, *68*(1), 4–23.

Mackenzie, S. (2011). "Yes, but…": Rhetoric, Reality and Resistance in Teaching Assistants' Experiences of Inclusive Education. *Support for Learning*, *26*, 64–71.

Maguire, M., Ball, S. and Braun, A. (2010). Behaviour, Classroom Management and Student 'Control': Enacting Policy in the English Secondary School. *International Studies in Sociology of Education*, *20*(2), 153–170.

Mansaray, A. (2006). Liminality and In/Exclusion: Exploring the Work of Teaching Assistants. *Pedagogy, Culture & Society*, *14*(2), 171–187.

McVittie, E. (2005). The Role of the Teaching Assistant: An Investigative Study to Discover if Teaching Assistants are Being Used Effectively to Support Children with Special Educational Needs in Mainstream Schools. *Education 3–13*, *33*(3), 26–31.

Mistry, M., Burton, N. and Brundrett, M. (2004). Managing LSAs: An Evaluation of the Use of Learning Support Assistants in an Urban Primary School. *School Leadership & Management*, *24*(2), 125–137.

Moran, A. and Abbott, L. (2002). Developing Inclusive Schools: The Pivotal Role of Teaching Assistants in Promoting Inclusion in Special and Mainstream Schools in Northern Ireland. *European Journal of Special Needs Education*, *17*(2), 161–173.

Morris, E. (2001). *Professionalism and Rust – The Future of Teachers and Teaching*. London: DfES.

O'Brien, T. and Garner, P. (2002). Tim and Philip's Story: Setting the Record Straight. In O'Brien, T. and Garner, P. (Eds.), *Untold Stories – Learning Support Assistants and Their Work* (pp. 1–10). Stoke on Trent: Trentham Books Ltd.

Ofsted. (2004). *Reading for Purpose and Pleasure an Evaluation of the Teaching of Reading in Primary Schools*. London: Ofsted.

Porter, A. (1989). External Standards and Good Teaching: The Pros and Cons of Telling Teachers What to Do. *Educational Evaluation and Policy Analysis, 11*(4), 343–356.

Quicke, J. (2003). Teaching Assistants: Students or Servants? *FORUM, 45*(2), 71–74.

Radford, J., Bosanquet, P., Webster, R. and Blatchford, P. (2015). Scaffolding Learning for Independence: Clarifying Teacher and Teaching Assistant Roles for Children with Special Educational Needs. *Learning and Instruction, 36*, 1–10.

Rose, R. and Forlin, C. (2010). Impact of Training on Change in Practice for Education Assistants in a Group of International Private Schools in Hong Kong. *International Journal of Inclusive Education, 14*(3), 309–323.

Sharples, J., Webster, R. and Blatchford, P. (2015). *Making Best Use of Teaching Assistants: Guidance Report*. London: Educational Endowment Foundation.

Smith, P., Whitby, K. and Sharp, C. (2004). *The Employment and Deployment of Teaching Assistants*. Slough: NFER.

Thomas, G. (1992). *Effective Classroom Teamwork: Support or Intrusion?* London: Routledge.

Trent, J. (2014). 'I'm Teaching, but I'm Not Really a Teacher'. Teaching Assistants and the Construction of Professional Identities in Hong Kong Schools. *Educational Research, 56*(1), 28–47.

Tucker, S. (2009). Perceptions and Reflections on the Role of the Teaching Assistant in the Classroom Environment. *Pastoral Care in Education, 27*(4), 291–300.

UNISON. (2013). *The Evident Value of Teaching Assistants: Report of a UNISON Survey*. Retrieved from www.unison.org.uk/content/uploads/2013/06/Briefings-and-CircularsEVIDENT-VALUE-OF-TEACHING-ASSISTANTS-Autosaved3.pdf

Watkins, C. and Wagner, P. (2000). *Improving School Behaviour*. London: Paul Chapman Publishing Ltd.

Webster, R., Blatchford, P. and Russell, A. (2013). Challenging and Hanging How Schools Use Teaching Assistants: Findings from the Effective Deployment of Teaching Assistants Project. *School Leadership and Management, 33*(1), 78–96.

TAs supporting children's behaviour – advantages and limitations

In the previous chapter, we discussed some of the reasons why TAs' role has evolved, and continues to evolve, in schools and other settings. We considered some of the advantages and disadvantages of trying to clearly define TAs' role in schools and began to reflect on how the fluid nature of TAs' work might impact on teachers. Following on from that, this chapter will consider why, in their unique position, TAs might be well placed to offer support to those children with behavioural difficulties. We will also think about some of the challenges TAs might experience in relation to their role in schools in offering this sort of support.

This chapter will:

■ Consider why many TAs are placed to work with children with behaviour problems in an unplanned way and the issues arising from this

■ Share some of the challenges and opportunities the TA role presents when working with children whose behaviour may be challenging

 What does the research tell us?

Aside from my own study (the findings of which are discussed in detail in Part 4 and Chapter 14 of this book), there is no research that explicitly focuses on how TAs manage behaviour. However, how TAs manage behaviour is included in some studies as part of the data gathered and an overview to some of the key findings from these studies will be introduced here. One of the key issues is that TAs are often deployed to manage behaviour in unplanned rather than actively planned ways, for example by working largely with children with SEND and those with other non-standard needs. As a result, TAs may not have the time, training or opportunities to develop this hidden aspect of their role. Despite this, the range of ways in which they work and the differences between TAs' and teachers' roles may be advantageous when managing behaviour.

Galton and MacBeath (2008) suggested that 'containment and curricular differentiation' were two of the key roles fulfilled by TAs. Their concept of 'containment' could be seen to be linked with managing behaviour, whilst differentiation is often associated with their work supporting children with SEND. Despite this research being over a decade old, it still reflects much that happens in current practice. TAs remain the main educator for the most needy pupils and in the main, teaching responsibility for children with a statement of SEND continues to fall to TAs (Webster, 2014). It was suggested that TAs have become almost exclusively *the* way to support children with SEND, opposed to simply *a* way (Giangreco, 2013).

As noted, research has shown that although TAs can be deployed in a number of different roles, they mostly continue to work supporting children SEND including those with behavioural difficulties (Groom and Rose, 2005; Ofsted, 2008; Sharples, Webster and Blatchford, 2015; UNISON, 2013; Webster and Blatchford, 2013; Webster, Blatchford and Russell, 2012). In primary schools, TAs have been shown to spend on average 29 per cent of their time working on a one-to-one basis supporting individual children and 15 per cent working with a group of children; in Key Stage Two half of all TAs are used to support children with SEND (Blatchford, Russell, Bassett, Brown and Martin, 2007).

The DfE (2012) highlighted the link between pupils identified as having SEND with 'higher levels of self-reported or observed misbehaviour' and significantly higher rates of both fixed-term (nine times more likely) and permanent (eight times more likely) exclusions. Deploying TAs in this way means that in most schools they are most likely to be spending the majority of their time supporting children with a range of behaviour problems and wider non-standard needs. This additional aspect is often not considered deeply, as TAs' main role when working children with SEND is to support them academically and their role is usually framed in this way. For example, this can be seen where discussions with teachers may focus on the work or intervention intended, rather than specifically discussing strategies to manage behaviour and so on.

Advantages of TAs managing behaviour

Findings (Blatchford, Russell and Webster, 2012; Galton and MacBeath, 2008; Sharples et al., 2015) have suggested that teachers particularly value TAs' contributions in terms of working with small groups, or specific children. This is felt to decrease incidents of low-level disruption, where teachers stated that TAs' increased on-task learning behaviour, and a 'simultaneous reduction in off-task behaviour', with pupils being both less distracted and less disruptive (Blatchford et al., 2012; Sharples et al., 2015). This mirrored an earlier HMI (2002) report which also found that the quality of teaching was improved by TAs managing what they described as minor behavioural issues and encouraging pupil's attention and concentration by increasing levels of engagement and focusing on task behaviour.

More informally, it has been suggested that TAs provide invaluable support for behaviour issues, in part due to their ability to be an extra set of eyes and ears for teachers (Blatchford et al., 2012; Mansaray, 2006; Neill, 2002; Sharples et al., 2015). Groom and Rose's (2005) study suggested that schools had an overwhelming perception that part of TAs' role is supporting the management of behaviour. It was also suggested that even when TAs were used to support in the classroom more broadly, this was still associated with managing behaviour;

> Implicit in this role is the support for promoting classroom rules, reminding pupils of expectations, dealing with conflict and keeping individual pupils on task.
>
> (Groom and Rose, 2005, p.25)

Indeed, in England, the government has explicitly referred to managing behaviour as part of the TA role in a wide range of publications and polices, both historically and more recently (DfE, 2010, 2013, 2016; DfES, 2001, 2003, 2006; HMI, 2002; Ofsted, 2004).

The TA role has also been portrayed as bridging a link between pupils and teachers in managing class behaviour (Cajkler and Tennant, 2009) and of 'connecting and mediating' (Howes, 2003). These views resonate with a relatively large body of research that shows TAs are able to form less formal and more intimate relationships with pupils, taking on the role of a friendly adult or even significant other, in a way that the class teacher cannot (Armstrong, 2008; Blatchford et al., 2007; Clarke and Visser, 2016; Fraser and Meadows, 2008; Mansaray, 2006; HMI, 2002; Rubie-Davies, Blatchford, Webster, Koutsoubou and Bassett, 2010; Whittaker and Kikabhai, 2008). Kerry's (2005) research identified a number of different labels that were used to describe TAs' work, with the 'carer/mentor' label defining the TA as:

> an adult critical friend, not seen as tainted by the 'authority of schooldom', but wise in the ways of the world beyond school and able to act as a human shield.
>
> (p.378)

This illustrates the difference in the type of relationships TAs are able to form with children compared to teachers.

Associated with this, Mackenzie (2011) noted how the caring aspect of TAs' role, often associated with being female, resulted in the perception that the largely female population of TAs were more suited to working with children who had behaviour issues. This supported Ofsted's (2008) contention that TAs' range of experiences may be specifically beneficial to 'engage successfully with disaffected students'. These soft skills and the nurturing roles, which are often associated with women and specifically to mothers, are recurring themes in TA research and are viewed by some as indicative of the mothering identity which has been described by many as intrinsic to TAs (Barkham, 2008; Bland and Sleightholme, 2012; Blatchford, Russell, Bassett, Brown and Martin, 2004; Galton and MacBeath, 2008; Kerry, 2005; Mackenzie, 2011; Watson, Bayliss and Pratchett, 2013).

Pause point

What additional advantages might there be for TAs managing challenging behaviour?

■ Can you make a list? As the chapters progress, more advantages will be discussed; check as you progress through the book whether the ideas here and your own agree.

■ What have you seen work well in your own setting? Think also about *who* it worked well for – was it the child, TA, teacher, parent, school or a combination of the above?

Disadvantages of TAs managing behaviour

Despite suggestions that TAs played a pivotal role in managing behaviour (Groom and Rose, 2005) understanding how they actually do manage behaviour is challenging. This is because, as we have discussed, defining the TA's evolving role has been, and continues to be, fraught with difficulties. Despite suggestions that TA support is helpful in managing behaviour, there are contradictions in some of the evidence. Although the findings considered in the previous section proposed that TAs' caring role was supportive in managing behaviour, this is not as simple as it may seem at first glance. Understanding TAs' role as motherly highlights issues related to status and power (Devecchi, Dettori, Doveston, Sedgwick and Jament, 2011; Mansaray, 2006). Graves (2013) argued that these maternal associations at times made TAs' work both invisible and peripheral – highlighting possible challenges for them in managing behaviour. In line with this, research (Cajkler and Tennant, 2009) showed that TAs were less of an authority figure in comparison with teachers, with children reacting differently to TAs depending on the role that they were fulfilling. For example, TAs experienced more difficulties in managing behaviour on duty at playtime than they did working with a group in the classroom (Blatchford et al., 2007). This may be due to their supporting role in reinforcing previously set rules and expectations within the classroom, as opposed to an inherent expectation of authority (Devecchi and Rouse, 2010). This supported Graves's (2013) view that TAs were only viewed as '*not* teachers' rather than having their own distinct professional role and status, and Blatchford, Russell and Webster (2013) described how this, at times, resulted in children 'playing the teacher's seniority off against the TA's relatively weaker position'.

 Pause point

Is this idea of TAs being *not* teachers something you have seen or experienced?

■ Why might this be the case in your experience or setting?

■ What messages might children either implicitly or explicitly receive that suggests TAs are *not* teachers?

■ How might these messages impact on TAs' ability to manage behaviour?

HMI (2002) acknowledged that high levels of tailored behaviour support were not always easy for TAs, suggesting that most were 'able to manage the behaviour of four or five pupils' only, and that the support provided could be ineffective where there were problems for TAs in 'maintaining discipline'. Mansaray (2006) also believed that working with a TA could actually increase behavioural issues, as children interpreted working with a TA to mean they were lower achievers, as both historically and in some schools and settings, this form of deployment is common practice. This suggests that managing behaviour can be a challenge for TAs due to assumptions made by schools and children, including their caring rather than assertive role as well as their legacy of supporting specific groups of children.

In addition to these issues, role creep or the blurring of the roles between teacher and TA can cause tension in what TAs' role in managing behaviour is. Research (Butt and Lowe, 2011) found that TAs wanted more training in managing behaviour, yet teachers in their interviews were clear that this was not TAs' role or responsibility and considered managing behaviour a facet of the teachers' job only. Conversely, the government, children, parents and TAs themselves did view managing behaviour as part of TAs' role (Butt and Lowe, 2011; DfE, 2013, 2016; DfES, 2002, 2003, 2006; Tucker, 2009). Important differences have also been illustrated by research in the interactions teachers and TAs had with pupils when managing behaviour. Research (Rubie-Davies et al., 2010; Sharples et al., 2015) found that whilst teachers set 'clear expectations' or used 'strong statements' to manage behaviour, they suggested TA talk focused on 'requests for compliance' and 'weaker statements'. These tensions and differences in expectations can make TAs' role in managing behaviour even more challenging and complex.

 Pause point

Why might there be differences in teacher and TA interactions with children?
- How many reasons for these differences can you list?
- What could TAs do to address some of these reported differences?
- What could teachers do to address some of these reported differences?
- What might school leaders do to address these differences?
- If some of these differences were addressed how might it support (or not) TAs to manage behaviour?

What this might mean in school

As we have seen from the research, a common picture is emerging – one of disagreement! This makes interpreting the findings difficult. However, there are some steps that can be taken, despite the lack of agreement in research.

First, there is a lack of clarity, overall in TAs' roles in schools, as we discussed in the previous chapter (Chapter 5) and will do in Chapters 7 and 9, and this extends to whether they are supporting children in a given context and setting, and at a given time, either explicitly academically, behaviourally or both.

1. **Teachers and TAs need time to discuss the specific type(s) of support – either academic or behavioural – they anticipate TAs giving to specific groups or children, as well as help for TAs to develop a range of supportive strategies to fulfil this.**

Findings also suggest that because of differences between teachers' and TAs' roles and status in school children may be able to form supportive and more informal relationships with TAs and that the caring aspects of their role can be valuable for children with behaviour difficulties. However, as we noted in the previous chapter, what used to be automatic links between TAs and mums have been challenged and are seen as pejorative. Attention needs to be given to how to balance these.

2. **Drawing on TAs' soft skills and different forms of relationships with children to support their behaviour can be advantageous but this should not be at the detriment of TAs' professional identity.**

For a number of reasons, TAs in schools are often perceived to have less power and status than teachers. Although this can help form different relationships, it can also disadvantage TAs and make it more difficult for them to manage behaviour. Schools need to actively consider how to either develop TAs' status or consider the roles they are asked to fulfil to ensure this is not an issue. This can also be addressed to some extent in the school's behaviour policy (as will be discussed in Chapters 7and 10).

3. **Schools need to consider supporting TAs to develop their professional status within their setting to ensure status does not make TAs managing behaviour problematic. One way to do this is to make the actions they can take explicit in the whole-school behaviour policy.**

Research suggests that TAs manage behaviour through asking for compliance rather than setting clear expectations as teachers were reported to. It would be worth bearing in mind that TAs might have received little or no training on managing behaviour and may ask for compliance as they are unsure of any other strategies.

4. **TAs may well need or benefit from specific training in managing behaviour as well as being included in any whole-school training opportunities to enable them to develop their skills.**

 ## Reflection activity

Begin to think about how TAs are used in your setting, or where you have observed their work in schools. What makes them well placed to manage behaviour in these

TAs managing behaviour in schools			
When and where?	What makes them well placed to manage behaviour?	What limits them in managing behaviour?	How could the issues be resolved?
In the playground whilst on duty.	They might know the child better than other staff due to close work with them.	They might not have the opportunity after break to follow-up with the child. They might need to 'pass it on' to a teacher.	Could 5 minutes be built into end of lessons so TA can revisit issues with child(ren) if needed? End of lesson would ensure they had time to let teacher they were working with know.

Figure 6.1 TA deployment and impact on behaviour management

situations? What might make it difficult for them to manage behaviour in these contexts? Are there any changes that can be made to maximise these strengths?

Can you start to put your ideas down in the table shown in Figure 6.1? You will be able to add to this if you chose to as the chapters progress and more challenges and opportunities are discussed.

 **Summary**

In this chapter we have looked at some of the advantages and disadvantages TAs may experience when managing behaviour. We have again returned to issues of lack of clarity in their roles and suggested that this ability to work 'between' in schools may actually support them. This is because it can allow them to develop different sorts of professional relationships with children, possibly less formal and more 'caring', which might support the management of some children's behaviour.

On the other hand, we have also seen how the uncertainly over roles can be a contributing factor to reduced status and power and make it challenging to manage some children's behaviour. Despite the pedagogical work TAs undertake, which now accounts for their largest contribution to schools, their role may not regularly include managing the behaviour of whole classes, but instead focus on small groups or individuals, or being in a supporting role. This idea of positioning TAs in a supporting role may have implications for their status in school and as a result for their ability to manage behaviour.

We have also seen that guidance from the British government has been consistent in expectations that TAs play a role in managing behaviour in English schools and that it is suggested that all transactions with children, in whichever supporting or pedagogical capacity, will have some association with managing behaviour. Indeed, it has even been suggested that TAs' role in managing behaviour is pivotal.

 ## Key points

This chapter has:

■ Considered how and why managing behaviour might be part of TAs' role

■ Investigated research around the role of TAs and how assumptions about their caring and motherly role can influence schools and children's views of them in relation to managing behaviour.

■ Discussed why expectation of TAs managing behaviour can be implicit and the issues that might arise from this

■ Reflected on why TAs are well placed to manage behaviour and how they may be able to support children's behaviour in a way teachers might not

■ Considered why TAs might be in a challenging position in relation to managing behaviour and how teachers', children's and schools' assumptions may hinder them.

 ## Further reading

■ Blatchford, P., Russell, A. and Webster, R. (2012). *Reassessing the Impact of Teaching Assistants*. Oxon: Routledge.

■ Clarke, E. and Visser, J. (2016). Teaching Assistants Managing Behaviour – Who Knows How They Do It? A Review of Literature. *Support for Learning, 31*(4), 266–280.

■ UNISON. (2013). The Evident Value of Teaching Assistants: Report of a UNISON Survey. www.skillsforschools.org.uk/media/1075/unison-evident-value-of-tas.pdf

References

Armstrong, F. (2008). Inclusive Education. In Richards, G. and Armstrong, F. (Eds.), *Key Issues for Teaching Assistants: Working in Diverse Classrooms* (pp. 7–18). London: Routledge.

Barkham, J. (2008). Suitable Work for Women? Roles, Relationships and Changing Identities of 'Other Adults' in the Early Years Classroom. *British Educational Research Journal*, *34*(6), 839–853.

Bland, K. and Sleightholme, S. (2012). Researching the Pupil Voice: What Makes a Good Teaching Assistant? *Support for Learning*, *27*(4), 172–176.

Blatchford, P., Russell, A., Bassett, P., Brown, P. and Martin, C. (2004). *The Role and Effects of Teaching Assistants in English Primary Schools (Years 4 to 6) 2000 – 2003: Results from the Class Size and Pupil Adult Ratios (CSPAR) project. Final Report. (Research Report 605).* London: DfES.

Blatchford, P., Russell, A., Bassett, P., Brown, P. and Martin, C. (2007). The Role and Effects of Teaching Assistants in English Primary Schools (Years 4 to 6) 2000–2003. Results from the Class Size and Pupil–Adult Ratios (CSPAR) KS2 Project. *British Educational Research Journal*, *33*(1), 5–26.

Blatchford, P., Russell, A. and Webster, R. (2012). *Reassessing the Impact of Teaching Assistants*. Oxon: Routledge.

Blatchford, P., Russell, A. and Webster, R. (2013). *Maximising the Impact of Teaching Assistants: Guidance for School Leaders and Teachers*. Oxon: Routledge.

Butt, R. and Lowe, K. (2011). Teaching Assistants and Class Teachers: Differing Perceptions, Role Confusion and the Benefits of Skills-Based Training. *International Journal of Inclusive Education*, *16*(2), 207–219.

Cajkler, W. and Tennant, G. (2009). Teaching Assistants and Pupils' Academic and Social Engagement in Mainstream Schools: Insights from Systematic Literature Reviews. *International Journal of Emotional Education*, *1*(2), 71–90.

Clarke, E. and Visser, J. (2016). Teaching Assistants Managing Behaviour – Who Knows How They Do It? A Review of Literature. *Support for Learning*, *31*(4), 266–280.

Department for Education. (2010). *The Importance of Teaching: The School's White Paper 2010*. London: DfE.

Department for Education. (2012). *Pupil Behaviour in Schools in England*. In Research Report DFE-RR218. London: DfE.

Department for Education. (2013). *Behaviour and Discipline in Schools: Guidance for Governing Bodies*. London: DfE.

Department for Education. (2016). *Behaviour and Discipline in Schools: Advice for Headteachers and School Staff*. London: DfE.

Department for Education and Skills. (2001). *Schools Achieving Success*. London: DfES.

Department for Education and Skills. (2002). *Developing the Role of School Support Staff: The Consultation*. London: DfES.

Department for Education and Skills. (2003). *Developing the Role of Support Staff – What the National Agreement Means for You*. London: DfES.

Department for Education and Skills. (2006). *Raising Standards and Tackling Workload Implementing the National Agreement*. London: DfES.

Devecchi, C., Dettori, F., Doveston, M., Sedgwick, P. and Jament, J. (2011). Inclusive Classrooms in Italy and England: The Role of Support Teachers and Teaching Assistants. *European Journal of Special Needs Education, 27*(2), 171–184.

Devecchi, C. and Rouse, M. (2010). An Exploration of the Features of Effective Collaboration between Teachers and Teaching Assistants in Secondary Schools. *Support for Learning, 25*(2), 91–99.

Fraser, C. and Meadows, S. (2008). Children's Views of Teaching Assistants in Primary Schools. *Education 3–13, 36*(4), 351–363.

Galton, M. and MacBeath, J. (2008). *Teachers under Pressure.* London: SAGE Publications Ltd.

Giangreco, M. (2013). Teacher Assistant Supports in Inclusive Schools: Research, Practices and Alternatives. *Australasian Journal of Special Education, 37*(02), 93–106.

Graves, S. (2013). New Roles, Old Stereotypes – Developing a School Workforce in English Schools. *School Leadership & Management, 34*(3), 255–268.

Groom, B. and Rose, R. (2005). Supporting the Inclusion of Pupils with Social, Emotional and Behavioural Difficulties in the Primary School: The Role of Teaching Assistants. *Journal of Research in Special Educational Needs, 5*(1), 20–30.

HMI. (2002). *Teaching Assistants in Primary Schools an Evaluation of the Quality and Impact of Their Work.* London: Ofsted.

Howes, A. (2003). Teaching Reforms and the Impact of Paid Adult Support on Participation and Learning in Mainstream Schools. *Support for Learning, 18*(4), 147–153.

Kerry, T. (2005). Towards a Typology for Conceptualizing the Roles of Teaching Assistants. *Educational Review, 57*(3), 373–384.

Mackenzie, S. (2011). "Yes, but...": Rhetoric, Reality and Resistance in Teaching Assistants' Experiences of Inclusive Education. *Support for Learning, 26*, 64–71.

Mansaray, A. (2006). Liminality and In/Exclusion: Exploring the Work of Teaching Assistants. *Pedagogy, Culture & Society, 14*(2), 171–187.

Neill, S. (2002). *Teaching Assistants: A Survey Analyed for the NUT.* London: University of Warwick/National Union of Teachers.

Ofsted. (2004). *Reading for Purpose and Pleasure: An Evaluation of the Teaching of Reading in Primary Schools.* London: Ofsted.

Ofsted. (2008). *The Deployment, Training and Development of the Wider School Workforce.* London: Ofsted.

Rubie-Davies, C. M., Blatchford, P., Webster, R., Koutsoubou, M. and Bassett, P. (2010). Enhancing Learning? A Comparison of Teacher and Teaching Assistant Interactions with Pupils. *School Effectiveness and School Improvement, 21*(4), 429–449.

Sharples, J., Webster, R. and Blatchford, P. (2015). *Making Best Use of Teaching Assistants: Guidance Report.* London: Education Endowment Foundation.

Tucker, S. (2009). Perceptions and Reflections on the Role of the Teaching Assistant in the Classroom Environment. *Pastoral Care in Education, 27*(4), 291–300.

UNISON. (2013). *The Evident Value of Teaching Assistants: Report of a UNISON Survey.* Retrieved from www.unison.org.uk/content/uploads/2013/06/Briefings-and-CircularsEVIDENT-VALUE-OF-TEACHING-ASSISTANTS-Autosaved3.pdf

Watson, D., Bayliss, P. and Pratchett, G. (2013). Pond Life that 'Know Their Place': Exploring Teaching and Learning Support Assistants' Experiences through Positioning Theory. *International Journal of Qualitative Studies in Education, 26*(1), 100–117.

Webster, R. (2014). 2014 Code of Practice: How Research Evidence on the Role and Impact of Teaching Assistants Can Inform Professional Practice. *Educational Psychology in Practice, 30*(3), 232–237.

Webster, R. and Blatchford, P. (2013). *The Making a Statement Project Final Report. A Study of the Teaching and Support Experienced by Pupils with a Statement of Special Educational Needs in Mainstream Primary Schools.* London: Institute of Education.

Webster, R., Blatchford, P. and Russell, A. (2012). Challenging and Changing How Schools Use Teaching Assistants: Findings from the Effective Deployment of Teaching Assistants Project. *School Leadership & Management, 33*(1), 78–96.

Whittaker, J. and Kikabhai, N. (2008). How Schools Create Challenging Behaviours. In Richards, G. and Armstrong, F. (Eds.), *Key Issues for Teaching Assistants: Working in Diverse Classrooms* (pp. 120–130). London: Routledge.

7 TAs, teachers and school behaviour policies

In the previous chapters, we have considered what strengths TAs, and the TA role, have that make them particularly suited to managing behaviour, as well as shared some of the factors that might limit their contributions to managing behaviour. This chapter will consider how policies, and a school's behaviour policy specifically, can additionally either help or hinder TAs in managing behaviour. We will look at what issues might arise in writing polices and with general aspects of policy implementation.

This chapter also marks the end of the first part of the book before we move on to examining the specific in-school and wider factors that support and constrain TAs in managing behaviour.

This chapter will:

■ Investigate the role of policies and their impact on managing behaviour

■ Consider how policy content influences teachers and TAs

■ Present the arguments for consistency in policy implementations

■ Discuss problems that frequently arise in policy implementation

 ## What does the research tell us?

Research has suggested that are three different types of rights; legal, civil and human (Visser and Stokes, 2010) and that all three need to be addressed in a school's framework for managing behaviour – which places great importance on a school's behaviour policy. Despite this, Ball, Hoskins, Maguire and Braun (2011) argued that policies were a particularly English preoccupation, describing them as 'composites' and 'unstable, synthetic entities'. Ball et al. (2011) proposed that these behaviour policies presented specific and unusual challenges to schools, supporting Thomas and Loxley's (2001) earlier view that without revision of the 'odd collection of rules and practices' that behaviour policies contained, issues with children's behaviour were almost an inevitable consequence.

Policy broadly has been defined as a set of normative guidelines for action that governs how things should be done (Thomas and Loxley, 2001). From this it would be easy to assume that policy and policy implementation were straightforward and essentially for the greater good. Yet, much of the literature typifies it as messy, with inconsistent approaches and variability from implementer to implementer and school to school (Carrington, 1999; Coburn and Stein, 2006; Datnow and Castellano, 2000; Datnow and Stringfield, 2000; McLaughlin, 1991; Odden, 1991; Thomas and Loxley, 2001).

Research has also suggested that policy implementation exists on a continuum ranging from strict conformity at one end to complete modification at the other, with acquiescence, compromise, avoidance and defiance residing somewhere in between (Datnow and Stringfield, 2000; Thomas and Loxley, 2001). In their research, Datnow and Stringfield (2000) found that a variety of responses to policy were actually ubiquitous and the norm, rather than the exception. Discrete or specific policies (like behaviour policies) often ignore systemic and interconnected factors that influence classroom practice (McLaughlin, 1991) – and as a result, can be problematic to implement.

Further issues can occur that can affect how it is implemented. Datnow and Stringfield (2000) warned against the view that policy could be implemented identically anywhere, at any time and suggested that this flew in the face of both research and common sense. McLaughlin (1991) also believed that what he termed 'episodic interventions' – such as some behaviour polices – were only likely to be implemented in the interim as they were short-term priorities which quickly become replaced with another short-term priority. A continuous wave of new and at times conflicting demands, as well as by government policies in what McLaughlin (1991) described as being in a constant state of flux, only compounds difficulties. Datnow and Stringfield (2000) defined schools as being awash with new policies and suggested that as a result of balancing multiple issues with new policies school change was rarely a linear process.

 Pause point

It has been suggested here that schools are at times 'awash' with a raft of polices and that not all of them are working towards the same end. Think about:

■ Can you list all of the current policies your setting or school is implementing? If you are not in a school, how many are you aware of from wider reading?

■ Do the policies in your list complement or contradict each other?

■ Where does your policy implementation fit on the 'conformity to modification' scale?

■ What has made you conform, modify or ignore the selected policy?

■ What would the impact be if there were a range of approaches to implementing a whole school behaviour policy?

■ What might the disadvantages be and to whom?

■ What might the advantages be and to whom?

Datnow's (2000) research highlighted the difficulties of achieving real commitment to any externally imposed or mandated policy and confirmed findings from Odden's (1991) earlier research that proposed these polices 'were doomed to failure on the beaches of local policy implementation resistance'. This reflects the previous views of schools being awash with policy; Thomas and Loxley (2001) stated in relation to policy, 'we can ignore it, extend it, subvert it and rewrite it, but we cannot escape it'. If behaviour policies, rather than supporting a consistent and cohesive approach to managing behaviour, are considered, as some research suggested, episodic interventions with consistent implication-defying common sense and are doomed to resistance from staff, problems arise for TAs' management of behaviour.

It was suggested that policies, and specifically behaviour policies, should aim to be part of the oral tradition of the school and be enmeshed within the organisation's culture (Thomas and Loxley, 2001), as opposed to a stand-alone bureaucratic procedure. This mirrored Rowe's (2006) views about the importance of internalising the values in a behaviour policy rather than simply complying with it, and echoed O'Brien's (1998) statement that 'a policy cannot be allowed to decay on a shelf – it should be alive in practice'. These views supported research that showed that the behaviour policy must be integral to the school (Clarke and Murray, 1996; DfE, 2013; Lund, 1996; Porter, 2000; Visser, 2007; Watkins and Wagner, 2000). However, despite these assertions, research shows there is often a lack of collective responsibility for policies, with surprisingly few staff aware of key influential government documents on behaviour, or even their own school's policy (DfE, 2014; Holland and Hammerton, 1994; Maguire, Ball and Braun, 2010; Turner, 2003). Ofsted (2014) reported that a sixth of the teachers they surveyed found their school's behaviour policy to be unhelpful and only around 50 per cent applied it consistently.

The influence of policy content on TAs and teachers

A range of published work suggests that the very best behaviour policies change the focus from misbehaviour to good behaviour and have an emphasis on positive behaviour management strategies that benefits all pupils (DfE, 2014; Hallam, 2007; Visser, 2003). In line with this, Lund (1996) stated that behaviour policies should also ensure the development of high self-esteem and value, not only for pupils but also for all members of the school community, and that behaviour management and any focus on discipline should only form a small part of the school's overall policy. Even though Lund's research is over twenty years old it resonates with new English agendas on addressing well-being and mental health in schools. This was also seen in the British government's previous concerns over pupil resilience, where they pointed to school's importance in being a safe and affirming place in which children developed a sense of belonging and feel able to trust and talk openly and one where resilience was promoted (DfE, 2014).

A behaviour policy can also be framed either as reactive or proactive. Reactive approaches are those that are corrective, post-incident responses and have often been suggested to precipitate negative teacher reactions. Despite this, they remain commonly used and detailed in behaviour policies, despite evidential research on the effectiveness of proactive strategies (Clunies–Ross, Little and Kienhuis, 2008; Holland and Hammerton, 1994; Watkins and Wagner, 2000). A reactive policy can be exemplified by a tariff-or-sanction–based behaviourist approach in whatever form this may take – merits and de-merits, moving up or down a scale of some form or receiving red and yellow cards and so on. The main purpose of these tariff systems is to codify a set of responses to particular student behaviours, either positive or negative – with the emphasis more often than not on the latter (Watkins and Wagner, 2000). This tariff approach has been implicated in the increasing number of school exclusions, as the reactive strategies they promote have been shown to 'encourage rule-laden inflexibility' in some staff, which in turn can lead to various forms of 'disaffection' in the children they are applied to (Watkins and Wagner, 2000).

One of the key issues with reactive behaviourist policies is that they necessarily advocate a hierarchy of sanctions and punishments. These graded responses, where many of the sanctions can fall outside the remit of the teacher, and almost all outside the remit of the TA, can result in members of the school's senior leadership team being seen as people to send naughty children to. This then takes the place of most of the routine behaviour management being handled in the classroom by the teachers and TAs (Watkins and Wagner, 2000). This mirrors Lund's (1996) earlier research which found autonomy from a rigid hierarchy of rewards and sanctions was important, and that it was a teacher's or a TA's belief and confidence in an approach that made it effective. Goodman (2006) also argued for much greater autonomy in respect to discipline, stating that staff – teachers and TAs – were the ones who knew and understood best both the child and the context. He suggested that as a result, they should be given more authority to handle issues rather than automatically progressing up a pre-arranged set of sanctions. This freedom from rigidly following a policy might be very important if a child has additional, non-standard needs, has experienced adverse childhood experiences, is under a time of intense stress, for example a bereavement and so on. Gray and Noakes (1994) had previously contended that providing prescribed strategies or detailed guidance to support staff suggested they could not be trusted to make professional judgements.

This follows views that the behaviourist framework of rewards and sanctions was seen by staff as emotionally safe, whereas less-structured policies which required teachers and TAs to consider their own views and feelings about behaviour were seen as emotionally loaded (Radford, 2000).

It has been argued that British government policy in relation to behaviour has resulted in English schools' compulsory adoption of policies centred on rewards and sanctions, despite this form of behaviourist focus being all but lost in wider aspects of education (Payne, 2015). Indeed, as we noted in Chapters 3 and 4, Payne (2015) stated the behaviourist ideas which were required to form the foundation of schools' behaviour polices represented 'a potentially confused set of aims and theoretical principles'. Despite these views, schools' and staffs' autonomy in managing behaviour has continued to be challenged in a wide range of government publications in England (DfE, 2010, 2011, 2013, 2016; House of Commons Education Committee, 2011; Steer, 2005; Taylor, 2011).

 Pause point

Find a range of school behaviour policies (these are all obliged to be freely accessible on school web-sites). Think about:

■ Does it use a system of rewards and sanctions to manage behaviour?

■ Are there opportunities for teachers and TAs to apply their professional judgement?

■ Are the roles of teachers, TAs and other support staff made clear?

Think about your own experiences of managing behaviour:

■ Were there times when a hierarchy of rewards and sanctions would have been supportive? For whom? Why?

■ Were there times when a hierarchy of rewards and sanctions would not have been helpful? For whom? Why?

Consistency in policy implementation

One of the most challenging issues surrounding behaviour and behaviour policies is that of consistency, where a consensus-based message which comes from the school as an institution rather than the teacher as an individual is seen as important (Galvin and Costa, 1995). Visser (2007) found that a critical mass of professionals within the school, either in number or influence, were required for consistent policy application. Without consistency in application, children reported that the management of behaviour was unfair and without coherence. Ofsted (2005) also suggested that a lack of consistency was linked to increased behaviour problems and cautioned that unclear boundaries and inconsistent application could cause resentment in children who recognise the importance of rules and sanctions being consistently applied. These findings were replicated in an Ofsted report (2014) almost ten years later, showing the entrenched nature of the problem. This, as we saw in Chapters 3 and 4, can raise issues of 'fairness' from a behaviourist perspective when the same behaviours from different children are either rewarded or sanctioned differently. The Elton Report (DfES, 1989) had earlier suggested that on a larger scale the policy itself ensured that a whole range of processes are consistent with one another. It warned that a lack of consistent application could result in the school becoming a 'mere collection of classrooms' with contrasting disciplinary regimes that resulted in fragmentation and demoralisation for teachers and pupils alike. Research also showed that unless pupils were involved in the consultation process and were able to voice their opinions regarding the policy, they could reject it out of hand (DfES, 1989; Haroun and O'Hanlon, 1997; Turner, 2003; Wright, Weekes and McGlaughlin, 2004; 2CV Research, 2010).

To complicate matters, however, there have been inconsistent views on the importance of consistency. Much research has espoused whole-school consistency as absolutely essential (Bennett, 2017; Canter, 2010; DfE, 2014; Ofsted, 2008, 2014; Taylor, 2011; Visser, 2007). Despite this, others saw consistency as impossible and undesirable (DfES, 1989; Goodman, 2006; Watkins and Wagner, 2000). Watkins and Wagner (2000) believed that consistency in itself was not valuable; they advised that it could lead to a reduction in staff coherence and suggested that perpetuating the belief that consistency was necessary for children was not only inaccurate but actually 'likely to be damaging'. They argued rather that part of children's development process was learning how to respond in various situations (Watkins and Wagner, 2000). Nonetheless, it was noted that the consequences of inconsistency meant that pupils needed a 'great degree of sophistication' to deal with conflicting teacher expectations (Wright et al., 2004). The Elton Report (DfES, 1989) also found that complete uniformity in the implementation of behaviour policies was both impossible and undesirable, and the later White Paper (DfE, 2010), focused on the significance of professional judgement in addition to knowledge of the child when unacceptably poor behaviour was dealt with. In support of this, Galton and MacBeath (2008) proposed that a substantive body of evidence existed that illustrated how compliance stifles creativity and initiative and consensus can close down creative alternatives.

Power can also be seen in the process of policy implementation, or non-implementation. Power is an issue that affects TAs in a number of different ways and can be seen particularly in views which consider the lack of power and autonomy school staff and TAs in particular have in the face of policy dictates. Coburn (2005) proposed that rather than the high degree of professional autonomy previously assumed for some, staff in schools instead had what she termed 'bounded autonomy'. This is where professional judgements, autonomy and freedom are 'bounded', or constrained by outside (or sometimes within-school) factors, including factors such as Ofsted, curriculum constraints and government policy for example. She considered that this range of regulative pressures limited teachers' decision-making capabilities, but at the same time forced then to take some form of action as this was what was expected or required (Coburn, 2005). This supported Datnow's (2000) earlier research where she found teachers rarely experienced free, fully informed choice about policy adoption. If it has been suggested that teachers lack the opportunity for this free and informed decision-making it can be assumed that TAs will have even fewer opportunities to make informed decisions towards policy. TAs usually occupy positions that are associated with much less power than those that teachers occupy, so it could be suggested that if these problems exist for teachers they are likely to be magnified for TAs (the influence of power on TAs will be explored further in Chapters 9 and 11).

It has been suggested that behaviour policies should be 'assertive, appropriate, watchful, supportive and conflict avoiding' (Sproson, 2004). However, these are at odds with the British governments' increasingly behaviourist tone and its current guidance reinforcing a focus on discipline, control and authority in English schools (Bennett, 2017; DfE, 2010; DfE & Rt Hon Nicky Morgan, 2015). Cole (2004) argued, in relation to behaviour, that there had been little consistent guidance about whether policies should achieve the qualities Sproson (2004) cited through 'control, therapy, welfare or education', all of which have been proposed at certain times.

 Pause point

The discussion has considered whether behaviour polices could or should be implemented consistently. Think about:

■ What advantages are there in consistency implementing a behaviour policy?

■ How could it support children?

■ How could it support TAs?

■ What disadvantages might there be for these two groups?

Cole (2004) highlighted a range of suggested strategies for developing behaviour through the policy: control, therapy, welfare or education.

■ Which of these categories do the polices you have seen fall under?

■ What might the strengths and limitations of these approaches be?

■ How might these different approaches impact on the way TAs are included in and can enact the policy?

What this might mean in school

Again, the research we have looked at shows (unsurprisingly now!) a conflicting picture. There are tensions in what should be in a behaviour policy, how it should be applied and who is able to apply it. Whilst the absence of clear guidance from research could be seen as frustrating again, it gives schools and settings a degree of freedom – or bounded autonomy – to make decisions that meet the needs of the children they support.

One of the issues levelled at policy generally is that it has no real lasting impact in school because it is just one of many. Staff who have worked in education for a number of years may also have seen many policies come and go and as a result do not always implement them as intended, or show any great commitment to them. Clearly, a behaviour policy should be given lasting priority in a school but this is challenging given the shifting educational landscape in England. For the behaviour policy in your school or setting to be given the required importance and status it needs to be a 'living' document which is regularly revisited, discussed and owned by all staff.

1. **Care needs to be given to training, reviewing and discussing the behaviour policy regularly with all staff to ensure it is part of the school culture and owned by staff and children.**

Another key issue is that of consistent policy implementation. This links back to the type of perspective your school or setting has on how behaviour should be managed (as discussed in Chapters 3 and 4). However, it is reasonable to assume, as the British government expect rewards and sanctions to be detailed in a behaviour policy, that this is what most schools will do. This needs to be written with great thought to either allow some flexibility and professional judgement in application of rewards and sanctions which it has been suggested is advantageous or to encourage consistency by applying them rigidly.

2. **The rewards and sanctions detailed in the policy (if this is the perspective used) need great thought to either allow flexibility or encourage consistency depending on the ethos of the school and content of the policy.**

If consistent application is seen as important, then regular training and support needs to be given to ensure that all staff have the same reading of the policy and understanding of how and when to apply it.

3. **Training and support needs to be given to all staff to support implementation of the behaviour policy.**

As noted, some believe that flexibility and adaptability where staff can use their knowledge of the context is required when addressing and supporting children's behaviour. This is much more challenging to detail in a behaviour policy, particularly when written to meet the needs of a range of staff with a range of experience and training. If professional autonomy is to be encouraged significant discussion and training will need to accompany it to ensure it is sustainable and workable. In whichever way the policy is written, particularly if using rewards and sanctions, it is essential to give thought to who has access to the range of responses. For example, if a reward is a postcard home, can TAs also send these? If a sanction is to be put on some form of formal report card or monitoring system is this something TAs can do independently? If there is a need to refer to the class teacher, this may well negatively impact on TAs' power, status and willingness or ability to implement a policy that they are excluded from.

4. **When writing the policy ensure (if this is desired) that TAs and other non-teaching staff are not excluded from the strategies to manage behaviour. If they are, discussions need to be held with these staff so they understand the reasons for this.**

This penultimate point reflects the lack of trust it has been suggested some behaviour polices show in staff. If staff in your school or setting are trusted to manage behaviour positively and professionally, this should be reflected in the policy. If staff, or some groups of staff, are not trusted to manage behaviour in a way that is purposeful and in line with the school's ethos, this needs addressing in a range of ways, rather than in a constraining behaviour policy.

5. **All staff need time to discuss behaviour and attend training and then be trusted by the school or setting to manage behaviour.**

 ## Reflection activity

In this chapter we have looked at what a behaviour policy might include and the tensions there may be in applying it. Can you reflect on the activities you may have completed (or not!) as this chapter progressed. Can you annotate the diagram in Figure 7.1 to show what, if you were able to write or rewrite the policy for your school or setting, would be key to include to show that you trusted all staff to manage behaviour? What might be the implications of this trust?

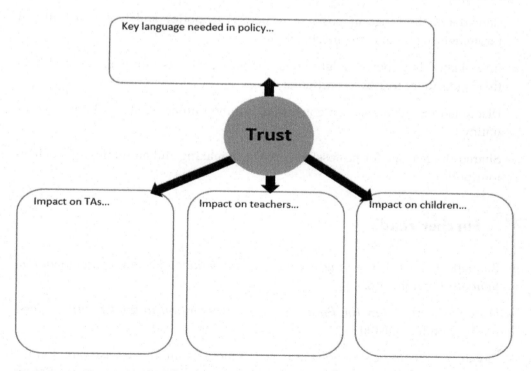

Figure 7.1 How 'trust' in stakeholders can be written into a behaviour policy

Summary

In this chapter, we have considered some of the issues with behaviour policies. These have included the fact that almost all policies are applied idiosyncratically – if they are applied at all. We have seen that policy implementation ranges between total avoidance to total compliance with many staff existing somewhere in the middle. We discussed how the influx of policies in schools means many staff are not as committed to, or aware of, key school polices, such as the behaviour policy, as they could be. The importance of the policy as a living document was noted so it becomes part of the culture and ethos of the school.

The debate between the importance of consistent application and autonomy and professional decision-making were reviewed, with issues of fairness and trust in staff highlighted as key issues to negotiate. When policies expect consistent application by all staff it is essential, if they are based on rewards and sanctions, that all staff can access these equally and easily. If professional decision-making is required, staff need time for discussion and training, particularly TAs who may not have previous training in this area.

 Key points

This chapter has:

- Considered the range of possible responses to policy and that variability in implementing them is the most common

- Investigated how power might affect the way policy is implemented and how this is pertinent to TAs in particular

- Discussed the advantages of consistency in the implementation of a behaviour policy

- Shared the reasons for professional decision-making and autonomy in a behaviour policy

 Further reading

- Bennett, T. (2017). *Creating a Culture: Independent Review of Behaviour in Schools*. London: DfE.

- Ofsted. (2014). *Below the Radar: Low-level Disruption in the Country's Classrooms*. London: Ofsted.

- Payne, R. (2015). Using Rewards and Sanctions in the Classroom: Pupils' Perceptions of their Own Responses to Current Behaviour Management Strategies. *Educational Review, 67*(4), 483–504.

■ Porter, L. (2000). *Behaviour in Schools: Theory and Practice for Teachers.* Buckingham: Open University Press.

References

Ball, S., Hoskins, K., Maguire, M. and Braun, A. (2011). Disciplinary Texts: A Policy Analysis of National and Local Behaviour Policies. *Critical Studies in Education, 52*(1), 1–14.

Bennett, T. (2017). *Creating a Culture: Independent Review of Behaviour in Schools.* London: DfE.

Canter, L. (2010). *Assertive Discipline* (4th ed.). Bloomington: Solution Tree Press.

Carrington, S. (1999). Inclusion Needs a Different School Culture. *International Journal of Inclusive Education, 3*(3), 257–268.

Clarke, D. and Murray, A. (1996). *Developing and Implementing a Whole-School Behaviour Policy.* London: David Fulton Publishers.

Clunies–Ross, P., Little, E. and Kienhuis, M. (2008). Self-reported and Actual Use of Proactive and Reactive Classroom Management Strategies and Their Relationship with Teacher Stress and Student Behaviour. *Educational Psychology, 28*(6), 693–710.

Coburn, C. (2005). The Role of Nonsystem Actors in the Relationship between Policy and Practice: The Case of Reading Instruction in California. *Educational Evaluation and Policy Analysis, 27*(1), 23–52.

Coburn, C. and Stein, M. (2006). Communities of Practice Theory and the Role of Teacher Professional Community in Policy Implementation. In Honig, M. (Ed.), *New Directions In Education Policy Implementation: Confronting Complexity* (pp. 25–47). Albany: State University of New York Press.

Cole, T. (2004). The Development of Provision for Children and Young People "with EBD": Past, Present and Future. In Wearmouth, J., Glynn, T., Richmond, R. and Berryman, M. (Ed.), *Inclusion And Behaviour Management In Schools: Issues And Challenges* (pp. 17–33). London: David Fulton Publishers.

Datnow, A. (2000). Power and Politics in the Adoption of School Reform Models. *Educational Evaluation and Policy Analysis, 22*(4), 357–374. doi:10.3102/01623737022004357

Datnow, A. and Castellano, M. (2000). Teachers' responses to Success for All: how beliefs, experiences, and adaptations shape implementation. *American Educational Research Journal, 37*(3), pp. 775–799.

Datnow, A. and Stringfield, S. (2000). Working Together for Reliable School Reform. *Journal of Education for Students Placed at Risk (JESPAR), 5*(1–2), 183–204.

Department for Education. (2010) *The Importance of Teaching: The Schools White Paper 2010.* London: DfE.

Department for Education. (2011) *Ensuring Good Behaviour in Schools.* London: DfE.

Department for Education. (2013) *Behaviour and Discipline in Schools: Guidance for Governing Bodies.* London: DfE.

Department for Education. (2014) *Mental Health and Behaviour in Schools.* (March). London: DfE.

Department for Education. (2016) *Behaviour and Discipline in Schools: Advice for Headteachers and School Staff.* London: DfE.

Department for Education and Rt Hon Nicky Morgan. (2015). *New Reforms to Raise Standards and Improve Behaviour.* London: DfE.

Department of Education and Science. (1989). *Discipline in Schools. Report of the Committee of Enquiry (Chairman: Lord Elton).* London: DfES.

Galton, M. and MacBeath, J. (2008). *Teachers under Pressure*. London: SAGE Publications Ltd.

Galvin, P. and Costa, P. (1995). Building Better Behaved Schools: Effective Support at the Whole School Level. In Gray, P., Miller, A. and Noakes, J. (Ed.), *Challenging Behaviour in Schools* (pp. 145–163). London: Routledge.

Goodman, J. (2006). School Discipline in Moral Disarray. *Journal of Moral Education, 35*(2), 213–230.

Gray, P. and Noakes, J. (1994). Providing Effective Support to Mainstream Schools: Issues and Stragegies. In Gray, P., Miller, A. and Noakes, J. (Ed.), *Challenging Behaviour in Schools* (pp. 79–90). London: Routledge.

Hallam, S. (2007). Evaluation of Behavioural Management in Schools: A Review of the Behaviour Improvement Programme and the Role of Behaviour and Education Support Teams. *Child and Adolescent Mental Health, 12*(3), 106–112.

Haroun, R. and O'Hanlon, C. (1997). Do Teachers and Students Agree in Their Perception of What School Discipline Is? *Educational Review, 49*(3), 237–250.

Holland, P. and Hammerton, P. (1994). Balancing School and Individual Approaches. In Gray, P., Miller, A. and Noakes, J. (Ed.), *Challenging Behaviour in Schools* (pp. 244–261). London: Routledge.

House of Commons Education Committee. (2011). *Behaviour and Discipline in Schools*. (February), 83. London: DfE.

Lund, R. (1996). *A Whole-School Behaviour Policy: A Practical Guide*. London: Kogan Page Limited.

Maguire, M., Ball, S. and Braun, A. (2010). Behaviour, Classroom Management and Student "Control": Enacting Policy in the English Secondary School. *International Studies in Sociology of Education, 20*(2), 153–170.

McLaughlin, M. (1991). The Rand Change Agent Study: Ten Years Later. In Odden, A. (Ed.), *Educational Policy Implementation* (pp. 143–156). Albany: State University of New York Press.

O'Brien, T. (1998). *Promoting Positive Behaviour*. London: David Fulton Publishers.

Odden, A. (1991). The Evolution of Educational Policy Implementation. In Odden, A. (Ed.), *Educational Policy Implementation* (pp. 1–12). Albany: State University of New York Press.

Ofsted. (2008). *The Deployment, Training and Development of the Wider School Workforce*. London: Ofsted.

Ofsted. (2014). *Below the Radar: Low-level Disruption in the Country's Classrooms*. London: Ofsted.

Payne, R. (2015). Using Rewards and Sanctions in the Classroom: Pupils' Perceptions of Their Own Responses to Current Behaviour Management Strategies. *Educational Review, 67*(4), 483–504.

Porter, L. (2000). *Behaviour in Schools: Theory and Practice for Teachers*. Buckingham: Open University Press.

Radford, J. (2000). Values into Practice: Developing Whole School Behaviour Policies. *Support for Learning, 15*(2), 86–89.

Rowe, D. (2006). Taking Responsibility: School Behaviour Policies in England, Moral Development and Implications for Citizenship Education. *Journal of Moral Education, 35*(4), 519–531.

Sproson, B. (2004). Some Do and Don't: Teacher Effectiveness in Managing Behaviour. In Wearmouth, J., Glynn, T., Richmond, R. and Berryman, M. (Ed.), *Inclusion And Behaviour Management In Schools: Issues And Challenges* (pp. 311–321). London: David Fulton Publishers.

Steer, A. (2005). *Learning Behaviour: The Report of the Practitioners' Group on School Behaviour and Discipline.*London: DfES.

Taylor, C. (2011). *Good Behaviour in Schools: Checklist for Teachers.* London: DfE.

Thomas, G. and Loxley, A. (2001). *Deconstructing Special Education and Constructing Inclusion.* Buckingham: Open University Press.

Turner, C. (2003). How Effective and Inclusive Is the School's Behaviour Policy? *Emotional and Behavioural Difficulties, 8*(1), 7–18.

Visser, J. (2003). *A Study of Children and Young People Who Present Challenging Behaviour – Literature Review.* London: Ofsted.

Visser, J. (2007). Key Factors that Enable the Successful Management of Difficult Behaviour in Schools and Classrooms. *Education 3–13, 33*(1), 26–31.

Visser, J. and Stokes, S. (2010). Is Education Ready for the Inclusion of Pupils with Emotional and Behavioural Difficulties: A Rights Perspective? *Educational Review, 55*(1), 65–75.

Watkins, C. and Wagner, P. (2000). *Improving School Behaviour.* London: Paul Chapman Publishing Ltd.

Wright, C., Weekes, D. and McGlaughlin, A. (2004). Teachers and Pupils – Relationships of Power and Resistance. In Wearmouth, J., Richmond, R., Glynn, T. and Berryman, M. (Ed.), *Understanding Pupil Behaviour in Schools: A Diversity of Approaches* (pp. 67–88). London: David Fulton Publishers.

2CV Research. (2010). *Customer Voice Behaviour and Discipline Powers in Schools.* DfE: London.

Part I

conclusion

The ongoing evolution, and, it could even be said, revolution, of TAs' role has the potential to make significant changes to the way they are used in schools and the types of work they undertake. One of the key changes in TAs' role has been, as Bach, Kessler and Heron (2006) suggested, a move away from ancillary and support roles to curriculum delivery and pedagogical roles. This change from 'paint-pot washers' to 'para-professionals' has had an impact on the expectations of TAs in managing behaviour. Government publications have continued to formalise expectations that with their increasingly pupil-focused, direct teaching work TAs will also play a direct role in behaviour management (DfE, 2012, 2016; DfES, 2006). As we have discussed, these expectations can be difficult to fully incorporate or contextualise due to the pervasive lack of clarity surrounding what TAs actually do; what their role is and is not, and how the roles they do undertake overlap with those expected of a qualified teacher.

Over ten years ago, Kerry (2005) stated that the roles of TAs were not clearly delineated, and that the definitions provided of TAs' expectations were pragmatic and functional rather than grounded in professional appropriateness or a philosophy of education. This remains the case, with much confusion remaining currently about how best to use TAs and manage issues of role-creep. Devecchi, Dettori, Doveston, Sedgwick and Jament (2011) argued that TAs inhabited a 'professional liminal space', the confines of which were 'marked by fluid and contentious personal boundaries'. Blatchford, Russell, Bassett, Brown and Martin (2004) also noted that boundary issues between TAs' pedagogical and other roles was a grey area, with a UNISON survey (2013) more recently describing the complex mix of responsibilities TAs undertake, which included a range of contrasting roles and an overlap between pastoral, pedagogical and administrative duties.

The biggest change, and the one which impacts most on TAs' role in managing behaviour, is their increasing teaching role. A growing range of research (Blatchford, Russell, Bassett, Brown and Martin, 2007; Calder and Grieve, 2004; Trent, 2014; Warhurst, Nickson, Commander and Gilbert, 2014) has demonstrated that in England and Scotland, TAs' 'direct pedagogical role' has – for the last ten years – become greater than time spent helping either the teacher or the school. This suggestion of the delegation of teaching tasks to HLTAs specifically as well as TAs more widely (Blatchford et al., 2007) is not without concerns (Galton and MacBeath, 2008). This blurring of roles between teacher and TA was seen by some as producing a decline in teachers' professional status and this form of 'role creep' has been viewed as a threat to teachers (Blatchford et al., 2007). Blatchford, Russell and Webster (2013) cautioned that much of the expansion of TAs' numbers and role in school had happened in an unplanned way that has not been research-informed. This suggests that, as Kerry (2005) and more recently Graves (2013) and Giangreco (2010) suggested, TAs have been used pragmatically and to buffer the numerous constraints and challenges schools work under rather than through a strategic, informed and considered plan.

Despite, as discussed, a wholesale shift in the role and expectations of TAs, the semantics associated with them have remained, as O'Brien and Garner (2002) suggested, a 'language of domination, manipulation and exclusion'. More recently, Lehane's (2016) study demonstrated that this was still largely the case. Armstrong (2008) had also noted that a marginalisation existed both in schools and in research, with 'devaluing or instrumental' language used to describe TAs' work. This can be seen in some of the research linked to TAs' efficacy in supporting children's academic attainment with suggestions that they were not 'value for money' (Sharples, Webster and Blatchford, 2015), which was challenged by Roffey-Barentsen and Watt (2014) who stated rather, that TAs were 'undervalued for the money they represent'. Although research about efficacy like this can be a very useful source for schools, some crucial thinking is needed before wholly subscribing to it. For example, if TAs only role in the school is to drive academic achievement for specific groups of children, then maybe they are not representing value for money – although one could argue that, in this scenario, neither is the teacher. If the TA role is considered more holistically, the concept of 'value-for-money' might look different. Using alternative definitions of the TA role as 'gluing' a range of people and processes together in schools, or just one of Kerry's (2005, p.378) categories of the TA role where they were expected to be a 'team player, ear lender, achiever, comforter, investigator, negotiator, supervisor, inspirer, story-teller, task setter, analyser, nurturer', makes the idea of not providing 'value-for-money' seem absurd.

 ## Reflection activity

At the end of the first part of the book we have covered a wide range of topics and focused on a broad understanding of who TAs are, what work they might do in relation to managing behaviour and why this could be advantageous and disadvantageous. We have considered how different perspectives on behaviour may cause it to be managed in different ways and how schools' behaviour policies might elicit a range of responses from TAs that could affect how they manage behaviour.

Before we move on to the next part, which considers how key aspects of role definition, role-creep and boundary crossing, as well as how others' views influence the TA role, take some time out to reflect on these questions:

■ Have you read anything that has surprised you?

■ Are there any aspects covered that you would like to find out more about?

■ Are there any of the references you are interested in following up?

■ Have you read anything that has echoed the experiences in your setting or that you have seen or read elsewhere?

■ Are there any changes you would make in your setting or to your own practice in light of anything you have read so far?

References

Armstrong, F. (2008). Inclusive Education. In Richards, G. and Armstrong, F. (Eds.), *Key Issues for Teaching Assistants: Working in Diverse Classrooms* (pp. 7–18). London: Routledge.

Bach, I., Kessler, S. and Heron, P. (2006) Changing Job Boundaries and Workforce Reform: The Case of Teaching Assistants. *Industrial Relations Journal, 37*(1), 2–21.

Blatchford, P., Russell, A. and Webster, R. (2013). *Maximising the Impact of Teaching Assistants: Guidance for School Leaders and Teachers.* Oxon: Routledge.

Blatchford, P., Russell, A., Bassett, P., Brown, P. and Martin, C. (2004). *The Role and Effects of Teaching Assistants in English Primary Schools (Years 4 to 6) 2000–2003: Results from the Class Size and Pupil Adult Ratios (CSPAR) Project. Final Report. (Research Report 605).* London: DfES.

Blatchford, P., Russell, A., Bassett, P., Brown, P. and Martin, C. (2007). The Role and Effects of Teaching Assistants in English Primary Schools (Years 4 to 6) 2000–2003. Results from the Class Size and Pupil–Adult Ratios (CSPAR) KS2 Project. *British Educational Research Journal, 33*(1), 5–26.

Calder, I. and Grieve, A. (2004). Working with Other Adults: What Teachers Need to Know. *Educational Studies, 30*(2), 113–126.

Department for Education and Skills. (2006). *Raising Standards and Tackling Workload Implementing the National Agreement.* Note 17. London: DfES.

Department for Education. (2012). *Pupil Behaviour in Schools in England. Research Report DFE-RR218.* London: DfE.

Department for Education. (2016). *Behaviour and Discipline in Schools: Advice for Headteachers and School Staff.* London: DfE.

Devecchi, C., Dettori, F., Doveston, M., Sedgwick, P. and Jament, J. (2011). Inclusive Classrooms in Italy and England: The Role of Support Teachers and Teaching Assistants. *European Journal of Special Needs Education, 27*(2), 171–184.

Galton, M. and MacBeath, J. (2008). *Teachers under Pressure.* London: SAGE Publications Ltd.

Giangreco, M. (2010). Utilization of Teacher Assistants in Inclusive Schools: Is It the Kind of Help that Helping Is All about? *European Journal of Special Needs Education, 25*(4), 341–345.

Graves, S. (2013). New Roles, Old Stereotypes – Developing a School Workforce in English Schools. *School Leadership & Management*, *34*(3), 255–268.

Kerry, T. (2005). Towards a Typology for Conceptualizing the Roles of Teaching Assistants. *Educational Review*, *57*(3), 373–384.

Lehane, T. (2016). "Cooling the Mark Out": Experienced Teaching Assistants' Perceptions of Their Work in the Inclusion of Pupils with Special Educational Needs in Mainstream Secondary Schools. *Educational Review*, *68*(1), 4–23.

O'Brien, T. and Garner, P. (2002). Tim and Philip's Story: Setting the Record Straight. In O'Brien, T. and Garner, P. (Eds.), *Untold Stories – Learning Support Assistants and Their Work* (pp. 1–10). Stoke on Trent: Trentham Books Ltd.

Roffey-Barentsen, J. and Watt, M. (2014). The Voices of Teaching Assistants (Are We Value for Money?). *Research in Education*, *92*(1), 18–31.

Sharples, J., Webster, R. and Blatchford, P. (2015). *Making Best Use of Teaching Assistants: Guidance Report*. London: Education Endowment Foundation.

Trent, J. (2014). 'I'm Teaching, but I'm Not Really a Teacher'. Teaching Assistants and the Construction of Professional Identities in Hong Kong Schools. *Educational Research*, *56*(1), 28–47.

Warhurst, C., Nickson, D., Commander, J. and Gilbert, K. (2014). 'Role Stretch': Assessing the Blurring of Teaching and Non-teaching in the Classroom Assistant Role in Scotland. *British Educational Research Journal*, *40*(1), 170–186.

Part 2

Part 2

 **8**

A clearly defined TA role and its impact on managing behaviour

The first chapter in Part 2 of this book follows on from the previous sections and will begin to look at some of the specific challenges and opportunities for TAs understanding their role and working with others in school. We will investigate TAs' role and whether the boundaries between what is their own and what is the teachers' work can act to support or constrain their ability to manage behaviour. In the first chapter in this section, we will consider how developing a clear understanding of the work that TAs do and how their role is defined can be advantageous and disadvantageous in relation to managing behaviour. This chapter builds on the discussions begun in Part 1 of the book, and will lead into the third section of the book where we will put together all of the research and theory and in the final section consider what your school or setting can do. In these and the final sections of the book, I will also share what my own research highlighted and how the views of the TAs I worked with and researched resonated with those in other studies.

This chapter will:

- Examine what the term role clarity means
- Investigate how and why TAs' roles in school have been described as multifaceted, and how this can help and hinder TAs' management of behaviour
- Share the challenges in providing TAs with explicit job descriptions
- Review the British government's guidance on TAs' role in English schools

 ## What does the research tell us?

Role clarity relates to a clear and unambiguous understanding of TAs' roles. This includes how they differ, or are discrete from teachers' roles, or where overlaps occur between their roles making an explicit acknowledgement of these. From our discussions in the previous chapters of this book, it has already been suggested that this aspect is far from as simple as it sounds! Although TAs in schools are provided with job descriptions and are employed within a range of pay bands which *should* define the key tasks and roles they are expected to undertake, this does not always translate in practice. Trent (2014) has argued that comprehending what it means to be a TA 'was a challenging task'.

 Pause point

Research suggests there are a range of challenges in outlining all the tasks a TA might undertake as part of their role:

- How many tasks can you list that a TA might fulfil?
- Look at your list – how many of these might a teacher also do?
- How many tasks are you left with that a TA would be asked to do but not a teacher?
- Does this suggest the roles can/should be separated?
- What issues might this overlap or 'role creep' cause?
- What opportunities might this overlap or 'role creep' provide?

To add to the complexity, it is possible that TAs might be employed under a range of pay bands or job titles. For example, it is possible that a TA might be employed (and or deployed) to support a class teacher generally for the first lesson, which might involve working with a group in the classroom under the direction of the teachers to support children consolidating a key skill in maths. In the second lesson of the day, the same TA might work on a specialist one-to-one basis in a range of capacities, for example delivering a specific intervention designed by a speech therapist, with a child until lunchtime. At lunchtime this same TA might take on an additional role working as a mid-day supervisor. After lunch this same TA might work alone with a whole class as a higher level TA (HLTA) delivering a planned lesson, whilst the teacher is working elsewhere as part of their planning, preparation and assessment (PPA) time. For the final lesson of the day, the TA might return to being employed to support a teacher and these duties might include general preparation such as photocopying resources. This wide range of deployments, all of which might happen in a single day make it very difficult to pin down definitively what a TA's role is. In fact, there have been suggestions, which we will consider, that it is not possible to clearly define the role due to this variety. In line with this, it was also argued (Blatchford, Russell and Webster, 2016; Radford, Bosanquet, Webster and Blatchford, 2015) that the British government has purposefully avoided providing explicit guidance in relation to TA and teacher roles, possibly for this very reason.

Advantages and disadvantages of role clarity

The fluidity, as it has been described, in the roles TAs take on has been argued to be a blessing and key advantage; nevertheless, it also has associated disadvantages. Groom and Rose (2005) noted that the greater the uncertainty about the TA role, the less effective the TA was. Moran and Abbott (2002) stated that a crucial ingredient of team success in the working relationship between teachers and TAs was a clear definition of the TA role. Mansaray (2006) suggested that policies devolved to schools can often attempt to impose order on the complexity of both place and space within schools, serving to control and maintain boundaries between teachers and others professionals, including TAs. Thomas (1992) believed that when considering classroom teams, it could be 'downright impossible to discover how roles were formulated'. Tucker (2009) also suggested that TAs' roles were self-determined with a discernible tension felt in discussions to agree future developments of the role. Hancock, Hall, Cable and Eyres's (2010) research similarly found a lack of clear definition of TAs' roles, with their involvement in schools being personally and socially constructed, rather than externally mandated either by policy or, internally, by the senior leadership team (SLT). Additionally, they noted TAs as what they called 'boundary crossers' and stated that within a week or even a day they were repeatedly moving in and out of their own and teachers' roles (Hancock et al., 2010). These views regarding the tensions in defining TAs' role in schools were supported by other research which also showed little uniform understanding, or definition, of teacher–TA role boundaries, despite their significance to the success of the relationship between the two (Butt and Lowe, 2011; Cockroft and Atkinson, 2015; Devecchi and Rouse, 2010; Gerschel, 2005; Mansaray, 2006; Radford et al., 2015; Rose, 2000; Rose and Forlin, 2010; Webster, Blatchford and Russell, 2012).

Sharples, Webster and Blatchford (2015) called for schools to rigorously define the TA role, with Graves (2012) in England, and Giangreco (2010) in the US, asserting that a concomitant redefinition of the teacher role was axiomatic to the discussion. However, it can be seen that providing a clear, unequivocal and fixed definition of the role or roles TAs are anticipated to fulfil in a complex, social and varied school environment is not an easy task. If views that TAs act like the glue holding different people (staff, children, parents) and parts of the school together are to be acted on this might negate writing a black and white list of roles that TAs can undertake. Mansaray (2006) described TAs' role as transitional, incomplete, ambiguous and incoherent, which indicates why producing a clear definition is challenging. Graves (2013) supported this and suggested that TAs' roles, and specifically HLTAs' roles, were chameleon-like, which, she proposed worked against the development of a distinct professional identity. Indeed, Graves (2013) suggested that the role was defined only in the negative; that TAs were *not* teachers which, she argued, obscured what exactly the role *is*.

Pause point

Can you find, either online or from your own setting, a job description for a TA position? Using that, think about:

- How do their roles differ from a teacher?
- Does the job description take into account the 'transitional and ambiguous' aspects of the TA role?
- What improvements might you make?
- What problems and/or opportunities might this create?

Role boundaries, teachers and role-creep

The research currently available may be able to help us consider what the TA role is *not*, but could currently be less helpful when thinking about what the role *does* encompass. Viewing the definition of TAs' role as research has described it, as transitional or chameleon-like, throws into sharp relief some of the issues in defining it. It has been argued that role boundaries between the teacher and the TA should be clear, yet research showed that this was usually not the case (Anderson and Finney, 2008; Blatchford, Russell and Webster, 2013; Devecchi and Rouse, 2010; Mansaray, 2006; Moran and Abbott, 2002; Rose, 2000; Thomas, 1992). The lack of shared or agreed understanding between teachers (and schools more broadly) and TAs, and of TAs' assumed role in school, was suggested to constrain the development of effective relationships with teachers, affecting both TAs' efficacy and status in the classroom (Blatchford et al, 2013; Cajkler and Tennant, 2009; Devecchi and Rouse, 2010; Graves, 2013; Groom and Rose, 2005; Moran and Abbott, 2002).

If expectations over what is the teachers' role and what is the TAs' role when managing behaviour are not clear for either party, it can be suggested that this makes it challenging for TAs to manage behaviour, as they do not have clarity on what their role is, or if managing behaviour is *even* their role. When TAs are working in a range of contexts and with a range of teachers this lack of clarity is compounded. The discussions in published literature and research regarding the lack of role clarity highlights that the absence of a clear, agreed and widely disseminated understanding of the TA role is an issue for both TAs and teachers. Indeed, the lack of role clarity and the associated issues of 'role creep', where teachers' and TAs' roles overlap, were highlighted in much research as a persistent issue for TAs (including, but not only Blatchford et al., 2013, 2016; Devecchi and Rouse, 2010; Harris and Aprile, 2015; Kerry, 2005; Mansaray, 2006; Rose, 2000).

This was a central theme in my own research and had a significant influence on the agency of, and the ability to manage behaviour for the TAs in my study. In line with Blatchford, Russell, Bassett, Brown and Martin's (2007) findings, fluidity in definitions and boundaries within TAs' role caused tensions and was associated with what has been described as the 'messiness of identity construction' (Tucker, 2009). Soini, Pietarinen, Toom and Pyhältö (2015) proposed that for teachers, agency could be understood as identities in motion, where schools offer particular positions and identities for individuals to inhabit. It was argued these positions influenced how teachers acted and engaged (Soini et al., 2015). In their discussion of teacher identity, Biesta, Priestley and Robinson (2015) highlighted how this motion (Soini et al., 2015) resulted in teachers regularly being left confused about their role. This view of the teachers' role as being in motion tallies with previous discussions of TAs' role being fluid and transitional. However, if it is proposed that this is how teachers understand their role, then perhaps defining the TA role is even more problematic, as it experiences even more motion!

TAs have arguably been exposed to substantially more incremental change in their role which, as Giangreco (2010) proposed, has not built upon a theoretically defensible foundation. Tensions in role creep and the boundaries between what is considered teachers' and TAs' roles can be seen to be linked with problems in TAs' agency. From Soini et al.'s (2015) perspective the positions and identities given to TAs by schools and teachers cause them to act in, and engage with, certain ways of managing behaviour. These positions and identifies are in flux, or are unclear, as is the suggestion, it does not support TAs in knowing how they are expected to manage behaviour.

 Pause point

Reflect on the idea of a distinct TA identity:

- How might, or does, your setting support a clear TA identity?
- How has the TA identify changed in your own experience or in your own setting?
- Is having a clearly defined role or identity necessary to manage behaviour?
- Why?
- What might be the issues and opportunities around TA identity?

Burke (2004) suggested that the means of understanding your identity were provided by your location in the social structure. For TAs, we have argued, without clarity or an understanding of their role in the social structure of the school or setting, gaining a clear understanding of their professional identity, and as a result, their role in aspects such as managing behaviour, becomes very difficult. Burke (2004) argued than an understanding of your group identity, of where you fit, professionally and socially, actively helped to sustain the group and maintained the division between in-group and out-group – which in this case would be teachers and TAs. The lack of a clear understanding of their role, and how it relates to that of the teacher, may well, therefore, exacerbate role creep and limit their agency in managing behaviour due to uncertainties about what is expected from them. Challenges in terms of establishing a group identity for TAs were noted as an area where tension exists, both in a wide range of published research as well as in my own findings (Anderson and Finney, 2008; Blatchford et al., 2013; 2016; Devecchi and Rouse, 2010; Devecchi et al., 2011; Graves, 2013; Hancock et al., 2010; Mansaray, 2006; Moran and Abbott, 2002; Roffey-Barentsen and Watt, 2014; Rose, 2000; Thomas, 1992).

In my own research, one of the participating TAs called for clarity in the distinction between the teacher and TA role, whilst another suggested that even within the TA identity there is, as discussed, a great range of variation. She argued that your identity as a TA depends on whether it 'is written down on a piece of paper defining your pay bracket, or whether it's actually what your role is within the school that year'. She went on to highlight the movement within her understanding of her identity, because more changes were made by the school every year and her TA role and identity continued to develop and be fluid. This variable and context-dependent characterisation of the role was a significant site of tension for TAs in my study. Here my TAs suggested this constant motion, where the role changed incrementally or substantially year by year, and for some, term by term, was problematic for them. This meant they never really knew what their role was or could be.

The TAs who took part in my study suggested that the inconsistency they experienced in understanding their role placed them in an awkward position, particularly in relation to managing behaviour. This awkwardness was in part due to challenges in defining their identity and position in managing behaviour relative to that of the teacher when it had been in motion (Biesta et al., 2015; Burke, 2004; Soini et al., 2015; Tucker, 2009). The lack of clear boundaries and consistency between teachers' and TAs' roles in managing behaviour meant that some of the participants in my research felt very responsible for the children they worked with. One TA described herself as taking on aspects of the teacher's role, but repeated that she was a TA, *not* a teacher. This linked with Graves's (2013) research noting the TA role was defined by what it was not – *not* a teacher – rather than what it might be. This was also repeated in the data I collected, where TAs noted that they were very aware their role was not that of a teacher, but did not manage to actually define what their TA role was. This made the clear demarcations TAs in Trent's (2014) research wanted between TAs' and teachers' identities and roles very challenging.

The findings from my research also demonstrated a parallel lack of consistency in TAs' perceptions of how the teachers they worked with understood TAs' role in managing behaviour. In support of Mackenzie's (2011) research showing teachers' views of classroom roles lacked congruence with each other, participants in my research suggested that teachers were largely unaware of the challenges for TAs in managing behaviour. Wenger-Trayner and Wenger-Trayner (2015) also highlighted the potential misunderstandings that resulted from these incongruent and inconsistent perceptions by teachers and others in the school of TAs' role. Conflict was additionally noted in my research with no consistent understanding emerging about what TAs felt their own role in managing behaviour was, supportive of suggestions that definitions of TAs' role were pragmatic (Kerry, 2005) and assumed, as opposed to distinct (Thomas, 1992). It was suggested (Mansaray, 2006) that although the lack of role clarity and boundary-crossing between the teacher and TA role was a site of tension for both TAs and teachers, it was not seen as problematic for children, with the suggestion that distinctions between the roles go largely unnoticed in the classroom.

 Pause point

Why might teachers and TAs have different understandings of the TA role in managing behaviour?

- Have you seen any examples of this in your setting?
- What issues might this lack of understanding have?
- How might this impact on the teacher(s)?
- How might this impact on the TA(s)?
- How might it impact on the children's behaviour?

What this might mean in school

In this chapter we have consolidated our understanding of TAs' roles. We have seen that it is very difficult to capture the range and complexity of their roles in a job description. We have also seen how roles change incrementally year by year, or even term by term for some TAs in some contexts.

1. **Job descriptions can rarely encompass the diversity of roles TAs fulfil in schools. Care needs to be given to how TAs understand what is expected of them if their job descriptions are only part of the picture or are out of date.**

In line with this, we also discussed how the TAs in my own research saw their job descriptions as unreflective of the range of roles they were expected to undertake in school and as not keeping up with the evolution of their roles year on year.

2. **Annual reviews can be useful for TAs to give them a platform to discuss their progress and needs as well as reviewing and discussing expectations of their role(s) in school if these have changed or developed over the year.**

It has been suggested that many TAs' roles in school are socially, as opposed to institutionally, constructed and that within the same day they may move in and out of the 'teacher' role. Schools need to consider how they see the TA role, and whether this changes from individual to individual or is a static and fixed identity. When ideas about what it means to be a TA in the context of this school, year group, one-to-one and so on have been considered, careful thought needs to be given to how this message is shared both directly and indirectly with all staff.

3. **It has been suggested that TAs often understand their role from social rather than institutional information. Consideration needs to be given to what the school sees TAs' role to be strategically and how social interactions support and develop this strategic vision.**

In order for TAs to receive consistent messages from all staff about the range of roles they could fulfil, even when these are variable or context dependent, time needs to be provided for teachers and TAs to meet together and discuss these expectations to ensure they all have an agreed understanding of the way the school may ask TAs to work.

4. **Time needs to be protected for teachers and TAs to meet together and develop a shared understanding, guided by the school, about the roles TAs may undertake.**

 Reflection activity

This chapter builds on the discussion that we began in Chapter 5, on the boundaries of what is and what is not a TAs' work. Can you add some ideas to the diagram shown in Figure 8.1 about where the boundaries between the roles a teacher undertakes and the roles a TA undertakes lie and where crossovers might occur?

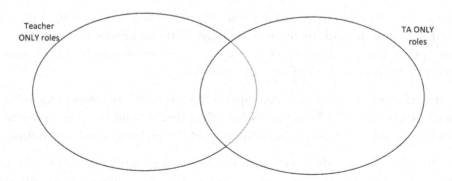

Figure 8.1 The differences and similarities between the teacher and TA role

It would be interesting, if possible, to work with friends and colleagues in other age phases, classes or settings to see if the boundaries they identify are different. For example, would the boundaries of each professional's role be the same or different in a Reception class, a class in a special school (i.e. one for children with profound and multiple learning difficulties, a pupil referral unit etc.) and a Year 6 class?

If you have identified differences between settings, colleagues' ideas, teacher's and TAs' views what steps might need to be taken – if any – to move forward?

 ## Summary

In this chapter we have looked in more detail about the issues in defining TAs' roles, specifically when working with or 'under the direction' of the teacher (DfE, 2011). We have developed the discussion we began back in Chapter 5 and I have included the voices of the TAs in my research to add a personal aspect to the wider body of research findings.

We have discussed the impact of what has been argued to be a necessary flexibility, or motion in definitions, of the TA role. However, although this allows them to work between the spaces or formal structures in schools, gluing different groups together, it also has challenges. The key challenges my TAs reported, and which were also shown in research, is that when their role keeps changing and flowing it makes it difficult to develop a professional identity and know where they fit in schools. This also makes it very difficult to understand how their role is separate and different from that of teachers. Without a clear understanding of their identity as TAs and what their role is they find it difficult to know who they are as professionals and, as a result, what they can do.

 ## Key points

This chapter has:

- Investigated why role clarity can be so difficult to define for TAs

- Discussed the advantages and disadvantages of a static definition of TAs' roles in schools

- Revisited the tensions TAs might experience in working across boundaries

- Shared problems in the construction of a clear TA identity

- Considered the issues that inconsistent understandings of their role in school may create in terms of TAs' actions to manage behaviour

Further reading

- Blatchford, P., Russell, A. and Webster, R. (2016). *Maximising the Impact of Teaching Assistants: Guidance for School Leaders and Teachers* (2nd ed.). London: Routledge.

- Richards, G. and Armstrong, F. (Eds.), *Key Issues for Teaching Assistants: Working in Diverse Classrooms*. London: Routledge.

- Webster, R., Blatchford, P. and Russell, A. (2012). Challenging and Changing How Schools Use Teaching Assistants: Findings from the Effective Deployment of Teaching Assistants Project. *School Leadership & Management*, 33(1), 78–96.

References

Anderson, V. and Finney, M. (2008). I'm a TA Not a PA! In Richards, G. and Armstrong, F. (Eds.), *Key Issues for Teaching Assistants: Working in Diverse Classrooms* (pp. 73–83). London: Routledge.

Biesta, G., Priestley, M. and Robinson, S. (2015). The Role of Beliefs in Teacher Agency. *Teachers and Teaching: Theory and Practice*, *21*(6), 624–640.

Blatchford, P., Russell, A. and Webster, R. (2013). *Maximising the Impact of Teaching Assistants*. London: Routledge.

Blatchford, P., Russell, A. and Webster, R. (2016). *Maximising the Impact of Teaching Assistants: Guidance for School Leaders and Teachers* (2nd ed.). London: Routledge.

Blatchford, P., Russell, A., Bassett, P., Brown, P. and Martin, C. (2007). The Role and Effects of Teaching Assistants in English Primary Schools (Years 4 to 6) 2000–2003. Results from the Class Size and Pupil–Adult Ratios (CSPAR) KS2 Project. *British Educational Research Journal*, *33*(1), pp. 5–26.

Burke, P. (2004). Identities and Social Structure: The 2003 Cooley-Mead Award Address. *Social Psychology Quarterly*, *67*(1), 5–15.

Butt, R. and Lowe, K. (2011). Teaching Assistants and Class Teachers: Differing Perceptions, Role Confusion and the Benefits of Skills-based Training. *International Journal of Inclusive Education*, *16*(2), 207–219.

Cajkler, W. and Tennant, G. (2009). Teaching Assistants and Pupils' Academic and Social Engagement in Mainstream Schools: Insights from Systematic Literature Reviews. *International Journal of Emotional Education*, *1*(2), 71–90.

Cockroft, C. and Atkinson, C. (2015). Using the Wider Pedagogical Role Model to Establish Learning Support Assistants' Views about Facilitators and Barriers to Effective Practice. *Support for Learning*, *30*(2), 88–104.

Department for Education. (2011). *Ensuring Good Behaviour in Schools*. London: DfE. Retrieved from Apps.Bps.Org.Uk.

Devecchi, C. and Rouse, M. (2010). An Exploration of the Features of Effective Collaboration between Teachers and Teaching Assistants in Secondary Schools. *Support for Learning*, *25*(2), 91–99.

Gerschel, L. (2005). The Special Educational Needs Coordinator's Role in Managing Teaching Assistants: The Greenwich Perspective. *Support for Learning, 20*(2), 69–76.

Giangreco, M. (2010). Utilization of Teacher Assistants in Inclusive Schools: Is It the Kind of Help that Helping Is All about? *European Journal of Special Needs Education, 25*(4), 341–345.

Graves, S. (2012). Chameleon or Chimera? The Role of the Higher Level Teaching Assistant (HLTA) in a Remodelled Workforce in English Schools. *Educational Management Administration & Leadership, 41*(1), 95–104.

Graves, S. (2013). New Roles, Old Stereotypes – Developing a School Workforce in English Schools. *School Leadership & Management, 34*(3), 255–268.

Groom, B. and Rose, R. (2005). Supporting the Inclusion of Pupils with Social, Emotional and Behavioural Difficulties in the Primary School: The Role of Teaching Assistants. *Journal of Research in Special Educational Needs, 5*(1), 20–30.

Hancock, R., Hall, T., Cable, C. and Eyres, I. (2010). 'They Call Me Wonder Woman': The Job Jurisdictions and Work-related Learning of Higher Level Teaching Assistants. *Cambridge Journal of Education, 40*(2), 97–112.

Harris, L. and Aprile, K. (2015). 'I Can Sort of Slot into Many Different Roles': Examining Teacher Aide Roles and Their Implications for Practice. *School Leadership & Management, 35*(2), 140–162.

Kerry, T. (2005). Towards a Typology for Conceptualizing the Roles of Teaching Assistants. *Educational Review, 57*(3), 373–384.

Mackenzie, S. (2011). "Yes, but…": Rhetoric, Reality and Resistance in Teaching Assistants' Experiences of Inclusive Education. *Support for Learning, 26*, 64–71.

Mansaray, A. (2006). Liminality and In/Exclusion: Exploring the Work of Teaching Assistants. *Pedagogy, Culture & Society, 14*(2), 171–187.

Moran, A. and Abbott, L. (2002). Developing Inclusive Schools: The Pivotal Role of Teaching Assistants in Promoting Inclusion in Special and Mainstream Schools in Northern Ireland. *European Journal of Special Needs Education, 17*(2), 161–173.

Radford, J., Bosanquet, P., Webster, R. and Blatchford, P. (2015). Scaffolding Learning for Independence: Clarifying Teacher and Teaching Assistant Roles for Children with Special Educational Needs. *Learning and Instruction, 36*, 1–10.

Roffey-Barentsen, J. and Watt, M. (2014). The Voices of Teaching Assistants (Are We Value for Money?). *Research in Education, 92*(1), 18–31.

Rose, R. (2000). Using Classroom Support in a Primary School: A Single School Case Study. *British Journal of Special Education, 27*(4), 191–196.

Rose, R. and Forlin, C. (2010). Impact of Training on Change in Practice for Education Assistants in a Group of International Private Schools in Hong Kong. *International Journal of Inclusive Education, 14*(3), 309–323.

Sharples, J., Webster, R. and Blatchford, P. (2015). *Making Best Use of Teaching Assistants: Guidance Report.* London: Education Endowment Foundation.

Soini, T., Pietarinen, J., Toom, A. and Pyhältö, K. (2015). What coCntributes to First-year Student Teachers' Sense of Professional Agency in the Classroom? *Teachers and Teaching, 21*(6), 641–659.

Thomas, G. (1992). *Effective Classroom Teamwork: Support or Intrusion?* London: Routledge.

Trent, J. (2014). 'I'm Teaching, but I'm Not Really a Teacher'. Teaching Assistants and the Construction of Professional Identities in Hong Kong Schools. *Educational Research, 56*(1), 28–47.

Tucker, S. (2009). Perceptions and Reflections on the Role of the Teaching Assistant in the Classroom Environment. *Pastoral Care in Education, 27*(4), 291–300.

Webster, R., Blatchford, P. and Russell, A. (2012). Challenging and Changing How Schools Use Teaching Assistants: Findings from the Effective Deployment of Teaching Assistants Project. *School Leadership & Management, 33*(1), 78–96.

Wenger-Trayner, E. and Wenger-Trayner, B. (2015). Learning in a Landscape of Practice. In Wenger-Trayner, E., Fenton-O-Creevy, M., Hutchinson, S., Kubiak, C. and Wenger-Trayner, B. (Eds.), *Learning in Landscapes of Practice: Boundaries, Identity and Knowledgeability in Practice-based Learning* (pp. 13–30). Oxon: Routledge.

Others' views of the TA role and their impact on TAs

In the previous chapter (Chapter 8), we considered the challenges in categorically defining TAs' role(s), particularly now that TAs are often defined – in research at least – as para-professionals. Recurring issues around role clarity, role-creep and the boundaries in general between what is, and what is not, TAs' work, have not been made any clearer by this more up-to-date view of TAs. Watson, Bayliss and Pratchett (2013) suggested that the term papa-professional, rather than being advantageous, in fact alluded to TAs as *not* professional. This is because they suggested 'para' implies '*be-coming* or *not-quite* professional' rather than helping TAs to be seen as professionals in their own right. This chapter will continue and develop the points from the previous chapters (Chapters 5 and 7) looking at how TAs' unclear and challenging professional boundaries influence their work with others, including children and teachers. We will consider how the lack of clear limits to what is the TA's role and what is the teacher's, influences TAs' ability to manage behaviour in a range of significant ways – both positively and negatively.

This chapter will:

■ Consider how children view the role of the TA

■ Investigate how any differences children identify impact on TAs' ability to manage behaviour

■ Develop previous discussions on issues of role-creep and how it can influence the teacher and the TA when managing behaviour

■ Discuss how teachers might perceive the role of the TA

■ Reflect on how teacher's understandings might impact on TAs' role in managing behaviour

What does the research tell us?

Children's views on TAs

Research (Blatchford, Russell, Bassett, Brown and Martin, 2004) suggests that children were able to identify differences between the roles of teachers and TAs by working patterns, often thinking of TAs as working solely with individuals or groups, whilst the teacher worked with the whole class. In Bland and Sleightholme's (2012) research, these differences were evident, with children noting not TAs' pedagogical or other roles but that they were required to 'fetch coffee and biscuits for the teacher' as well as 'keep an eye on them [the teacher] all the time'! Other research (Eyres, Cable, Hancock and Turner, 2004; Fraser and Meadows, 2008) found that all children, even if they had trouble articulating it, were aware of differences, not only in roles, but in status and power, between the teacher and other adults – who they viewed as '"just" assistants'. This was differentiated by children's view of the class teacher's role as a manager and that 'teachers "tell" while TAs "help"' (Eyres et al., 2004; Fraser and Meadows, 2008). However, despite their understanding of difference between teachers and TAs, Eyres et al. (2004) suggested that children did not see the delineation in roles as clear divisions in labour due to the 'great deal of overlap and interchange' between the teacher and TA roles (as we have discussed in Chapters 7 and 8).

The data collected from my research also suggested that some children could distinguish a difference between teachers' and TAs' status and power, if not roles. Data from my TA participants suggested that about half believed children saw the TA and teacher role with parity, whilst the other half suggested children were less respectful in their treatment of TAs compared to that of teachers. These views were split along Key Stage (KS) lines, with most responses attributing a lack of respect for TAs' role to older KS2 (seven- to eleven-year-old) children. Findings from Mistry, Burton and Brundrett (2004) also noted that TAs in their study showed a marked reluctance to being deployed with older children, due in part to what was perceived as their more challenging behaviour. This difference in status between the teacher and the TA may impact negatively on TAs' ability to manage behaviour, as research suggests they can be seen as less of an authority figure than the teacher (Cajkler and Tennant, 2009).

In my study when I asked TAs how they thought children perceived their role in relation to managing behaviour, one of my participating TAs noted that she was often called 'mum'. This supported Graves's (2013) findings that TAs assumed a maternal as opposed to a teaching role (something we began to discuss in Chapter 5). Other references to mothering were also made in my study, where a TA suggested that some of her behaviour management strategies were the same as those she used with her own children at home. This reflected Galton and MacBeath's (2008) findings, which suggested that TAs rely on maternal experience as opposed to any external behaviour specific training. The demographic of TAs participating in my research met the recruitment strategy noted by Bach, Kessler and Heron (2006) of mums making the shift to TAs. This alludes to further issues with a clearly defined professional role for TAs as this form of progression was perceived to constrain TAs' claims to being part of a professional community. This is due to their persisting historical (if inaccurate) identity as 'parent helpers' (Graves, 2013) as opposed to professionals who are part of the school culture. In addition, the gendered perspective that describes TAs' roles in research and their association with mothering, Graves (2013) argued, had associated issues in measuring their contributions. This difficulty in quantifying TAs' contributions without a clearly defined role or job description was evident in the dichotomies that existed, with schools suggesting they would be unable to function without TAs (Cockroft and Atkinson, 2015; UNISON, 2013), yet research calling into question their 'value for money' (Sharples, Webster and Blatchford, 2015).

 Pause point

Some research has questioned whether TAs are 'value for money'. Think about:

- What are the issues in thinking about a group of staff in this way?

- Why might it be necessary to justify 'value for money'?

- How might you begin to provide a rationale to an outside stakeholder in how TAs' work in school might be 'value for money'?

It was also suggested schools cannot function without TAs. If your setting (or a setting you know of) suddenly lost all its TAs:

- What would be the first changes that might be seen?

- What aspects of school life would be most affected?

Teachers' views on TAs

Hammersley-Fletcher and Qualter (2009) found that how teachers choose to see themselves influenced their expectations of the TAs they worked with. This ranged from teachers either viewing themselves as the only ones who could meet pupils' needs by being in control of the classroom, or by taking, as suggested by Hammersley-Fletcher and Qualter (2009), a more 'expanded view of professionalism'. This 'expanded' view included an openness to teamwork and collaboration. It can be suggested that if teachers saw themselves as ultimately in control of their classroom they might intentionally limit, or specifically direct, what they expected TAs to do. Conversely, if they were working with an 'expanded view' they might see themselves and the TA working together as a team and being open to TAs taking a more active role alongside the teacher. This reflects the findings from research by Quicke (2003) and Cockroft and Atkinson (2015) who considered teachers' own views were a key influence on the roles TAs were able to fulfil. This also mirrors our previous discussions about the variation in roles TAs fulfil and how these are more often socially and relationally constructed – devised either explicitly or implicitly between the TA and the people they work with – than made clear through job descriptions. Thomas (1992) suggested that collaboration and team-work between the teacher and TA in the classroom was challenging due to their 'different backgrounds, ideologies, skills and interests'. He highlighted factors which mediated the success, or otherwise, of the team, including:

> the quality of leadership; role definition and role ambiguity; the nature of the task to be undertaken; the mix of team members; the ease with which team members can communicate.
>
> (Thomas, 1992, p.8)

 Pause point

Thomas (1992) suggested that successful teamwork between teachers and TAs relied on a range of factors which are difficult to centralise and legislate for. Think about:

■ Should teachers' and TAs' different skills be considered as part of whole-school planning when organising who works together?

■ Should teachers' ideologies impact on how they work with TAs?

■ What might the advantages of this be?

■ What might the disadvantages be?

Eteläpelto, Vähäsantanen and Hökkä (2015) found from their research that when coping with managing behaviour at the classroom level, teachers 'saw their colleagues as one of the most important resources'. This suggests that TAs can be seen by some teachers as a source of support in the classroom. Other research also found that as well as providing an improvement in children's learning outcomes, increased support for learning and teaching, and improved classroom management (Blatchford et al., 2004; Blatchford, Russell and Webster, 2012; Neill, 2002; Sharples et al., 2015), teachers stated that having a TA present increased their confidence and ability 'to cope' (Galton and MacBeath, 2008). Johnson's (2010) research on teacher collaboration also confirmed that teachers reported 'important emotional and psychological benefits' to working in teams, with respondents citing that the support given and received when working with TAs was important.

Johnson's (2010) research concluded that 'interpersonal relationships' were responsible for either 'inhibiting or promoting critical collaboration'. Eteläpelto et al. (2015) also found 'the quality of peer relations' impacted on 'professional agency'. This again suggests that the relationship the teacher is able to form with the TA or TAs they work with influences the role(s) they play in the classroom.

Barkham (2008) highlighted the importance of what she described as, 'personal friendships' in mediating any 'tensions' in teacher–TA collaboration. However, it could be argued that TAs should not need to rely on friendships to work with a range of teachers, or vice versa. This reliance on getting along with people would not be seen as an appropriate or professional response to other aspects of school life, but it perhaps serves to illustrate the lack of opportunities TAs have to engage in professional dialogue and could be seen as an example of their 'marginalisation' from schools, as noted previously.

Research indicates that TAs' role clarity, training and deployment as well as institutional factors such as whole-school approaches, social practices and power all influence the way in which teachers view TAs and, as a result, the way in which teachers and TAs collaborate and work together, if they work together at all. Although a simplistic model might be easy to produce to show how teachers view and therefore work with TAs, it may be more realistic to consider the research findings on teachers' views of TAs and TA–teacher relationships and models of working together as existing on a continuum or spectrum. At one end of this spectrum – a wide range of research shows, teachers' view TAs as a source of 'tension' and 'antagonism'. From this perspective working together is a burden, due to the complexity of interpersonal and professional uncertainties and the lack of clarity between roles and responsibilities (Anderson and Finney, 2008; Hammersley-Fletcher and Qualter, 2009; Johnson, 2010; Mackenzie, 2011; Tucker, 2009; Wilson and Bedford, 2008). Working with TAs at this end of the spectrum includes an increased workload because the teacher's view of the TA is hierarchical and managerialist, where they are working clearly under the direction of the teacher. This keeps the TA peripheral and at the margins, as an apprentice, or even 'servant' to the teacher (Dunne, Goddard and Woolhouse, 2008; HMI, 2002; Howes, 2003; Mansaray, 2006; Quicke, 2003; Wilson and Bedford, 2008). This view results in TAs often being passive and waiting for instructions and directions from the teachers as opposed to using their own initiative. At this extreme end of the continuum, TAs may struggle to take an active role in managing behaviour and their scope for making professional decisions in relation to behaviour would be highly constrained.

If the TA–teacher relationship was described at the other end of the continuum it would include the benefits of collaborative teamwork, a close working partnership and moral support, as well as enhancing children's behaviour (Blatchford et al., 2012; HMI, 2002; Johnson, 2010; Neill, 2002; Sharples et al., 2015; Webster, Blatchford, Bassett, Brown, Martin and Russell, 2010). Communication and time to reflect and involve TAs in planning and preparation would result in a meaningful understanding of TAs' role. As a result, the fuzzy boundaries between teachers' and TAs' roles and the fluidity to support both the teacher and children would be an advantage rather than a limitation (Devecchi, Dettori, Doveston, Sedgwick and Jament, 2011; Gerschel, 2005; Groom, 2006; Mansaray, 2006; Marr, Turner, Swann and Hancock, 2002; Rose, 2000; Sharples et al., 2015; Webster, Blatchford, Bassett,

Brown and Russell, 2011; Webster, Blatchford and Russell, 2012). This was rein-forced by Datnow (2011) who noted that truly collaborative working was defined by interactions that were 'knowledgeable and assertive' as opposed to being 'con-genial and complacent'. O'Brien and Garner (2002) believed, given the right cir-cumstances, co-operation between teachers and TAs could develop into an ideal relationship where TAs:

> were partners in a meaningful, formative enterprise rather than having a walk-on part in an educational drama (or in some regrettable cases being employed simply to paint the scenery).
>
> (p.3)

These two descriptions of how teacher's perceptions of TAs might influence their role in the classrooms are at the extreme ends of the continuum and in reality, many teachers will occupy much more of a middle ground between these two polar opposites. However, it is important to be aware how the perceptions of TAs and relationships between teachers and TAs can influence TAs' roles in the class-room and their ability to manage behaviour.

Reflection activity

The preceding discussion has considered how teachers' self-perception influences how they work with TAs – consciously or subconsciously. The Teachers' Standards (Department for Education, 2013) document that governs the professional expec-tation of all trainee and qualified teachers in England, refers to the teachers' role to 'deploy support staff effectively'. The word *deploy* here is open to a range of interpretations.

The table in Figure 9.1 details a range of management styles that a teacher might reasonably use to *deploy* a TA in their class. Using the table, begin to think, after read-ing this chapter, about what different outcomes each management style, or deploy-ment, might result in, and how these might influence TAs' professional agency and their actions to manage behaviour in the classroom. Whilst completing this table reflect on the TAs' aim in my research to help and support the teacher in managing behaviour. Which style of deployment might support TAs in meeting their aim?

What this might mean in school

The research considered in this chapter suggests that even though it is rarely made explicit by the teacher or TA, children are able to perceive differences in their roles. Although this is not specifically problematic it, can lead to issues of dimin-ished power and status for TAs, which can, in turn, mean it is more difficult for them to manage behaviour or that they are more reluctant to manage behaviour from this position.

Leadership style	Example	You might say...	You aim to develop...	Could this increase or decrease professional agency?	How might TAs approach to managing behaviour be affected?
VISIONARY	Vision focused and motivational	'Come with me on this'	Self-confidence, empathy and change		
COACHING	Developing capacity in people for the future	'Let's try this'	Developing others, self-awareness and empathy		
AFFILIATIVE	Developing harmony and personal relationships	'People come first'	Empathy, relationships and communication		
DEMOCRATIC	Develops consensus through encouraging participation	'What do you think?'	Collaboration, team leadership and communication		
PACESETTING	Develops rigorous standards for performance	'Do as I do'	Conscientiousness, drive and initiative		
COMMANDING	Demands immediate compliance	'Do what I tell you'	Drive, initiative and control		

Figure 9.1 The impact of leadership styles on TAs
Amended from Goleman, D. (2000) Leadership that Gets Results. *Harvard Business Review.* March–April. pp. 82–83.

1. **Care needs to be given to considering how messages about TAs' status are conveyed, both explicitly and implicitly. If TAs are only perceived as 'helpers' they may struggle to manage some behaviours.**

We also considered how teachers own views about their role in the classroom affect how they perceive TAs. This variation in perception of what is the TA's role and what is the teacher's, can make it challenging for TAs to develop a consistent understanding of what roles they can and should fulfil when working with different teachers.

2. **When working with a range of teachers, TAs and teachers need time to talk to together to develop an understanding of how best to work with each other and what roles the TA might fulfil.**

The research we have discussed in this chapter also points to some of the advantages of teachers working collaboratively with TAs. If TAs and teachers are to experience the emotional support and improvements in behaviour that research suggests can develop from working together, schools need to provide effective structures to enhance the collegial aspects of the TA–teacher relationship.

3. **Times and space need to be explicitly planned in for TAs and teachers to develop collegial relationships to effectively support improvements in behaviour as well as to offer support to each other.**

These suggestions are based on the assumption that the school or setting would like teachers and TAs to work as part of a team. Research suggest that there is often an automatic assumption that adults can work together and that when they do, it is a 'Good Thing'. Schools and settings need to make a clear decision (rather than an unspoken assumption) about how they would like adults to work together. This could be under the managerialist model where teachers actively deploy TAs and TAs take their lead from the teacher, or the collegial model where TAs and teachers make (some) joint decisions on classroom management. It might also be a pragmatic combination of these two models depending on teachers' and TAs' personalities, skills and dispositions. Each of these strategies comes with a range of advantages and disadvantages; however, if the school as a whole has a clear idea of how it expects adults to work together steps can be taken to limit the disadvantages and maximise the advantages. Problems are more difficult to manage when assumptions about working styles have been made but not clearly communicated with TAs and teachers.

4. **Schools need to clearly communicate expectations on how TAs and teachers will work together.**

 # Summary

In this chapter, we have considered how children's and teachers' understanding of the TA role impact on the working relationships formed and on the roles TAs undertake. We discussed how children might not be able to distinguish between teachers and TAs in terms of the roles they undertake but can see differences between them in terms of power and status. Children's views of TAs having less power and status than teachers can make it difficult for TAs to manage behaviour.

We also considered how teachers' beliefs about their own role influence the way in which they work with TAs. This was considered to be on a spectrum ranging broadly from the teacher being in control and directing the TA, to the TA and teacher working together as a team. When reflecting on what this might mean in school, we also noted the importance of not assuming that adults could work well, or easily, together and how explicit messages, rather than assumptions about ways of working, might be needed.

This chapter has:

- Investigated how children's and teacher's perception of TAs impact on the roles they undertake

- Considered how children's view of TAs as having less power and status than teachers might affect how they manage behaviour

- Reflected on how teachers' own understanding of their role affects how they work with TAs

- Discussed the continuum of teachers work with TAs as ranging from control to collaboration

📚 Further reading

- Blatchford, P., Russell, A. and Webster, R. (2012). *Reassessing the Impact of Teaching Assistants*. Oxon: Routledge.

- Goleman, D. (2000) Leadership that Gets Results. *Harvard Business Review*. March-April. pp. 82–83.

- O'Brien, T. and Garner, P. (2002). Tim and Philip's Story: Setting the Record Straight. In O'Brien, T. and Garner, P. (Eds.), *Untold Stories – Learning Support Assistants And Their Work* (pp. 1–10). Stoke on Trent: Trentham Books Ltd.

References

Anderson, V. and Finney, M. (2008). I'm a TA Not a PA! In Richards, G. and Armstrong, F. (Eds.), *Key Issues for Teaching Assistants: Working in Diverse Classrooms* (pp. 73–83). London: Routledge.

Bach, I., Kessler, S. and Heron, P. (2006). Changing Job Boundaries and Workforce Reform: The Case of Teaching Assistants. *Industrial Relations Journal*, *37*(1), 2–21.

Barkham, J. (2008). Suitable Work for Women? Roles, Relationships and Changing Identities of 'Other Adults' in the Early Years Classroom. *British Educational Research Journal*, *34*(6), 839–853.

Bland, K. and Sleightholme, S. (2012). Researching the Pupil Voice: What Makes a Good Teaching Assistant? *Support for Learning*, *27*(4), 172–176.

Blatchford, P., Russell, A., Bassett, P., Brown, P. and Martin, C. (2004). *The Role and Effects of Teaching Assistants in English Primary Schools (Years 4 to 6) 2000 – 2003: Results from the Class Size and Pupil Adult Ratios (CSPAR) Project. Final Report. (Research Report 605)*. London: DfES.

Blatchford, P., Russell, A. and Webster, R. (2012). *Reassessing the Impact of Teaching Assistants*. Oxon: Routledge.

Cajkler, W. and Tennant, G. (2009). Teaching Assistants and Pupils' Academic and Social Engagement in Mainstream Schools: Insights from Systematic Literature Reviews. *International Journal of Emotional Education*, *1*(2), 71–90.

Cockroft, C. and Atkinson, C. (2015). Using the Wider Pedagogical Role Model to Establish Learning Support Assistants' Views about Facilitators and Barriers to Effective Practice. *Support for Learning*, *30*(2), 88–104.

Datnow, A. (2011). Collaboration and Contrived Collegiality: Revisiting Hargreaves in the Age of Accountability. *Journal of Educational Change*, *12*(2), 147–158.

Department for Education. (2013). *Teachers' Standards*. (June), 1–11. London: DfE. Retrieved from https://www.gov.uk/government/publications/teachers-standards

Devecchi, C., Dettori, F., Doveston, M., Sedgwick, P. and Jament, J. (2011). Inclusive Classrooms in Italy and England: The Role of Support Teachers and Teaching Assistants. *European Journal of Special Needs Education*, *27*(2), 171–184.

Dunne, L., Goddard, G. and Woolhouse, C. (2008). Teaching Assistants' Perceptions of Their Professional Role and Their Experiences of Doing a Foundation Degree. *Improving Schools*, *11*(3), 239–249.

Eteläpelto, A., Vähäsantanen, K. and Hökkä, P. (2015). How Do Novice Teachers in Finland Perceive Their Professional Agency? *Teachers and Teaching*, *21*(6), 660–680.

Eyres, I., Cable, C., Hancock, R. and Turner, J. (2004). 'Whoops, I Forgot David': Children's Perceptions of the Adults Who Work in Their Classrooms. *Early Years*, *24*(2), 149–162.

Fraser, C. and Meadows, S. (2008). Children's Views of Teaching Assistants in Primary Schools. *Education 3-13*, *36*(4), 351–363.

Galton, M. and MacBeath, J. (2008). *Teachers under Pressure*. London: SAGE Publications Ltd.

Gerschel, L. (2005). The Special Educational Needs Coordinator's Role in Managing Teaching Assistants: The Greenwich Perspective. *Support for Learning*, *20*(2), 69–76.

Goleman, D. (2000) Leadership that Gets Results. *Harvard Business Review*. March-April. pp. 82–83.

Graves, S. (2013). New Roles, Old Stereotypes – Developing a School Workforce in English Schools. *School Leadership & Management*, *34*(3), 255–268.

Groom, B. (2006). Building Lelationships for Learning: The Developing Role of the Teaching Assistant. *Support for Learning*, *21*(4), 199–203.

Hammersley-Fletcher, L. and Qualter, A. (2009). Chasing Improved Pupil Performance: The Impact of Policy Change on School Educators' Perceptions of Their Professional Identity, the Case of Further Change in English Schools. *British Educational Research Journal*, *36*(6), 903–917.

HMI. (2002). *Teaching Assistants in Primary Schools an Evaluation of the Quality and Impact of Their Work*. London: HMI.

Howes, A. (2003). Teaching Reforms and the Impact of Paid Adult Support on Participation and Learning in Mainstream Schools. *Support for Learning*, *18*(4), 147–153.

Johnson, B. (2010). Teacher collaboration: Good for Some, Not so Good for Others. *Educational Studies*, *29*(4), 337–350.

Mackenzie, S. (2011). "Yes, but…": Rhetoric, Reality and Resistance in Teaching Assistants' Experiences of Inclusive Education. *Support for Learning*, *26*, 64–71.

Mansaray, A. (2006). Liminality and In/Exclusion: Exploring the Work of Teaching Assistants. *Pedagogy, Culture & Society*, *14*(2), 171–187.

Marr, A., Turner, J., Swann, W. and Hancock, R. (2002). *Classroom Assistants in the Pimary School: Employment and Deployment*. Milton Keynes: Open University.

Mistry, M., Burton, N. and Brundrett, M. (2004). Managing LSAs: An Evaluation of the Use of Learning Support Assistants in an Urban Primary School. *School Leadership & Management*, *24*(2), 125–137.

Neill, S. (2002). *Teaching Assistants: A Survey Analysed for the NUT*. London: University of Warwick/National Union of Teachers.

O'Brien, T. and Garner, P. (2002). Tim and Philip's Story: Setting the Record Straight. In O'Brien, T. and Garner, P. (Eds.), *Untold Stories – Learning Support Assistants And Their Work* (pp. 1–10). Stoke on Trent: Trentham Books Ltd.

Quicke, J. (2003). Teaching Assistants: Students or Servants? *FORUM*, *45*(2), 71–74.

Rose, R. (2000). Using Classroom Support in a Primary School: A Single School Case Study. *British Journal of Special Education*, *27*(4), 191–196.

Sharples, J., Webster, R. and Blatchford, P. (2015). *Making Best Use of Teaching Assistants: Guidance Report*. London: Education Endowment Foundation.

Thomas, G. (1992). *Effective Classroom Teamwork: Support or Intrusion?* London: Routledge.

Tucker, S. (2009). Perceptions and Reflections on the Role of the Teaching Assistant in the Classroom Environment. *Pastoral Care in Education*, *27*(4), 291–300.

UNISON. (2013). *The Evident Value of Teaching Assistants: Report of a UNISON Survey*. Retrieved from www.unison.org.uk/content/uploads/2013/06/Briefings-and-Circular-sEVIDENT-VALUE-OF-TEACHING-ASSISTANTS-Autosaved3.pdf

Webster, R., Blatchford, P., Bassett, P., Brown, P., Martin, C. and Russell, A. (2010). Engaging with the Question "Should Teaching Assistants Have a Pedagogical Role?" *European Journal of Special Needs Education*, *25*(4), 347–348.

Webster, R., Blatchford, P., Bassett, P., Brown, P. and Russell, A. (2011). The wider pedagogical role of teaching assistants. *School Leadership and Management*, 31(1), 3–20.

Webster, R., Blatchford, P. and Russell, A. (2012). Challenging and Changing How Schools Use Teaching Assistants: Findings from the Effective Deployment of Teaching Assistants Project. *School Leadership & Management*, *33*(1), 78–96.

Wilson, E. and Bedford, D. (2008). "New Partnerships for Learning": Teachers and Teaching Assistants Working Together in Schools – The Way Forward. *Journal of Education for Teaching*, *34*(2), 137–150.

Part 2
conclusion

Part 2 of this book has considered how TAs roles are defined, and how difficult it is to clearly identify what TAs do and how the role of the TA is distinct from that of the teacher. As we have noted previously, Watson et al. (2013) defined TAs' role as being the 'cultural and interpersonal glue between teachers, children, and families'. This shows their role in working with a range of school stakeholders and the importance of their 'boundary crossing' work, or ability to work with and relate to a range of different groups with different needs. Although Watson et al.'s (2003) definition might be considered the most complete, it also illustrates the difficulty of transforming the multifaceted, complex, flexible and context-dependent roles TAs fulfil into a definitive list. This lack of clarity surrounding TAs' evolving role has been the focus of concerns for teaching unions, teachers, schools, and TAs, with their increased pedagogical responsibility and diminishing gap between teachers' and TAs' roles implied, but not made explicit by the National Workforce Agreement (DfES, 2003). This ambiguity has left many confused (Blatchford, Russell, Bassett, Brown and Martin, 2007), and there have been suggestions that the lack of precision in TAs' roles has effectively ensured that they are 'by definition dependent' both on teachers and the school (Quicke, 2003) to decide their roles for them. Graves (2012) concurred, arguing that the lack of role definition has made TAs vulnerable to 'fit in with the predilections' of school staff rather than having a distinct professional identity – something which the findings from my research support in relation to TAs managing behaviour.

If TAs are already in a position where their roles in school in general are difficult to pin down and their expectations of managing behaviour remain largely unspoken, then working with a range of teachers whose own personal understandings influence how they manage behaviour can only make it even more challenging for TAs to understand their role. This additional variation shows how complex TAs' work can be. Part 3 of this book develops these ideas and looks in detail at how TAs' management of behaviour can be either constrained or facilitated by specific in-school factors such as role clarity, training, power, whole-school approaches and deployment.

Reflection activity

At the end of this second part of the book we have built on the broader factors discussed in Part 1 to consider how issues of understanding the work TAs do and how others view the role impact on TAs' ability to manage behaviour. We have considered the advantages and disadvantages of a clear and consistent definition of the role(s) TAs undertake. We have looked at the way in which teachers see how their own role impacts on how they work with TAs and the expectations they have of the roles they will undertake. We have also considered how power and status, rather than roles, might be seen by children as a key difference between teachers and TAs.

Before we move on to the next section, which considers how in-school and contextual factors influence TAs' work managing behaviour, take some time out to reflect on these questions:

- Have you read anything that has surprised you?

- Are there any aspects covered that you would like to find out more about?

- Are there any of the references you are interested in following up?

- Have you read anything that has echoed the experiences in your setting or that you have seen or read elsewhere?

- Are there any changes you would make in your setting or to your own practice in light if anything you have read so far?

References

Blatchford, P., Russell, A., Bassett, P., Brown, P. and Martin, C. (2007). The Role and Effects of Teaching Assistants in English Primary Schools (Years 4 to 6) 2000–2003. Results from the Class Size and Pupil–Adult Ratios (CSPAR) KS2 Project. *British Educational Research Journal*, *33*(1), 5–26.

Department for Education and Skills. (2003). *Developing the Role of Support Staff – What the National Agreement Means for You*. London: DfES.

Graves, S. (2012) Chameleon or Chimera? the Role of the Higher Level Teaching Assistant (HLTA) in a Remodelled Workforce in English Schools. *Educational Management Administration and Leadership*, *41*(1), 95–104.

Quicke, J. (2003). Teaching Assistants: Students or Servants? *FORUM*, *45*(2), 71–74.

Watson, D., Bayliss, P. and Pratchett, G. (2013). Pond Life that 'Know Their Place': Exploring Teaching and Learning Support Assistants' Experiences through Positioning Theory. *International Journal of Qualitative Studies in Education*, *26*(1), 100–117.

Part 3

Part 3

10 Training and the TA

In the previous part of this book, we considered how TAs' input in managing behaviour was influenced by how they and others understood their role. We discussed, as was touched on in Chapter 9, how difficulties in clearly delineating TAs' role has led to role creep and blurred boundaries which affect how they worked with teachers as well as children's views of TAs. The main focus of the preceding chapter was relationships and roles. This part of the book now moves that consideration on to look at how factors outside TAs' relationships with others mediate how they manage behaviour. The first of these factors we will look at is how training, or the lack of training, supports or constrains TAs in managing behaviour.

This chapter will:

■ Consider the access to and types of training available to TAs

■ Share how formal and informal learning impact on TAs' ability to manage behaviour

■ Discuss the current arrangements for training and expectations of TAs

■ Discuss how workplace learning, rather than formal training, often occurs and how this can support and constrain TAs' managing behaviour

 ## What does the research tell us?

Over twenty years ago, the DfEE (1997) cautioned that many TAs had little or no training for the work they did and, over ten years later, it was also conceded by Ofsted (2008) that weaknesses continued to remain in TAs' training and deployment. The same point was again more recently highlighted by others, who continued to raise concerns about the level of training TAs have (Radford, Blatchford and Webster, 2011; Sharples, Webster and Blatchford, 2015; UNISON, 2013; Webster, Blatchford, Bassett, Brown and Russell, 2011).

The term 'training' as used here includes access both to school-based (for example, staff meetings, twilights, INSET) training as well as external courses and qualifications. It also incorporates the role of informal, or 'on-the-job' learning and inductions to the TA role the school or setting might provide. Training, in particular TA specific training, is a thorny issue, with a large body of research identifying what has been described as a mismatch between the level of training TAs usually receive and their increasingly demanding and pedagogical roles in school (Clarke and Visser, 2016; Gerschel, 2005; Groom and Rose, 2005; O'Brien and Garner, 2002; Sharples et al., 2015; Smith, Whitby and Sharp, 2004; Tucker, 2009; UNISON, 2013). The key suggestion from these studies is that TAs are being asked to do much more than their levels of training suggest they can confidently do. Galton and MacBeath (2008) found that although TAs in their study were described as being indispensable by schools – a sentiment echoed more recently by a UNISON (2013) survey – they were also asked to fulfil roles which 'exceed their expertise'.

Bach, Kessler and Heron (2006) had suggested that a 'drift-in', organic, as opposed to planned, informal method of recruitment existed for TAs – a parallel of which does not exist for teachers. They found that 'mums' had often made the unplanned transition from voluntary helper to TA. This was reflected by many head teachers historically prioritising personal qualities and experience over academic qualifications when recruiting to the TA role (Blatchford, Russell, Bassett, Brown and Martin, 2007). As a result of this, there was little or no formal induction or training programme in schools for long-standing TAs, with maternal experience relied upon instead to plug the gaps in the absence of training (Galton and MacBeath, 2008). It has been suggested that this lack of training or induction for TAs has caused related issues, as Graves (2013) suggested, and was discussed in the previous chapter (Chapter 9) in the development of a clear and distinct professional identity for TAs. It was argued that that attempts at 'professionalisation' of the TA role 'precluded inter-professional dialogue and joint decision making' and had resultant implications for teacher–TA relationships, where differences between TA and teacher status were highlighted, rather than reduced (Edmond and Price, 2009; Wilson and Bedford, 2008).

A key problem is not only the gap between the training for and subsequent expectations of TAs, but also the fact that if TAs do receive training it is often 'filtered' by the school. This 'filtering' is where the impact of any training provided, either internally by the school or externally by another agency or provider, is then mediated by a range of in-school factors. These factors can include the attitudes of, and support from, the senior leaderships team (SLT) and individual teachers, as well as the ways in which TAs are subsequently deployed and the types of learners they work with. This process means that the training gained is sadly not always utilised fully (Rose and Forlin, 2010; Rose and O'Neill, 2009; Tucker, 2009). One of my participants exemplified this when talking about specific training she had received for a mentoring role. She noted that she now felt well equipped to support children's behaviour through this mentoring process and had really enjoyed the training, citing a range of ways she felt it had developed her professional skill set.

However, the way in which she was deployed in school had not changed following the training and she was largely unable to use the ideas for one-to-one mentoring as she did not see children individually, or at times when she could usefully use those skills.

The fragmented and varied deployment TAs in my research, and more widely, experienced in schools can make implementing or organising training difficult. This resonated with the difficulties Trent (2014) found in addressing the training needs for the multiple roles TAs had, where he suggested that the role overload TAs experienced was associated with what he termed 'weakened efficiency'. These multiple and ill-defined TA roles, as we have discussed (Chapters 5, 8 and 9), raise a range of other concerns and tensions. Eraut and Hirsh (2007) argued that clarity and explicitness was needed to develop and support links being made between actions and outcomes. If we think back to the previous discussion of TAs' role clarity and relationships (Chapters 6 and 8 specifically) the implicit and unspoken nature of their role in managing behaviour also has consequences for the clarity research suggested is essential for making links between strategies used to manage behaviour and their outcomes in the classroom (Eraut and Hirsh, 2007).

Although just over half of the TAs in my research had received some form of training, interestingly, none related to it specifically when discussing behaviour. One of my participants acknowledged that she has received some training and learnt some strategies, but highlighted the importance of experience too. Another TA in my research also relied on experience, contending that wherever her understanding of strategies to manage behaviour came from, it certainly was not the behaviour policy. This shows that, even when some training has been given, it is not always used. This may be because it is not seen by the TAs as suitable or relevant in some way, or maybe that it does not include useful strategies for the classroom.

 Pause point

It has been suggested that, in the past (although some would say this was still the case) a TA's personal skills were most important when recruiting. Think about:

■ Would you agree or disagree with this view?

■ Why?

■ Are personal qualities or academic qualifications more important in relation to managing behaviour?

There are suggestions that TAs cannot always use the training they receive due to a range of in-school factors. We have mentioned the views of the SLT and deployment here:

■ How many others can you think of?

■ Have you seen or experienced this?

■ What could be done to limit the 'filtering' of training received by TAs?

Despite research (Marr, Turner, Swann and Hancock, 2002) that showed that although nearly all of the TAs they surveyed had an interest in training, almost half had difficulty attending courses either as a result of other commitments or through a lack of availability. These same issues were additionally highlighted in later research (Stoll and Seashore Louis, 2007; Webster et al., 2011). This suggests that it is not TAs who are reluctant to participate in training, but that the training is not available or not available at times or venues that that TAs can make. These issues may have been compounded by school budget cuts that means that buying into external training, or paying for cover to attend daytime training courses, is beyond the reach of many schools. Moves to improve the training available for TAs have been made previously, specifically with the introduction of thirty-one national professional standards for HLTAs (DfES, 2006). These standards in some respects mirrored those that govern teachers (DfE, 2011). Burgess and Mayes (2009) noted that despite TAs in their study stating that the training for this was very beneficial, the actual uptake nationally for the training programme was low. The issues for TAs accessing training were also compounded by the withdrawal of funding for some HLTA programmes (Brown and Devecchi, 2013; Burgess and Mayes, 2009; Graves, 2013). For those without HLTA status there was less additional training available, which had associated repercussions (Brown and Devecchi, 2013; Galton and MacBeath, 2008), with Graves (2013) stating the lack of any national pay or career structure had resulted in ad hoc, and often absent, training opportunities and had actively hampered TAs' progression.

In 2016 'Professional Standards for Teaching Assistants' (Dethridge, 2016) were published. These were originally produced for the DfE in England who, after a series of delays, finally withdrew entirely from the project at the last minute. The schools minister at that time, Nick Gibb, stated that the standards remained unpublished in order to give schools freedom in how they deployed TAs (Scott, 2015). The Minister's statement reinforced views (Blatchford, Russell and Webster, 2016; Radford, Bosanquet, Webster and Blatchford, 2015) about the uncharacteristically 'quiet and hands off' government position which was at odds with, for example, the government's position on behaviour at the time, which moved towards increased micromanagement (Maguire, Ball and Braun, 2010) and the churning out of a large range of documentation (for example: DfE, 2014, 2015; DfE and Nick Gibb MP, 2014; DfE and The Rt Hon Michael Gove MP, 2014; DfE and The Rt Hon Nicky Morgan, 2015; Ofsted, 2014). The standards the group produced are available, but not endorsed by the British government, and free to access.

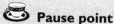 **Pause point**

Access the teaching standards for TAs:

Available on the maximising TAs website (maximisingtas.co.uk) under the resources tab.

Now access the Teacher Standards: (available at gov.uk)

Compare the standards for TAs (pages 6–8 in the document) to those for teachers.

- How do they link together? Can you see any parallels between the two standards? Are there clear separations of roles within the two documents?

If you think about TAs in your own setting or in your own:

- Are there any additional requirements you would add to the published standards for TAs, or any you would remove?

- Do you think there would be differences across settings, types of provisions and year groups?

Think back to the diagram you might have begun in the previous reflection point (page x) where you identified different (or not!) roles for teachers and TAs. Compare your thoughts to those outlined in the standards for the two groups.

- Does that ally with your earlier thoughts?

- Are there any differences?

- Has your view of the roles changed in this case?

- Why or why not?

The types of training and availability of training for TAs – specifically for HLTAs who are more likely to have whole-class teaching roles and, therefore, greater responsibility for managing behaviour – highlights a number of difficulties. It was proposed that basing the HLTA standards on competence indicators, rather than on any form of further education or training, made for the worrying assumption that all the necessary training could be gained 'on the job'. This was opposite to the view of professional development for others in the wider children's workforce and could be seen as another example of the marginalisation of TAs (Edmond and Price, 2009; Graves, 2013). It was suggested that this contrast between occupational or 'on the job learning' and professional training varied considerably in effectiveness, with 'induction, training and appraisal' rated as being 'unsatisfactory' in half of the schools Ofsted (2008) visited at that time. There is a clear issue here, if this is the main way in which TAs are supported and developed by the schools or settings they work in.

The tensions in the availability of, and access to, training may be suggested to impact on TAs' ability to manage behaviour. This lack of training is problematic particularly when behaviour management was identified by TAs as an area they required more training in (Butt and Lowe, 2011; Cockroft and Atkinson, 2015; Rose and Forlin, 2010). Managing behaviour is often a key worry for qualified teachers (as discussed in Chapters 2, 3 and 4) and feeling unsafe in the classroom was cited as a key reason preventing undergraduates training as teachers (House of Commons Education Committee, 2011). If managing behaviour is significant for those who will or have received training, it is unusual, to say the least, to expect those who have not received training, but who have requested it, to work with the same children with the same confidence as qualified teachers do. Without any training Galton and MacBeath (2008) found that TAs in their study resorted to using common sense and family experience, with one respondent in their study (reflecting the views of my participants) suggesting that she had drawn on her experience as a mum to plug the gaps in training.

 Pause point

Participants in my research also highlighted their maternal experience and use of common sense to manage behaviour. Think about:

- What advantages might this have?
- What disadvantages might this have?
- Which TAs might be able to rely on these skills and which might not?
- Can this personal experience and on-the-job experience take the place of training (either internal or external)?

This reliance on TAs' own experience and on their common sense reflected Spillane, Reiser and Reimer's (2002) findings that people construct 'intuitive models from their experience' rather than relying solely on formal training or courses. This also links with Eraut's (2007) conclusions that most learning was within the workplace itself. TAs in my research suggested that their own experiences, rather than training, were commonly used to manage behaviour. Eraut (2004) proposed that much in-school training was the result of informal learning within the workplace and described this type of interpersonal learning as a complementary partner to the personal – or 'learning through experience' – that TAs often made reference to. It could be suggested that if TAs have had a broad experience of working with a range of children with a range of needs in numerous settings, then this reliance on their own previous experience might at times be a workable solution to a lack of training. However, when TAs are new to the job or have had few previous experiences working with children whose behaviour might be challenging, or whose personal experience does not match what the school, child, teacher or parent might want, then there could be significant problems.

This can also be seen echoed in van der Heijden, Geldens, Beijaard and Popeijus's (2015) arguments about the role that knowledge and mastery play in influencing agency as well as understanding of the professional self. The lack of training and ability to implement new skills may reduce TAs' sense of mastery in managing behaviour and could result in negative perceptions of their professional self. This allies with considerations of TAs' reduced professional status and limited ability to exercise professional agency as a limiting factor in their ability to manage behaviour (Edwards, 2012; Eteläpelto, Vähäsantanen and Hökkä, 2015; Quinn and Carl, 2015; van der Heijden et al., 2015). Associated with this is Edwards (2012) perception of the importance of common knowledge in what she described as, 'interprofessional' work, such as that between teachers and TAs in managing behaviour. Eraut and Hirsh (2007) highlighted relationships as a key factor that influence the quality of on-the-job learning that can take place for TAs when working with teachers. This reliance on good relationships between the two can be seen as problematic when considering the range of tensions (previously discussed in Chapter 9) that can occur when teachers and TAs work closely together.

Philpott (2014) had suggested that professional learning was enhanced through frequent feedback and 'access to tacit knowledge'. If these are considered in relation to TAs, it is difficult to see how most could regularly access these. Teachers in schools have observations and performance management reviews at least annually, where feedback about their practice can be discussed and they have a wide range of opportunities to access others' knowledge, not least during their years in teacher education. These same opportunities do not often exist for TAs. Informal observation has been identified as one of the main methods through which HLTAs received professional development and gained some sense of other people's tacit knowledge (Eraut, 2007; Graves, 2011). However, as has been discussed, if teachers' own management of behaviour relies in some part on their own views and the behaviour policy is interpreted in a range of ways, it is possible that these TAs are receiving conflicting advice. Philpott (2014) also found that professional learning was developed through both working alongside others and observing them, but also importantly through opportunities to talk about their own work and others work. The required time for TAs and teachers to talk together effectively is difficult to ring-fence in many schools and settings. Nevertheless, time has been highlighted by many as necessary (Gerschel, 2005; Marr et al., 2002; Rose, 2000; Sharples et al., 2015; Thomas, 1992; Webster et al., 2011, Webster, Blatchford and Russell, 2012) to give teachers the opportunity to reflect on, and discuss their practice with TAs – which was noted as an important aspect of additional training (Eraut, 2004, 2007). This in turn can enable teachers to develop a meaningful understanding of the TA role and how they influence TA effectiveness – either positively or negatively – and as a result begin to, or continue to, cultivate positive relationships (Rose, 2000; Webster et al., 2012).

Any time available for teachers and TAs to talk together is often very limited and precious, and usually urgent matters, such as expectations for the next lesson, might be the only topic of discussion. The forms of professional development Philpott considered would need more than a five-minute chat over a biscuit at playtime – which is the reality for many teachers and TAs. Reflecting this, Eraut and Hirsh (2007) acknowledged that in conversations between staff, any useful exchanges of knowledge were often a secondary consideration and were affected by the interpersonal relationship between the teacher and TA. As in other research (Groom, 2006; HMI, 2002; Houssart, 2013; Rose, 2010), Eraut and Hirsh (2007) noted the importance of time required for these trusting relationships where knowledge could be exchanged to develop, and how changes in the membership of these groups negatively affected the former. Edwards's (2011) view of relational expertise and relational agency is pertinent here as it is associated with an understanding of not only your own knowledge and skills, but how these can be used in a relationship with others. She suggested that relational agency:

> involves the ability to attune one's responses to … those being made by other professionals. Relational expertise is … based on confident engagement with the knowledge that underpins one's own practice, as well as a capacity to recognise and respond to what others might offer …
>
> (Edwards, 2011, p.33)

The research we have considered suggests that TAs may well not have this form of 'confident engagement' with teachers, and that teachers in turn do not always understand or acknowledge what TAs can 'offer' in relation to managing behaviour.

Wenger (1991) stated that it was participation in what have been termed communities of practice rather than training alone that affected not only peoples' actions but also 'who we are and how we interpret what we do'. Communities of practice will be considered in more detail in later chapters (Chapters 11 and 12) but briefly have been defined as:

> a group of individuals, who through joint enterprise have developed shared practices, historical and social resources and common practices.
>
> (Coburn and Stein, 2006, p.28)

In a school setting this might be a group or community of TAs, of teachers and TAs, of only teachers, of only members of the SLT or it might have a mixed and flexible membership. Although there was no evidence of TAs discussing and supporting each other with managing behaviour in my research, this may have taken place very informally. It could be that actually little exchange of knowledge or sharing of practice exits between TAs in most schools, and that rather than learning from each other they might learn from the teachers they work with through observation and mimesis. A participant in my research suggested that her fragmented deployment, rather than being a disadvantage, actually gave her an opportunity to observe a wide range of varied practice in managing behaviour, and to 'pick out the best parts that you like'. She suggested that this strategy of copying what she had seen was an active process, and that observation was used as a method to develop her practice. She noted that 'tends to be how I've done it ... you adopt good practice. So it's been a process of observing others, as opposed to training'. However, although this might seem positive and may well be very supportive for some TAs, concerns were raised that without discussion, simply reproducing teachers' practice did not help to develop an understanding of the underlying knowledge base teachers possessed, and did not develop TAs' practice (Graves, 2011). Despite being seen as problematic, Graves (2011) found that TAs' personal assessment of teachers and other colleagues in the way described by my participants was their primary source of induction, enculturation and training in schools.

 Pause point

Finding time in schools for meaningful conversations between teachers and TAs is often a challenge. Think about:

- If talking about practice is a key step in professional learning, when could this take place?

- What constraints are there in your experience or setting which might make this problematic?

- What steps might need to be taken to facilitate these forms of learning conversations?

- Is difficulty in finding time the only reason stopping these types of conversations between teachers and TAs? What other reasons might there be?

Armstrong's (2014) overview of research noted how training positively affected educators' attitudes when working with children with challenging behaviour. This was supported by Arbuckle and Little's (2004) earlier survey of primary and secondary school teachers that suggested training, as well as length of experience and confidence, significantly impacted on their perceptions and understandings of disruptive behaviour. Length of experience may not constrain TAs in managing behaviour, as research suggests that almost half of TAs have nine or more years' experience (Blatchford et al., 2007), but lack of training – and by association confidence – may negatively affect their views of challenging behaviour. Given the paucity of training available for most TAs, particularly in behaviour, this could affect their perception of the behaviour of children they are deployed with. Cockroft and Atkinson (2015) found in their study that limited training led to inaccurate implementation of interventions, highlighting additional issues for TAs who may have relied on their school's behaviour policy to support them in managing behaviour.

Linked to this, Spillane, Reiser and Gomez (2006) also suggested that the experience and expertise of TAs and teachers affected how they implemented policies. They suggested that the more expertise a person had in the specific area the policy related to, the greater their understanding, allowing them to see the bigger picture and reducing reliance on what they described as superficial similarities with other previous policies. If we think about TAs and teachers from this perspective, most would agree that teachers have a greater understanding due to their training and experience working with whole classes and, as a result, could see the bigger picture, or context of their school's behaviour policy. This overview allows teachers to focus on the more important conceptual differences (Spillane et al., 2006) between policies. Coburn and Stein's (2006) work supported this, suggesting that members of the school community grafted new approaches onto what they already understood, and that surface manifestations might be relied on, as opposed to the deeper pedagogical principles. It would be reasonable to assume that teachers overall occupied the expert role, as they have day-to-day experience of managing the behaviour of their classes as well as historical knowledge and understanding and theoretical knowledge from university courses or professional development opportunities. TAs are likely to have less experience in managing behaviour, as their role may not include managing the behaviour of whole classes, instead focusing on small groups or individuals, or being in a supporting role. This was supported by research findings (Blatchford et al., 2007) that showed TAs in their sample spent on average, 29 per cent of their time working on a one-to-one basis supporting individual children, 16 per cent roving the classroom providing support to the children and teacher and 15 per cent working with a group of children.

It could be argued that a school's behaviour policy is an essential tool for TAs to develop a consistent understanding of managing behaviour and could begin to ameliorate the lack of formal (or informal) training they receive (as discussed in detail in Chapters 10 and 12). Firestone, Fitz and Broadfoot (1999) considered learning a key factor in policy implementation, suggesting that policies can often ask people at lower levels to carry out interventions or schemes that they do not know how to. However, in practice, behaviour policy documents were found to be instead a distillation of custom, practice and what works (Maguire et al., 2010). Spillane et al. (2002) suggested that a school or organisation's history was used as a way to understand or interpret a policy. Organisational histories may provide a sense of 'this is what we have always done' and influence how any new behaviour policies or issues surrounding new ways of managing behaviour are dealt with. Lund's (1996) research supported this, suggesting that although a consensus might be implied by a *whole-school* policy, there may in reality be lots of differing understanding and interpretations of exactly what has been agreed. As a result, it might be that rather than a clear and consistently applied behaviour policy to guide TAs in managing behaviour they might all have different interpretations of it, depending on what they know works and how they have always done things.

TAs' often tangential, rather than integral or purposeful, involvement in training or discussions around a school behaviour policy runs contrary to research which highlighted that for improved policy take-up, specific and extended training was needed with regular meetings and a high degree of participation in decision-making (Datnow, 2000; Datnow and Castellano, 2000; Firestone et al., 1999; Hill, 2001; McLaughlin, 1991). Kubiak, Cameron, Conole, Fenton-O'Creevy, Mylrea, Rees and Shreeve (2015) noted how a lack of participation and engagement in, for example drawing up the behaviour policy, resulted in participants being unable to make the practice their own. They described this as their responses to behaviour becoming like following a script rather than reconstructing practice in a way that reflects experience, knowledge and skills. Dual tensions can emerge from TAs' inconsistent relationships with the teachers they work with and a lack clarity in their role in managing behaviour which requires them to simultaneously adopt, and adapt to, both teachers' strategies for managing behaviour and the behaviour policy itself (Graves, 2013). This reflected research findings where, of the teachers who responded to a YouGov survey (Ofsted, 2014), almost 90 per cent stated that they confidently used their own behaviour management strategies to tackle disruption, rather than those dictated by policy.

The importance of leadership was also cited in a wide range of research as essential to supporting effective and consistent policy application (Canter, 2010; Derrington, 2008; Galvin and Costa, 1995; Ofsted, 2008; Watkins and Wagner, 2000). Steer (2005), who chaired the influential 'Learning Behaviour: The Report of the Practitioners' Group on School Behaviour and Discipline', cited one of the main barriers to consistent policy application as a lack of leadership and support from the head teacher and SLT. This was exemplified in data collected for my research, where a lack of confidence in support from the schools' SLT influenced the actions TAs took when managing behaviour. One of my participating TAs stated in reference to support from the SLT, 'those words are said but I don't feel it would be backed up with the actual support', echoing findings by the DfE (2012). It may be proposed, therefore, that any perceived lack of support from the SLT limits TAs being willing to, and agency in, behaviour management.

Coburn (2005) found in her research that 'non-system actors' such as independent professional development providers, reform organisations, publishers and universities and so on, exerted a greater influence on classroom practice than others, such as head teachers or members of the SLT. This is very interesting when we consider, as discussed, the challenges that exist for TAs in finding and accessing training from 'non-system actors'. It may then follow that what teachers do in the classroom and informal learning (Eraut, 2004) is of less influence on TAs' praxis than external factors. The conflict between a lack of formal, out-of-school training and opportunities for workplace learning to develop skills in managing behaviour has clear implications for TAs. Butt and Lowe (2011) also found a disparity between what teachers and TAs believed TA training needs actually were, which they suggested could be ameliorated by training teachers and TAs together, as others have also called for (Bedford, Jackson and Wilson, 2008; Radford et al., 2015).

What this might mean in school

This chapter has developed the understanding of one of the factors that can help or hinder TAs managing behaviour in schools. The focus of this chapter – training – can sometimes be seen to be outside schools' control. However, there are a number of actions that can be taken to limit some of the disadvantages noted in this chapter and maximise the opportunities for TAs.

Initially, the lack of training and induction provided for TAs by many schools was noted. Although there may be budgetary constraints in accessing training, induction is often provided 'in-house' by schools. A clear, well-planned induction programme for TAs could limit a number of the issues highlighted in this chapter.

1. **It is suggested that many TAs have drifted into the role and have not had a clear induction. Schools should plan a context- or setting-specific programme of induction to support new TAs that could also be offered to long-standing employees.**

The induction provided may include documentation with information about support and training, line-manager responsibilities, a programme of performance management, additional information about the job descriptions as well as an in-house CPD programme which might involve informal observation of others with discussion and feedback time built in.

It has been argued that due to the lack of formal (and informal) training TAs can access, they are often asked to fulfil roles that they have no experience in and are unsure about. This issue could be at least in part resolved through a programme of induction and performance management, either formally or informally. However, some method of evaluation for TAs and schools is needed to provide a channel for TAs to give feedback about a range of issues, including whether or not they feel prepared and confident fulfilling the roles they have been deployed to, or to identify the areas they need more support and/or training in.

2. **TAs and schools need clear, professional and regular two-way channels of communication to discuss training needs and confidence in fulfilling the wide range of roles they may be asked to perform.**

Historically, research suggests TAs have been recruited for their personal qualities. This may still be a factor in TA recruitment currently, particularly if they are employed with supporting children's behaviour in mind. Studies, and my own participants, reiterated the caring and maternal aspects of the role where family experience is often drawn upon. It cannot be assumed that just because a TA is female, or a parent, that they possess skills needed to support children with non-standard needs in school. It may be helpful to devise (or adapt a ready-made) skills audit to see what TAs in your school or setting already feel they have and which they would like to develop. This could be part of both the induction and or performance review.

3. **A skills audit may help to develop bespoke in-house training or CPD for TAs as well as understanding where they view their strengths.**

A key issue for schools highlighted by research was the concept of training that TAs received being filtered by schools. At times, it was suggested that even when schools paid for specific externally provided training, TAs were not able to use these new skills in their school or setting.

4. **Training for TAs needs to be part of whole-school strategic planning and care needs to be taken to ensure that TA deployment and management allows them to use the skills they gain from training attended.**

It is unrealistic to expect, as for teachers, that all training and skill development for TAs will be provided by external (and possibly expensive) training courses. Lots of valuable learning can take place in schools through observation. However, if this is used as a skill-development strategy it must be carefully planned. Research shows that although this informal learning can be very useful and varied if TAs work with a range of teachers, discussion is a key element of embedding and understanding what has been observed.

5. **If in-house and informal training is to be of value, there needs to be explicit time devoted to professional discussions about what has been seen and how and why it can be useful.**

 ## Summary

In this chapter we have considered the opportunities for TAs to engage in meaningful internal or external training. We have discussed how the limited training opportunities available to them may well have hampered perceptions of them as a professional group, as well as limited their professional development. We have also looked at research that suggests the levels of training people have received alter how they think about behaviour that is challenging, with more training resulting in less problematising views of this behaviours. The forms of training available to TAs, when they cannot access formal training, including forms of on-the-job training, as discussed, has been criticised due to great variation in the quality of it, as well as, if learning from the teachers they work with, the range of approaches TAs will be exposed to. Although this may seem positive, some research (Coburn and Stein, 2006; Spillane et al., 2006) has shown that TAs might use the actions they have observed teachers using to manage behaviour, without having the underpinning understanding of why certain actions have (or have not) been taken. It was argued that without this 'big-picture' knowledge these forms of managing behaviour were unlikely to be wholly successful.

Reflection activity

In the previous chapter (Chapter 9) we reflected on the issues of professional agency for TAs and how this is at times constrained by roles, relationships and other in-school and system-wide factors. We also considered how the TAs in my study and in the research that exists in this area showed that when agency was limited, so was action taken to manage behaviour. In this chapter we have looked at the issues around the availability of training for TAs and the types of informal learning that might occur instead. Using the diagram shown in Figure 10.1, can you begin to complete this list of the types of training most qualified teachers will have received and the types of training most TAs will have received? Begin then to think quite broadly about which aspects of the training would have supported the development of professional agency.

Looking at the likely training and the impact on agency, what might the next steps be to support TAs in managing behaviour? What would need to happen for these steps to become practice?

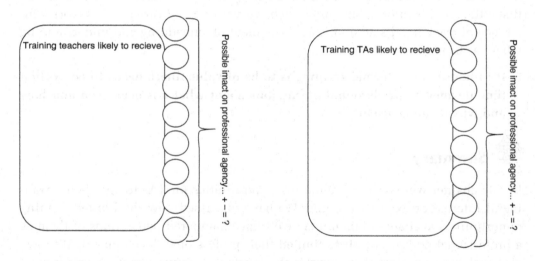

Figure 10.1 The impact of training for teachers and TAs on their professional agency

 Key points

This chapter has:

■ Examined the training available for TAs compared to the roles they undertake

■ Looked at how difficulties accessing training can leave them reliant on in-school learning

■ How school's induction and training procedures for TAs are often not as good as they need to be

■ Considered how the variety of practice TAs see from teachers and interpretations of the same school's behaviour policy may hinder rather than help their management of behaviour

■ Reflected on what training TAs receive in your own setting/school/experience and how this influences their ability to manage behaviour

Further reading

■ Blatchford, P., Russell, A. and Webster, R. (2016). *Maximising the Impact of Teaching Assistants: Guidance for School Leaders and Teachers* (2nd ed.). London: Routledge.

■ Dethridge, K. (2016) *Professional Standards for Teaching Assistants*. London: UNISON.

■ Watkins, C. and Wagner, P. (2000). *Improving School Behaviour*. London: Paul Chapman Publishing Ltd.

References

Arbuckle, C. and Little, E. (2004). Teachers' Perceptions and Management of Disruptive Classroom Behaviour during the Middle Years (Years Five to Nine). *Australian Journal of Educational and Developmental Psychology*, 4, 59–70.

Armstrong, D. (2014). Educator Perceptions of Children Who Present with Social, Emotional and Behavioural Difficulties: A Literature Review with Implications for Recent Educational Policy in England and Internationally. *International Journal of Inclusive Education*, 18(7), 731–745.

Bach, I., Kessler, S. and Heron, P. (2006). Changing Job Boundaries and Workforce Teform: The Case of Teaching Assistants. *Industrial Relations Journal*, 37(1), 2–21.

Bedford, D., Jackson, C. R. and Wilson, E. (2008). New Partnerships for Learning: Teachers' Perspectives on Their Developing Professional Relationships with Teaching Assistants in England. *Journal of In-Service Education*, 34(1), 7–25.

Blatchford, P., Russell, A., Bassett, P., Brown, P. and Martin, C. (2007). The Role and Effects of Teaching Assistants in English Primary Schools (Years 4 to 6) 2000–2003. Results from the Class Size and Pupil–Adult Ratios (CSPAR) KS2 Project. *British Educational Research Journal*, 33(1), 5–26.

Blatchford, P., Russell, A. and Webster, R. (2016). *Maximising the Impact of Teaching Assistants: Guidance for School Leaders and Teachers* (2nd ed.). London: Routledge.

Brown, J. and Devecchi, C. (2013). The Impact of Training on Teaching Assistants' Professional Development: Opportunities and Future Strategy. *Professional Development in Education*, 39(3), 369–386.

Burgess, H. and Mayes, A. (2009). An Exploration of Higher Level Teaching Assistants' Perceptions of Their Training and Development in the Context of School Workforce Reform. *Support for Learning*, 24(1), 19–25.

Butt, R. and Lowe, K. (2011). Teaching Assistants and Class Teachers: Differing Perceptions, Role Confusion and the Benefits of Skills-based Training. *International Journal of Inclusive Education, 16*(2), 207–219.

Canter, L. (2010). *Assertive Discipline* (4th ed.). Bloomington: Solution Tree Press.

Clarke, E. and Visser, J. (2016). Teaching Assistants Managing Behaviour – Who Knows How They Do It? A Review of Literature. *Support for Learning, 31*(4), 266–280.

Coburn, C. (2005). The Role of Nonsystem Actors in the Relationship between Policy and Practice: The Case of Reading Instruction in California. *Educational Evaluation and Policy Analysis, 27*(1), 23–52.

Coburn, C. and Stein, M. (2006). Communities of Practice Theory and the Role of Teacher Professional Community in Policy Implementation. In Honig, M. (Ed.), *New Directions In Education Policy Implementation: Confronting Complexity* (pp. 25–47). Albany: State University of New York Press.

Cockroft, C. and Atkinson, C. (2015). Using the Wider Pedagogical Role Model to Establish Learning Support Assistants' Views about Facilitators and Barriers to Effective Practice. *Support for Learning, 30*(2), 88–104. doi:10.1111/1467-9604.12081.

Datnow, A. (2000). Power and Politics in the Adoption of School Reform Models. *Educational Evaluation and Policy Analysis, 22*(4), 357–374.

Datnow, A. and Castellano, M. (2000). Teachers' Responses to Success for All: How Beliefs, Experiences, and Adaptations Shape Implementation. *American Educational Research Journal, 37*(3), 775–799.

Department for Education. (2011). *Teachers' Standards: Guidance for School Leaders, School Staff and Governing Bodies* (Vol. 2011). London: DfE.

Department for Education. (2012). Pupil Behaviour in Schools in England. In Research Report DFE-RR218. London: DfE.

Department for Education. (2014). *Behaviour and Discipline in Schools.* London: DfE.

Department for Education. (2015). *2010 to 2015 Government Policy: School Behaviour and Attendance.* London: DfE.

Department for Education and Employment. (1997). *Excellence in Schools. White Paper. 3681.* London: DfES.

Department for Education and Nick Gibb MP. (2014). *Thousands Fewer Pupils Excluded from School since 2010.* London: DfE. Retrieved from www.gov.uk/government/news/thousands-fewer-pupils-excluded-from-school-since-2010

Department for Education and Skills. (2006). Raising Standards and Tackling Workload Implementing the National Agreement. Note 17. London: DfES.

Department for Education and The Rt Hon Michael Gove MP. (2014). *Gove Gives Green Light to Teachers to Use Tough Sanctions to Tackle Bad Behaviour.* London: DfE. Retrieved from www.gov.uk/government/news/gove-gives-green-light-to-teachers-to-use-tough-sanctions-to-tackle-bad-behaviour

Department for Education & Rt Hon Nicky Morgan. (2015). *New Reforms to Raise Standards and Improve Behaviour.* London: DfE.

Derrington, C. (2008). *Behaviour in Primary Schools Final Report.* London: True Vision Productions.

Dethridge, K. (2016). *Professional Standards for Teaching Assistants.* London: UNISON.

Edmond, N. and Price, M. (2009). Workforce Re-modelling and Pastoral Care in Schools: A Diversification of Roles or a De-professionalisation of Functions? *Pastoral Care in Education, 3944*(November), 301–311.

Edwards, A. (2011). Building Common Knowledge at the Boundaries between Professional Practices: Relational Agency and Relational Expertise in Systems of Distributed Expertise. *International Journal of Educational Research, 50*(1), 33–39.

Edwards, A. (2012). The Role of Common Knowledge in Achieving Collaboration across Practices. *Learning, Culture and Social Interaction, 1*(1), 22–32.

Eraut, M. (2004). Informal Learning in the Workplace. *Studies in Continuing Education, 26*(2), 247–273.

Eraut, M. (2007). Learning from Other People in the Workplace. *Oxford Review of Education, 33*(4), 403–422.

Eraut, M. and Hirsh, W. (2007). *The Significance of Workplace Learning for Individuals, Groups and Organisations.* Retrieved from www.voced.edu.au/content/ngv:58866

Eteläpelto, A., Vähäsantanen, K. and Hökkä, P. (2015). How Do Novice Teachers in Finland Perceive Their Professional Agency? *Teachers and Teaching, 21*(6), 660–680.

Firestone, W., Fitz, J. and Broadfoot, P. (1999). Power, Learning, and Legitimation: Assessment Implementation across Levels in the United States and the United Kingdom. *American Educational Research Journal, 36*(4), 759–793.

Galton, M. and MacBeath, J. (2008). *Teachers under Pressure.* London: SAGE Publications Ltd.

Galvin, P. and Costa, P. (1995). Building Better Behaved Schools: Effective Support at the Whole School Level. In Gray, P., Miller, A. and Noakes, J. (Eds.), *Challenging Behaviour In Schools* (pp. 145–163). London: Routledge.

Gerschel, L. (2005). The Special Educational Needs Coordinator's Role in Managing Teaching Assistants: The Greenwich Perspective. *Support for Learning, 20*(2), 69–76.

Graves, S. (2011). Performance or Enactment? the Role of the Higher Level Teaching Assistant in a Remodelled School Workforce in England. *Management in Education, 25*(1), 15–20.

Graves, S. (2013). New Roles, Old Stereotypes – Developing a School Workforce in English Schools. *School Leadership & Management, 34*(3), 255–268.

Groom, B. (2006). Building Relationships for Learning: The Developing Role of the Teaching Assistant. *Support for Learning, 21*(4), 199–203.

Groom, B. and Rose, R. (2005). Supporting the Inclusion of Pupils with Social, Emotional and Behavioural Difficulties in the Primary School: The Role of Teaching Assistants. *Journal of Research in Special Educational Needs, 5*(1), 20–30.

Hill, H. (2001). Policy Is Not Enough: Language and the Interpretation of State Standards. *American Educational Research Journal, 38*(2), 289–318.

HMI. (2002). *Teaching Assistants in Primary Schools an Evaluation of the Quality and Impact of Their Work.* London: HMI.

House of Commons Education Committee. (2011). *Behaviour and Discipline in Schools. Vol 1. HC 516 – 1.* London: DfE.

Houssart, J. (2013). 'Give Me a Lesson and I'll Deliver It': Teaching Assistants' Experiences of Leading Primary Mathematics Lessons in England. *Cambridge Journal of Education, 43*(1), 1–16.

Kubiak, C., Cameron, S., Conole, G., Fenton-O'Creevy, M., Mylrea, P., Rees, E. and Shreeve, A. (2015). Membership and Identification. In Wenher-Trayner, E., Fenton-O'Creevy, M., Hutchinson, S., Kubiak, C. and Wenger-Trayner, B. (Eds.), *Learning in Landscapes of Practice: Boundaries, Identity and Knowledgeability in Practice-based Learning* (pp. 64–80). Oxon: Routledge.

Lund, R. (1996). *A Whole-School Behaviour Policy: A Practical Guide.* London: Kogan Page Limited.

Maguire, M., Ball, S. and Braun, A. (2010). Behaviour, Classroom Management and Student 'Control': Enacting Policy in the English Secondary School. *International Studies in Sociology of Education, 20*(2), 153–170.

Marr, A., Turner, J., Swann, W. and Hancock, R. (2002). *Classroom Assistants in the Pimary School: Employment and Deployment.* Milton Keynes: Open University.

McLaughlin, M. (1991). The Rand Change Agent Study: Ten Years Later. In Odden, A. (Ed.), *Educational Policy Implementation* (pp. 143–156). Albany: State University of New York Press.

O'Brien, T. and Garner, P. (2002). Tim and Philip's Story: Setting the Record Straight. In O'Brien, T. and Garner, P. (Eds.), *Untold Stories – Learning Support Assistants and Their Work* (pp. 1–10). Stoke on Trent: Trentham Books Ltd.

Ofsted. (2008). *The Deployment, Training and Development of the Wider School Workforce.* London: Ofsted.

Ofsted. (2014). *Below the Radar: Low-Level Disruption in the Country's Classrooms.* London: Ofsted.

Philpott, C. (2014). *Theories of Professional Learning: A Critical Guide for Teacher Educators.* Northwich: Critical Publishing.

Quinn, R. and Carl, N. (2015). Teacher Activist Organizations and the Development of Professional Agency. *Teachers and Teaching, 21*(6), 745–758.

Radford, J., Blatchford, P. and Webster, R. (2011). Opening up and Closing down: How Teachers and TAs Manage Turn-taking, Topic and Repair in Mathematics Lessons. *Learning and Instruction, 21*(5), 625–635.

Radford, J., Bosanquet, P., Webster, R. and Blatchford, P. (2015). Scaffolding Learning for Independence: Clarifying Teacher and Teaching Assistant Roles for Children with Special Educational Needs. *Learning and Instruction, 36,* 1–10.

Rose, R. (2000). Using Classroom Support in a Primary School: A Single School Case Study. *British Journal of Special Education, 27*(4), 191–196.

Rose, R. (2010). Understanding Inclusion: Interpretations, Perspectives and Cultures. In Rose, R. (Ed.), *Confronting Obstacles to Inclusion* (pp. 1–7). Oxon: Routledge.

Rose, R. and Forlin, C. (2010). Impact of Training on Change in Practice for Education Assistants in a Group of International Private Schools in Hong Kong. *International Journal of Inclusive Education, 14*(3), 309–323.

Rose, R. and O'Neill, Á. (2009). Classroom Support for Inclusion in England and Ireland: An Evaluation of Contrasting Models. *Research in Comparative and International Education, 4*(3), 250–261.

Scott, S. (2015, October 15). The Teaching Assistants Standards Report that Nicky Morgan Doesn't Want You to See. *Schools Week.*

Sharples, J., Webster, R. and Blatchford, P. (2015). *Making Best Use of Teaching Assistants: Guidance Report.* London: Education Endowment Foundation.

Smith, P., Whitby, K. and Sharp, C. (2004). *The Employment and Deployment of Teaching Assistants.* Slough: NFER.

Spillane, J., Reiser, B. and Gomez, L. (2006). Policy Implementation and Cognition: The Role of Human, Social and Distributed Cognition in Framing Policy Implementation. In Honig, M. (Ed.), *New Directions In Education Policy Implementation: Confronting Complexity* (pp. 47–64). Albany: State University of New York Press.

Spillane, J., Reiser, B. and Reimer, T. (2002). Policy Implementation and Cognition: Reframing and Refocusing Implementation Research. *Review of Educational Research, 72*(3), 387–431.

Steer, A. (2005). *Learning Behaviour: The Report of the Practitioners' Group on School Behaviour and Discipline.* London: DfES.

Stoll, L. and Seashore Louis, K. (2007). *Professional Learning Communities: Divergence, Depth and Dilemmas.* Maidenhead: McGraw-Hill Education.

Thomas, G. (1992). *Effective Classroom Teamwork: Support or Intrusion?* London: Routledge.

Trent, J. (2014). 'I'm Teaching, but I'm Not Really a Teacher'. Teaching Assistants and the Construction of Professional Identities in Hong Kong Schools. *Educational Research*, *56*(1), 28–47.

Tucker, S. (2009). Perceptions and Reflections on the Role of the Teaching Assistant in the Classroom Environment. *Pastoral Care in Education*, *27*(4), 291–300.

UNISON. (2013). *The Evident Value of Teaching Assistants: Report of a UNISON Survey*. Retrieved from www.unison.org.uk/content/uploads/2013/06/Briefings-and-Circular-sEVIDENT-VALUE-OF-TEACHING-ASSISTANTS-Autosaved3.pdf

van der Heijden, H., Geldens, J., Beijaard, D. and Popeijus, H. (2015). Characteristics of Teachers as Change Agents. *Teachers and Teaching*, *21*(6), 681–699.

Watkins, C. and Wagner, P. (2000). *Improving School Behaviour*. London: Paul Chapman Publishing Ltd.

Webster, R., Blatchford, P., Bassett, P., Brown, C. and Russell, A. (2011). The Wider Pedagogical Role of Teaching Assistants. *School Leadership and Management*, *31*(1), 3–20.

Webster, R., Blatchford, P. and Russell, A. (2012). Challenging and Changing How Schools Use Teaching Assistants: Findings from the Effective Deployment of Teaching Assistants Project. *School Leadership & Management*, *33*(1), 78–96.

Wenger, E. (1991). *Communities of Practice: Learning, Meaning, and Identity*. Cambridge: Cambridge University Press.

Wilson, E. and Bedford, D. (2008). "New Partnerships for Learning": Teachers and Teaching Assistants Working Together in Schools – The Way Forward. *Journal of Education for Teaching*, *34*(2), 137–150.

Power and the TA

This chapter will continue, as the previous one did, to look at some of the in-school factors and how these can either support or hamper TAs' skills and agency in managing behaviour. The last chapter considered how a lack of formal, or even informal, training can be challenging when TAs manage behaviour. This chapter moves on to look at issues of power, both with regard to the TA role more broadly and to issues of status and power as part of the school workforce. We will reflect on how power impacts on TAs' agency to manage behaviour and how this might affect what actions they take in the classroom, with groups and with individual children.

This chapter will:

■ Consider TAs' status compared to others in the school workforce

■ Reflect on how power is exercised over TAs in schools

■ Discuss how gender and power might impact on TAs

■ Share how status can affect TAs' ability to manage behaviour

■ Investigate how power impacts TAs' relationships with children and teachers

■ Look at links between behaviour policies and power

 ## What does the research tell us?

Power is a very emotive word; most of us want to feel powerful in some way and feeling powerless is often uncomfortable. Power, as I will use the word in this chapter, relates to the position and status of TAs in schools compared to other members of staff, including teachers and the SLT. It also considers not only the comparative power that TAs possess but how power is exercised *over* them. At the individual level, TAs often remain relatively voiceless in schools and there are problems in defining a distinct professional identity (as we have discussed in Chapters 5 and 8). This lack of power compounds issues of being peripheral and invisible which much research suggests TAs have been and continue to remain (Ball, 1987; Galton and MacBeath, 2008; Gilbert, Warhurst, Nickson, Hurrell and Commander, 2012; Graves, 2013; Kerry, 2005; Lehane, 2016; Mackenzie, 2011; Trent, 2014; Watson, Bayliss and Pratchett, 2013). Roffey-Barentsen and Watt (2014) noted that if the importance of voice was acknowledged for teachers then the same recognition should also be given to TAs, not least as they account for one third of the primary workforce, yet they continued to be quiet and un-heard in research and wider educational discussions.

If we pause to think about research into the work TAs do, despite an increasing number of studies since the seminal Deployment and Impact of Support Staff (DISS) report (Blatchford, Russell and Webster, 2012) there still remains a gap in research which specifically focuses on TAs' voice and perspective, despite many calls to address this over at least the last thirty years (Ball, 1987; Gilbert et al., 2012; Lehane, 2016; Trent, 2014; Watson et al., 2013). Indeed, the DISS report – which was, and still is, the largest study of TAs worldwide, being described as 'formidably extensive' (Fletcher-Campbell, 2010), collecting thousands of individual pieces of data over a number of years – did not specifically highlight data collected from TAs. Blatchford et al. (2012) justified their exclusion of the TA voice in this study by suggesting that their aim was to build a dialogue about TAs through discussion 'with staff with decision making responsibilities' rather than with TAs themselves.

It is key, therefore, to consider how the power and status attributed to TAs' role influences not only the way in which they work, but also what we are able to know from research about the way in which they work.

Research has shown time and time again that education, and the politics that go hand-in-hand with education, are linked by overarching issues of power (Datnow, 2000; Dumas and Anyon, 2006; Thomas and Loxley, 2001; Wenger-Trayner and Wenger-Trayner, 2015). Firestone, Fitz and Broadfoot (1999) proposed that power was enacted through what they described as 'games' at the various hierarchical levels of the institution – in this case schools and the wider environment, which could be government policy, the multi-academy trust (MAT) CEO and so on – through the provision or constraint of resources. If we cast our minds back to the previous chapter, it could be suggested that the government had restricted the resources available to TAs by removing funding for some HLTA training and withdrawing from formally producing the standards for TAs they commissioned. Examples of providing resources might be schools working with TAs to support them through HLTA assessments, or encouraging them to develop professionally through opportunities created by the school. Datnow (2000) characterised schools as places of 'hierarchical regulations of power and competing interests and ideologies' where power dynamics were present in all relationships. It is therefore important that we consider how these influence TAs and affect their work in managing behaviour.

Datnow (2000) noted that hierarchical power relations such as those in a top-down school model, where the headteacher was responsible for the majority of the leadership and decision-making, resulted in 'highly politicised' reactions to implementing policies. She suggested that this meant meanings in the policy, such as a behaviour policy, were not automatically shared due to the way power was distributed and applied within schools. This also led to what she described as 'disagreement or conflict'. This is important to consider due to the impact on TAs of either applying, partially applying or not applying at all, a behaviour policy. In relation to implementing a behaviour policy and managing behaviour, it was stated (Ball, 1987; Thomas and Loxley, 2001) that power was an issue which constrained TAs, with policies never being neutral but always containing 'underlying social relations of power'. It was argued (Watkins and Wagner, 2000) that without full consultation of all stakeholders, power, with all its associated ethical issues, was assumed by default.

Datnow (2000) suggested that discussions around policy and even training may give the presumption of buy-in from all staff, but that this actually was 'pseudo-democracy', which took no account of systematic power relations embedded in the school. It was argued that even teachers, who are proposed to be in a more powerful position than TAs, were 'relatively powerless' (Devecchi, Dettori, Doveston, Sedgwick and Jament, 2011; Graves, 2011; Mansaray, 2006; Stoll and Seashore Louis, 2007; Watson et al., 2013). This was echoed in other research (Datnow and Castellano, 2000) which found that when policies were mandated either internally or externally they resulted in a conflict between aims and purposes and those dominant in the school.

 Pause point

There are clear suggestions in research that schools are places of hierarchies, where power is pervasive in the relationships that exist. Think about:

- What clear hierarchies are there in schools – even if they are in name only?
- How do power relations manifest themselves in schools in your experience or setting?
- What benefits do these relationships that are regulated by power have?
- What disadvantages do they have?
- Who are usually the most powerful people in schools?
- Who are the least?

Looking back at Datnow's (2000) view about the pervasive nature of power relations in schools, it could be suggested that these may be magnified due to TAs' status within hierarchical school management structures, where they are typically not in a powerful position.

Gender issues have also been highlighted as affecting TAs' status and power. The workforce of TAs in English schools is almost all female and the percentage of women working as TAs in primary schools continues to rise, from 92 per cent of all primary TAs being women in 2014 (DfE, 2014b) to 95 per cent in 2017 (DfE, 2017). The average TA is suggested by a range of research (Bach, Kessler and Heron, 2006; Blatchford, Russell, Bassett, Brown and Martin, 2007; DfE, 2014b; HMI, 2002; Quicke, 2003; Smith, Whitby and Sharp, 2004) to be aged between forty-one and fifty, to have a lower level of formal education than teachers (the typical school leaving age of the population was sixteen) and have family responsibilities. Barkham (2008) suggested that lower wages and family commitments has led to the TA role becoming inescapably associated with of motherhood. Watson et al. (2013) noted how TAs in their research labelled themselves as mums first and TAs second as a strategy to add value to their role. Participants in my research also noted how they relied on their experience as a mum to manage behaviour. This maternal stereotype can also be seen in historic (hopefully) descriptions of TAs as a 'mum's army' where the role provided a 'bit of pocket money for housewives' (Smith et al., 2004).

The stereotypically female attributes of caring, nurturing and people skills TAs are expected to draw on to fulfil their multiple roles, particularly those related to managing behaviour, can be problematic, with gender stereotyping of the TA role cited in a wide range of research (Barkham, 2008; Butt and Lowe, 2011; Dunne, Goddard and Woolhouse, 2008; Fraser and Meadows, 2008; Graves, 2011, 2013; Mackenzie, 2011; Ofsted, 2008; Watson et al., 2013). Despite these qualities undoubtedly being valuable in a TA, viewing TAs' role as purely motherly denotes issues related to both reduced status and power (Devecchi et al., 2011; Mansaray, 2006). Graves (2013) argued that these maternal connotations also made TAs' work invisible and peripheral. This links with others' views, as discussed in previous chapters (Chapters 6, 8 and 9) that TAs' work was largely separate from larger concerns of teaching and learning and that the ways in which schools deployed them continued to make them invisible and peripheral, in terms of status as well as physically. For example, TAs can be deployed to work with groups of children outside the classroom and as a result are not physically present to develop relationships with the class or with the teacher.

Due to the wide and varied range of roles they undertake, TAs' contribution to schools can be difficult to clearly define or pin-down in wider educational discourses which often focus on value for money (Houssart and Croucher, 2013; Roffey-Barentsen and Watt, 2014; Sharples, Webster and Blatchford, 2015). One example of this is the widely used Educational Endowment Foundation's Teaching and Learning Toolkit (EEF, 2018) where TA support was argued to be high cost but low impact. The lack of clarity on what TAs' role encompasses aside from their contribution to children's academic performance, and the current focus in schools on performativity and external ranking such as league tables, as opposed to a focus on care (Graves, 2013, p.266), only compounds the continuing difficulties in both quantifying and recognising TAs' work:

The contribution of support staff in terms of emotional labour and caring work, which is an integral part of the socialisation of children ... needs to be acknowledged as, within the present discourse, it is often disregarded, devalued and dispatched to the periphery of educational experience

(Graves, 2013, p.266)

 Pause point

The TA role is dominated by women, many of whom are mums. Think about:

■ Do TAs in your school, setting or experience fit this pattern?

■ Is someone who is female and a mum expected to make a better TA?

■ What might that tell us about TAs' role?

We have considered the role power may play in the work TAs do and in the agency they may be able to exert over their work. Mansaray (2006) believed that TAs were in a structurally weaker position than teachers in schools while others argued that they were devoid of status and power (Devecchi, 2007; Devecchi et al., 2011). Yet, interestingly, these differences between teacher and TA status appear to have little impact on children's academic motivation. Fraser and Meadows (2008) found that only 20 per cent of boys and only 8 per cent of girls in their sample worked harder for the teacher than they would for a TA. Nevertheless, as we have discussed (in Chapters 6, 8 and 9) the differences in status TAs may well experience in schools impacts on the relationships they form as well as some of the ways in which they work with children. The TAs in my research highlighted how important they felt it was to 'know your place' and avoid crossing the line; this shows how power relations affected their relationships with teachers as well as the way they worked with them. Ideas about place will be revisited (in Chapter 14) and we will continue to investigate how a TA's status and power can affect how they are deployed and the work they do with children (Chapter 11).

Much research shows the importance of teachers and TAs collaborating in their work (Bedford, Jackson and Wilson, 2008; Devecchi, Dettori, Doveston, Sedgwick and Jament, 2011; Devecchi and Rouse, 2010; Gerschel, 2005; HMI, 2002; Johnson, 2010; O'Brien and Garner, 2002; Ofsted, 2008). However, although this co-operation has been shown to be important there are distinct barriers to it happening, with TAs' status and power in schools being a key reason. Trent (2014) argued in his research that without addressing what he described as the 'untouched relations of power' that existed between teachers and TAs, where TAs were often viewed as 'subordinate', these partnerships could not be effectively established. In my research, one of the TAs highlighted this issue, explaining how she felt that some teachers took their role 'far more seriously' and as a result saw themselves very differently to TAs. Her implication was that this difference was that teachers were 'above' TAs in terms of status and power. She noted that in her experience 'I think some teachers are like 'yeah I'm a teacher but I am willing to learn and I am open to ideas and suggestions' whereas other teachers were very clear that they were in charge'. This shows that, at least in her experience, not all teachers were open to the idea of collaborating with the TAs in their class.

The way the teacher views the TA, their role and their status, all influence how they choose to work with them (or not!). This was reflected in research, with Dunne et al. (2008) citing that the power and authority inherent in the teacher role often resulted in them working with TAs in a managerial and corporate way, almost by default. This also paralleled Quicke's (2003) concerns about teachers' assumed managerial role in the classroom which he suggested put TAs in the position of 'managed, trainees, novices', or possibly even 'servants'.

 Pause point

Have another look now at the leadership styles activity you might have considered in Chapter 9 (p. 106). Think about:

■ Can you match the suggestions of Quicke's (2003) perceptions of being managed to the different styles outlined in the grid? What style might make TAs feel;

a. Managed?

b. Like a trainee?

c. Like a novice?

d. Like a servant?

■ How might these feelings influence TAs' status and power?

■ How might it affect their relationship with the teacher?

■ How might it affect the actions they take to manage behaviour?

Following on from Quicke's (2003) views, Watson et al. (2013) discussed the contradiction they saw from their research on TAs' roles, which can usually be broadly categorised as either providing *support* for pupils or *assistance* for teachers. TAs providing support for pupils rather than teachers, which was TAs' highest-ranking priority in my research, might actually serve to mediate some of the tensions they experienced in teacher–TA relationships and also increase their power. This resonated with Riches' (1982, in Thomas, 1992) earlier beliefs that TAs actually actively eschewed teamwork in order to increase their power. Positioning themselves as primarily offering support to children, rather than assisting teachers, could, therefore, be perceived as a method for TAs to increase their status and power as well as agency and autonomy in managing behaviour.

Working directly with teachers in the classroom, rather than supporting pupils either in groups or individually inside or outside the classroom, can sometimes negatively highlight the difference in status and power between the two. Watson et al. (2013) argued that what they saw as 'working in the shadow of teachers' positioned TAs as 'less competent' than the teacher and requiring 'supervision'. Trent (2014) highlighted similar issues related to positioning of TAs, suggesting that identifying their role as providing support or aid effectively distanced them from teachers and from teaching, bringing us back to arguments that TAs have been marginalised to work on the edges or periphery of education (Howes, 2003; Mansaray, 2006). How power and status impacts on TAs' perceived roles was also identified by Harris and Aprile (2015) who suggested that hierarchical attitudes resulting from preconceived ideas and assumptions about TAs' competencies in specific roles – for example, managing behaviour – often devalued their contributions.

Roffey-Barentsen and Watt (2014) described the hierarchy they observed in schools, with the HLTA role perceived as having the highest status and TAs supporting a specific pupil or working one-to-one as having the lowest status. Although this contradicted TAs' positioning of themselves as supporting children in order to improve issues of power and agency, HLTAs exercised significant levels of autonomy and self-direction due to their increased pedagogical role compared to those who did not have the same qualification. Mackenzie (2011) and Lehane (2016) found that poor status was a generic and recurring issue for all of the TAs in their research. Their participants had described themselves as outsiders – a term also used by a TA in my research – and 'lesser' in the school hierarchy, as being 'at the bottom of the ladder' and even as 'a dumping ground' (Lehane, 2016; Mackenzie, 2011). Watson et al. (2013) found that descriptions even extended to the incredibly pejorative term 'pond life' to describe the very worst experiences of their participating TAs in the hierarchical arrangement of schools. This resonated with TAs in my own research, who noted a perception that both children and teachers viewed the TAs' role as below that of the teacher and as different. One participating TA simply stated that teachers had 'the upper hand ... the authority'.

This view of TAs as having less status impacts on what they feel able to do or feel is appropriate when managing behaviour. In Roffey-Barentsen and Watt's (2014) research, a peripatetic behaviour support assistant reported her status as very low, suggesting that as a result of this, teachers perceived her as interfering when she managed behaviour. This view of TAs as interfering when managing behaviour was also reflected in participants' responses in my research. One TA stated that she felt teachers 'don't necessarily want you to be butting in and controlling behaviour', or 'sticking my nose in', as another TA referred to it. These responses both show how TAs felt they had much less status and agency than the teachers they were working with. This was expressed by TAs in my research as them 'crossing the line' by managing behaviour. One of my participants supported this, stating that 'some teachers might not want you to have that input', suggesting instead that 'it's the teacher's job to discipline the child'. This resonated with the conflicts Butt and Lowe (2011) identified in their research, where some teachers did not see managing behaviour as part of TAs' remit, yet parents, children and TAs did. TAs' perception of teachers' ownership of the class – 'it's the teacher's class', as one of my TAs noted – was associated with Thomas's (1992) suggestions that teachers were territorial in the classroom, seeing it as their own space, and Hargreaves's (1994) classification of teachers' cultures conforming to either 'individualism', 'contrived collegiality' or 'balkanisation'.

 Pause point

Have another look now at the leadership styles activity you might have considered in Chapter 9 (p. 106). Hargreaves (1994) grouped teachers' cultures in a number of different styles. How might theses align with the leadership styles in the grid?

a. *Individualism* – here the teacher favours working autonomously, often in isolation from others.

b. *Collaboration* – the teacher values working together with others in a range of different ways, without this being externally controlled.

c. *Contrived collegiality* – the teacher works with others because it is compulsory, often at set times and places.

d. *Balkanisation* – teachers here are not isolated but do not work as a whole school. Instead smaller groups or even cliques form.

Adapted from – Stoll, L. (1998) School culture. *School Improvement Network's Bulletin*. 9.

■ How might these cultures affect TAs' status and power?

■ How might they influence TAs' relationship with the teacher?

■ How might it affect the actions TAs take to manage behaviour?

The blurred boundary between TAs' and teachers' roles in managing behaviour was highlighted in my research. There were a range of views as to whether it was the teacher or the TA who was responsible for managing behaviour, reflecting the lack of clarity much of the research shows on wider TA roles as we have discussed (see Chapter 8). The findings in my research support Butt and Lowe's (2011) in relation to TAs' understanding of their responsibility and may also echo their perception of teachers' views, with my participating TAs reiterating their own supporting role in managing behaviour. One TA noted:

> I'd feel it was the responsibility of the teacher to do that [manage behaviour] and if they were letting the class behaviour get out of control then I wouldn't feel as though I could do much about that ... I feel I am very much in a supporting role.

This view of the TA as a support for behaviour also resonates with Barkham's (2008) findings that TAs firmly believed that responsibility lies with a qualified teacher to manage behaviour. One of the key consequences of the TA's supporting role and the lack of clarity on what their role might be, is what my participating TAs described as the need to 'know your place'. In Watson et al.'s (2013) research, their TA respondents also noted 'I know my place', and when discussing issues in the classroom highlighted that 'I wouldn't dream of telling the teacher … that would be undermining'.

When considering power issues, the phrase TAs commonly used in my research was the importance of knowing their place. One of my participants clearly stated: 'in terms of place, I think that definitely is and has always been the case, even if you put personalities aside. I think there will always be a place for TAs and a place for teachers'. In their study, Watson et al. (2013) TAs also believed that knowing their place was a 'really good quality', something that was also noted by TAs participating in my study. Yet, it was suggested that:

> the importance placed by some members of school staff on TLSAs [TAs] *knowing their place* was a strong reminder … of how deeply entrenched the discourses of professionalism in schools are.
>
> (Watson et al., 2013, p.107, emphasis added)

Watson et al. (2013) argued that knowing your place was the result of TAs' title defining their role as a supporting or assisting one (Graves, 2013; Harris and Aprile, 2015; Roffey-Barentsen and Watt, 2014; Trent, 2014). The concept of 'know your place', therefore, carried with it an assumption that TAs' 'place' was implicit through understood rules and duties (Watson et al., 2013). However, this is rarely the case. Despite referring to the need to know your place, TAs are in the difficult position of *not* knowing their place, due to the implicit, unspoken and variable expectations of them in managing behaviour which they are often required to simply infer.

The research findings that we have considered here, as well as those in my own study, suggest that power and status have a significant impact on the ways in which TAs manage (or not) behaviour, and in their relationships with teachers, as well as the ways in which they are perceived in schools.

What this might mean in school

In this chapter, we have explored the relationship between TAs, power and managing behaviour. Understanding power and status from TAs' position in school when you are not a TA is challenging. It is important to ensure that TAs are included in any decision-making processes in the school as these decisions are likely to have a significant impact on them as they filter through the educational 'hierarchies' that naturally exist in all schools. When thinking about managing behaviour, an aspect that challenges some teachers, it is key to include TAs and provide the opportunities for discussions with different groups.

1. **Power relations in school tend to minimise the contributions TAs can make, particularly to managing behaviour. They need to be actively included in discussions around behaviour to support them and reduce some of these power issues.**

Research suggests that power is endemic in schools. This can influence TAs in a number of ways, but seems to have very few advantages for them and can make their role in managing behaviour even more difficult. One way in which this power can be acted out in schools is by making either overt or covert links between TAs and mums. It is important to consider how language, policy and day-to-day interactions with TAs sends messages about their position and status in the school or setting. Supporting TAs to develop a distinct professional identity is important.

2. **Being seen as a professional can support TAs in understanding their 'place' in managing behaviour in a positive way. Strategies to improve the professional standing of TAs may need to be implemented.**

One strategy to support TAs' professional standing and identity is to give careful consideration to the roles they fulfil and whether the term TA is an appropriate one to use. Although the term TA is used in formal policy documentation and so on, there is no reason they cannot be given a range of informal titles in individual schools or contexts. For example, would 'learning assistant' be more suitable for some TAs, or 'individual support' or 'intervention leader'? Although only a semantic change, it may cement changes in some children's and teacher's perceptions as well as making roles clearer for all.

3. **The language used to label and talk about TAs and the work they do holds implicit assumptions about power. Checking through in-school documentation and daily (formal or informal) language used about TAs can be a step to minimising power issues.**

Rethinking the term used to describe the work TAs do can be the start of a useful whole-school discussion which could lead on to further consideration of the roles TAs undertake, the expectations of them and their 'place', or 'places', in the whole-school system.

4. **TAs need to have a positive understanding of their 'place', or where they fit within the classroom and school. This will need time for TAs, teachers and staff more widely to talk about the unspoken expectations of TAs in relation to managing behaviour.**

It has been suggested in a range of research that time for TAs and teachers to talk together is vital. Ensuring time is planned in (as noted in Chapters 7, 8 and 9) is essential to support both TAs and teachers in positively determining TAs' 'place' and roles in managing behaviour. If TAs work with a range of teachers, they will need time with each teacher to negotiate these aspects of their work together.

5. **Not all teachers may have the same expectations of TAs managing behaviour in their classroom. TAs will need supporting in understanding what their different roles are when working with different teachers, or some consistent approach needs to be agreed upon as a whole school with all staff able to participate in the discussions.**

As we have seen in this chapter and others (Chapters 8 and 9), power relationships can influence policy implementation. Again, it is important that real buy-in is achieved for all staff, particularly those such as TAs who may not have the autonomy, agency, training or confidence to deviate from the behaviour policy.

6. **TAs' role needs to be clear and explicit in the policy. Automatic understanding and application of a behaviour policy cannot be assumed and TAs may need more support than others in implementing it due to the impact of their lower status and power in school.**

Reflection activity

When talking about their understanding of their role in school a key focus for my participating TAs was to 'know their place'. This sounded frighteningly pejorative and dismissive initially, but in my (and in other) research TAs saw it as a good thing. If you reflect now on TAs in your setting, school or experience, do they 'know their place'? How is this communicated to them – implicitly or explicitly?

Can you try to map your ideas about place and link them to our previous discussions on agency and professional standing. Look at the activity and, using the diagram shown in Figure 11.1, what ways might there be to support TAs in finding a 'place' positively or negatively? How will this impact on their professional identity, their agency and the actions they take (or not) to manage behaviour?

Summary

This chapter has begun to think about how TAs' status and power in school affects them. We have discussed how this can influence their relationships with the teachers and children they work with. We have also looked at the perspectives of existing research. We noted that the research that has been conducted on TAs has actually be *on* them, rather than *with* them, and that there are still gaps in research where TAs' voices are clearly heard. The impact of reduced power and status on the way in which TAs position themselves and view their role as a supporting one, was considered. From this we looked at the idea of TAs needing to 'know their place' and linked this to them developing a clear (if variable for the teachers they work

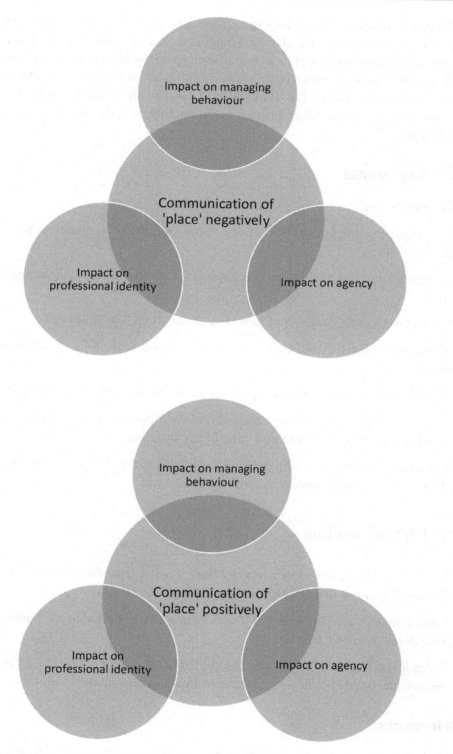

Figure 11.1 How 'place' might be communicated to TAs

with) understanding of their role in managing behaviour in the range of contexts that they might work in. We also investigated how TAs' need to know their place was seen as a keen desire not to undermine or upset the teacher they were working with by overstepping the mark or 'crossing the line'. A range of implications for school have been shared, but above all the need to purposefully and positively include TAs in discussions and decisions in relation to behaviour, role and policy in schools.

 Key points

This chapter has:

- Discussed the impact of TAs' lower status compared to others in the school workforce

- Examined the type of research that has been done and the issues that might exist in it

- Looked at the role gender and power might exert on TAs in schools

- Reflected on the ways in which power is consciously and unconsciously exercised over TAs

- Shared how the status of TAs negatively affects their ability to manage behaviour

- Investigated how power and a lack of understanding of 'place' impacts on TAs' relationships with children and specifically teachers

- Examined the links between behaviour policies and power and why TAs might find implementing a behaviour policy challenging

 Further reading

- HMI. (2002). *Teaching Assistants in Primary Schools an Evaluation of the Quality and Impact of their Work.* London: HMI.

- Ofsted. (2008). *The Deployment, Training and Development of the Wider School Workforce.* London: Ofsted.

- Sharples, J., Webster, R. and Blatchford, P. (2015). *Making Best Use of Teaching Assistants: Guidance Report.* London: Education Endowment Foundation.

References

Bach, I., Kessler, S. and Heron, P. (2006). Changing Job Boundaries and Workforce Teform: The Case of Teaching Assistants. *Industrial Relations Journal*, *37*(1), 2–21.

Ball, S. (1987). *The Micro-politics of the School: Towards a Theory of School Organisation.* London: Methuen.

Barkham, J. (2008). Suitable Work for Women? Roles, Relationships and Changing Identities of 'Other Adults' in the Early Years Classroom. *British Educational Research Journal, 34*(6), 839–853.

Bedford, D., Jackson, C. and Wilson, E. (2008). New Partnerships for Learning: Teachers' Perspectives on Their Developing Professional Relationships with Teaching Assistants in England. *Journal of In-Service Education, 34*(1), 7–25.

Blatchford, P., Russell, A., Bassett, P., Brown, P. and Martin, C. (2007). The Role and Effects of Teaching Assistants in English Primary Schools (Years 4 to 6) 2000–2003. Results from the Class Size and Pupil–Adult Ratios (CSPAR) KS2 Project. *British Educational Research Journal, 33*(1), 5–26.

Blatchford, P., Russell, A. and Webster, R. (2012). *Reassessing the Impact of Teaching Assistants.* Oxon: Routledge.

Butt, R. and Lowe, K. (2011). Teaching Assistants and Class Teachers: Differing Perceptions, Role Confusion and the Benefits of Skills-Based Training. *International Journal of Inclusive Education, 16*(2), 207–219.

Datnow, A. and Castellano, M. (2000). Teachers' responses to Success for All: how beliefs, experiences, and adaptations shape implementation. *American Educational Research Journal,* **37**(3), 775 –799.

Datnow, A. (2000). Power and Politics in the Adoption of School Reform Models. *Educational Evaluation and Policy Analysis, 22*(4), 357–374.

Department for Education. (2014a). *Behaviour and Discipline in Schools.* London: DfE.

Department for Education. (2014b). *Statistical First Release School Workforce in England: November 2014.* London: DfE.

Department for Education. (2017). *School Workforce in England November 2017.* London: DfE.

Devecchi, C. (2007). Teachers and teaching assistants working together: inclusion, collaboration, and support in one secondary school. *PhD diss.,* University of Cambridge.

Devecchi, C., Dettori, F., Doveston, M., Sedgwick, P. and Jament, J. (2011). Inclusive Classrooms in Italy and England: The Role of Support Teachers and Teaching Assistants. *European Journal of Special Needs Education, 27*(2), 171–184.

Devecchi, C. and Rouse, M. (2010). An Exploration of the Features of Effective Collaboration between Teachers and Teaching Assistants in Secondary Schools. *Support for Learning, 25*(2), 91–99.

Dumas, M. and Anyon, J. (2006). Towards a Critical Approach to Education Policy Implementation: Implications for the (Battle) Field. In Honig, M. (Ed.), *New Directions in Education Policy Implementation: Confronting Complexity* (pp. 149–168). Albany: State University of New York Press.

Dunne, L., Goddard, G. and Woolhouse, C. (2008). Teaching Assistants' Perceptions of Their Professional Role and Their Experiences of Doing a Foundation Degree. *Improving Schools, 11*(3), 239–249.

EEF (2018). *Teaching and Learning Toolkit.* London: Education Endowment Foundation. Available at: https://educationendowmentfoundation.org.uk/evidence-summaries/teaching-learning-toolkit/#closeSignup

Firestone, W., Fitz, J. and Broadfoot, P. (1999). Power, Learning, and Legitimation: Assessment Implementation across Levels in the United States and the United Kingdom. *American Educational Research Journal, 36*(4), 759–793.

Fletcher-Campbell, F. (2010). Double Standards and First Principles: Framing Teaching Assistant Support for Pupils with Special Educational Needs: A Response. *European Journal of Special Needs Education, 25*(4), 339–340.

Fraser, C. and Meadows, S. (2008). Children's Views of Teaching Assistants in Primary Schools. *Education 3-13, 36*(4), 351–363.

Galton, M. and MacBeath, J. (2008). *Teachers Under Pressure*. London: SAGE Publications Ltd.

Gerschel, L. (2005). The Special Educational Needs Coordinator's Role in Managing Teaching Assistants: The Greenwich Perspective. *Support for Learning, 20*(2), 69–76.

Gilbert, K., Warhurst, C., Nickson, D., Hurrell, S. and Commander, J. (2012). New Initiative, Old Problem: Classroom Assistants and the Under-Valuation of Women's Work. *Industrial Relations Journal, 43*(1), 22–37.

Graves, S. (2011). Performance or Enactment? The Role of the Higher Level Teaching Assistant in a Remodelled School Workforce in England. *Management in Education, 25*(1), 15–20.

Graves, S. (2013). New Roles, Old Stereotypes – Developing a School Workforce in English Schools. *School Leadership & Management, 34*(3), 255–268.

Hargreaves, A. (1994). *Changing Teachers, Changing Times; Teachers' Work and Culture in the Postmodern Age*. London: Cassell Educational Limited.

Harris, L. and Aprile, K. (2015). 'I Can Sort of Slot into Many Different Roles': Examining Teacher Aide Roles and Their Implications for Practice. *School Leadership & Management, 35*(2), 140–162.

HMI. (2002). *Teaching Assistants in Primary Schools an Evaluation of the Quality and Impact of Their Work*. London: HMI.

Houssart, J. and Croucher, R. (2013). Intervention Programmes in Mathematics and Literacy: Teaching Assistants' Perceptions of Their Training and Support. *School Leadership and Management, 33*(5), 427–439.

Howes, A. (2003). Teaching Reforms and the Impact of Paid Adult Support on Participation and Learning in Mainstream Schools. *Support for Learning, 18*(4), 147–153.

Johnson, B. (2010). Teacher Collaboration: Good for Some, Not so Good for Others. *Educational Studies, 29*(4), 337–350.

Kerry, T. (2005). Towards a Typology for Conceptualizing the Roles of Teaching Assistants. *Educational Review, 57*(3), 373–384.

Lehane, T. (2016). "Cooling the Mark Out": Experienced Teaching Assistants' Perceptions of Their Work in the Inclusion of Pupils with Special Educational Needs in Mainstream Secondary Schools. *Educational Review, 68*(1), 4–23.

Mackenzie, S. (2011). "Yes, but…": Rhetoric, Reality and Resistance in Teaching Assistants' Experiences of Inclusive Education. *Support for Learning, 26*, 64–71.

Mansaray, A. (2006). Liminality and In/Exclusion: Exploring the Work of Teaching Assistants. *Pedagogy, Culture & Society, 14*(2), 171–187.

O'Brien, T. and Garner, P. (2002). Tim and Philip's Story: Setting the Record Straight. In O'Brien, T. and Garner, P. (Eds.), *Untold Stories – Learning Support Assistants And Their Work* (pp. 1–10). Stoke on Trent: Trentham Books Ltd.

Ofsted. (2008). *The Deployment, Training and Development of the Wider School Workforce*. London: Ofsted.

Quicke, J. (2003). Teaching Assistants: Students or Servants? *FORUM, 45*(2), 71–74.

Roffey-Barentsen, J. and Watt, M. (2014). The Voices of Teaching Assistants (Are We Value for Money?). *Research in Education, 92*(1), 18–31.

Sharples, J., Webster, R. and Blatchford, P. (2015). *Making Best Use of Teaching Assistants: Guidance Report*. London: Education Endowment Foundation.

Smith, P., Whitby, K. and Sharp, C. (2004). *The Employment and Deployment of Teaching Assistants*. Slough: NFER.

Stoll, L. and Seashore Louis, K. (2007). *Professional Learning Communities: Divergence, Depth and Dilemmas*. Maidenhead: McGraw-Hill Education.

Thomas, G. (1992). *Effective Classroom Teamwork: Support or Intrusion?* London: Routledge.

Thomas, G. and Loxley, A. (2001). *Deconstructing Special Education And Constructing Inclusion*. Buckingham: Open University Press.

Trent, J. (2014). 'I'm Teaching, but I'm Not Really a Teacher'. Teaching Assistants and the Construction of Professional Identities in Hong Kong Schools. *Educational Research*, *56*(1), 28–47.

Watkins, C. and Wagner, P. (2000). *Improving School Behaviour*. London: Paul Chapman Publishing Ltd.

Watson, D., Bayliss, P. and Pratchett, G. (2013). Pond Life that 'Know Their Place': Exploring Teaching and Learning Support Assistants' Experiences through Positioning Theory. *International Journal of Qualitative Studies in Education*, *26*(1), 100–117.

Wenger-Trayner, E. and Wenger-Trayner, B. (2015). Learning in a Landscape of Practice. In Wenger-Trayner, E., Fenton-O-Creevy, M., Hutchinson, S., Kubiak, C. and Wenger-Trayner, B. (Eds.), *Learning in Landscapes of Practice: Boundaries, Identity and Knowledgeability in Practice-based Learning* (pp. 13–30). Oxon: Routledge.

12 Whole-school approaches and the TA

This chapter continues to build a picture of the influences that affect TAs broadly, and how they are able to manage behaviour more specifically. It will continue to weave the themes of power, training, role and broader aspects of policy and practice that have already been discussed (in Chapters 9, 10 and 11) to see how these, and aspects of whole-school approaches, influence TAs and affect how TAs choose to manage behaviour – if indeed they choose to.

In this chapter, the term whole-school approach is used to refer to a wide range of school-based systems, structures and ways of working. This includes aspects such as developing consistent approaches to managing behaviour through a behaviour policy, as well as TAs' levels of inclusion or marginalisation from aspects of school life. These school-wide approaches also include the schools' culture or their social practises. These include TAs' experiences of relationships and interactions in schools.

This chapter will:

- Consider what the concept of a whole-school community might look like

- Explore the challenges TAs might face in being part of a whole-school community

- Discuss how many whole-school approaches traditionally exclude TAs

- Investigate how a lack of inclusion can affect how TAs relate to others in school

- Share the principle of communities of practice

- Discuss how TAs' inclusion in a range of communities of practice could support or constrain their ability to manage behaviour

 ## What does the research tell us?

Spillane, Reiser and Reimer (2002) suggested from their research that being immersed as a member of a whole-school community through, for example, access to school-wide training, provided a cultural and contextual understanding that could become integrated into TAs' own personal views. From this, it was proposed that:

> tacit knowledge – actively acquired through participation in a culture – forms the basis of an individual's beliefs and expectations about how to act in certain situations.
>
> (p.410)

Here, Spillane and his colleagues are highlighting that without access to, or feeling included as part of, either a whole-school community or an approach, it is even more difficult for TAs to know how to act, to find their place in a positive way and to understand where they fit in the school culture. Even for those who are immersed as part of a whole-school approach or culture, there are still problems. Radford (2000) appreciated the inherent tensions that can occur between agreeing on a whole-school approach to a range of processes – including behaviour and an organisation made up of individuals. She cited the importance of sharing and respecting differences and each other's unique priorities and experiences when working towards goals. Groom and Rose (2005) also found in their research that involving TAs and valuing and recognising the contributions they made were paramount to effective practice. This supported Bedford, Jackson and Wilson's (2008) suggestions that team working was only possible in organisations where a culture of 'collaborative working, mutual support and professional learning amongst all staff' was embedded. Despite this, if we reflect back on discussions from previous chapters (Chapters 5, 8 and 9) we have seen that opportunities for TAs and teachers to meet and share their experiences and priorities is limited and even where it does exist, at times there is little learning that is achieved from these sorts of conversations. Blatchford, Russell and Webster (2012) found that three quarters of the teachers in their large-scale study had no formal time to plan with and talk to TAs, which resulted in brief and ad hoc discussions between the two.

The importance of working together (discussed in Chapters 8 and 9) is key to developing whole-school approaches and community. Symes and Humphrey (2011) in line with Smylie and Evans' (2006) earlier research, highlighted the importance of relationships within schools, as did Mackenzie (2011), who stated that as well as a strong commitment to their work she found that TAs in her study had an equally strong emotional connection to the people they worked with. Watkins and Wagner (2000) proposed that a proactive and collaborative community approach could enhance teamwork as well as allow for autonomy. Nias, Southworth and Yeomans (1989) earlier also found that collaborative staff were both happy and resilient, and defined the relationships between staff in these contexts as tough and flexible. This concept of working with others as part of a community supported other research (Gerschel, 2005; Ofsted, 2008) that asserted collaboration by TAs with other professionals, such as teachers, enhanced consistency and coherence when managing behaviour. Ofsted (2008) charged the school's leadership team with the responsibility for ensuring trust, openness and mutual support amongst staff, but provided little in the way of guidance in developing this. This is contradictory when issues such as the influence of leadership (discussed in Chapter 10 and 11) has been seen by research to be a source of a range of difficulties for TAs (Rose and Forlin, 2010; Rose and O'Neill, 2009; Tucker, 2009).

An important aspect of TAs' ability to manage behaviour is linked to social groupings within a school's culture. Datnow and Castellano (2000) stated that staff subcultures were based on ideological similarities or common interests. Coburn and Stein (2006) believed it was the professional communities that staff formed which were a crucial site for the implementation of policies – or not – and that these collaborative groups exerted a strong influence on both the degree to which, as well as how, a policy was implemented (Coburn and Stein, 2006; Smylie and Evans, 2006). One aspect of this social form of learning is known as the 'communities of practice' perspective, and as noted in Chapter 10, it is this community of practice where groups work together, formally or informally, to develop shared practices. It is the ongoing negotiation of meaning within these communities that influences the end product of, for example, a behaviour policy (Coburn and Stein, 2006) and, therefore, how behaviour might be managed.

 Pause point

The research we have just considered suggests that practices can be developed in these communities of professionals. We know that training opportunities are often limited for TAs. Think about:

- What might the advantages for TAs be in learning about managing behaviour in a community of practice?

- What might the disadvantages be of learning and developing in this way?

- If policy implementation is 'filtered' through these communities of practice, is that an advantage or disadvantage for a TA?

It has been suggested that interactions happen not only within communities of practice, but also between different communities and it is possible for individuals to belong to multiple, and at times competing, communities of practice resulting in what Kubiak, Fenton-O'Creevy, Appleby, Kempster, Reed, Solvason and Thorpe (2015) termed 'hybrid identities'. This is in part because these communities develop from personal and informal relationships, rather than in line with formal hierarchical power structures. For example, a TA may belong to one group made up exclusively of TAs and may also belong to a community made up of members of a specific Key Stage or year group. This could include teachers (some of whom may be members of the senior leadership team), other TAs and possibly ancillary staff. This results in exposure to a wide range of viewpoints and norms and therefore a range of different perspectives and understandings of a topic, for example behaviour. Coburn and Stein (2006) highlighted the multiple, overlapping communities that existed in schools, all of which had separate 'norms of mutual engagement, joint enterprise and repertoires of practice'. This means that TAs may well be exposed to a number of different views and understandings of behaviour and the behaviour policy if they participate in a range of communities of practice, but might have a more limited exposure if they only participate in one, or none at all.

As has been discussed (in Chapter 11), the status of TAs may also have had a bearing on their involvement in communities of practice and as a result, the way they manage behaviour. Coburn and Stein (2006) suggested that stronger teams were more likely to adapt or ignore a policy if it did not match with their beliefs and values and the converse also applied, that weaker communities were more likely to apply them. It is possible that TAs could belong to either strong or weak teams, or even both. TAs may be considered to be in strong teams due to their numbers and years of experience, but as a result of their relatively low status, they could be considered to be in weak teams. There is also the further possibility that they may concurrently be part of a strong and weak communities of practice. This might suggest then, that despite any training accessed, the people they work with in schools exerts an impact on the way in which TAs think about and manage behaviour, either constructively, or less constructively. This sort of informal learning is much harder to manage and understand than external training for example, as much may be tacit. Whichever the dominant influence, either a strong or weak community practice, or indeed both, it can be suggested that the interpersonal relationships in schools have the ability to influence how TAs implement a behaviour policy, and as a result how they manage behaviour. This is particularly pertinent when considering TAs' allegiance to specific communities and the effect this has on their understanding of policy. Coburn and Stein (2006) stated that these communities of practice, whilst neither being inherently good or bad, were places where learning unfolds and, as a result, where influence is exerted.

TAs' description in my own study of the variation they inferred in teachers' expectations of them in managing behaviour could also be seen as an aspect of social practices, following Coburn and Stein's (2006) and Datnow and Castellano's (2000) research, citing the importance of staff subcultures and professional communities in policy implementation. It was suggested that meanings were negotiated in these communities and that participation in them influenced 'who we are as well as what we do' (Coburn and Stein, 2006; Wenger, 1991). It can be argued that a lack of clarity in a school's behaviour policy could actively militate against the development of shared practices between teachers and TAs and may, as a result, actually increase variation in its implementation. Despite the presence of a behaviour policy, one of my participating TAs stated, teachers 'do their own thing'. This may be due to teachers communicating their own definitions of behaviour according to their particular view on the purposes of education, resulting in definitions that were more eclectic than standard (Haroun and O'Hanlon, 1997). Nevertheless, my participating TAs found their behaviour policy useful whether they implemented it wholly, partly or not at all. One of my TAs suggested that following the school's behaviour policy was important as it enabled her to 'do her part'. She suggested

> That is what you're there for to help the teacher, so I know that I follow the behaviour policy. I've got a copy in my bag and I feel like I know it now, but I carry a copy with me in my bag all the time so if I need to check something I can look. I can see where that fits in with sanctions how many times have they done that and I often referred to it.

The lack of consistent application of the behaviour policy on the part of the teachers' she worked with was excused by the TA's perception of them as being overloaded by constant low-level behaviour, among other workload burdens, and also not being as familiar with the policy as she felt she was. As we have seen (in Chapter 7), the idea of policy ownership is fraught with difficulties, and the lack of inclusion for all staff when drawing up a policy has been highlighted by a wide range of research as problematic (Coburn and Stein, 2006; Datnow and Castellano, 2000; Kubiak et al., 2015; McLaughlin, 1991). Within research, there also remains a lack of consensus on exactly who 'staff' are in relation to managing behaviour. The DfE's (2013) advice on 'behaviour and discipline' initially stated that all staff 'such as teaching assistants' were involved in managing behaviour which was later (DfE, 2016) amended to 'unless the head teacher says otherwise'. This makes clarifying TAs' role yet more challenging when a range of messages are given in external policies.

Visser (2003) stated that three 'c's were essential for a successful behaviour policy: consistency, consensus, and cohesion of purpose. Consistency and cohesion of purpose may have both also derived from another 'c': collaboration or 'collective commitment' (DfES, 1989). This process of collaboration involving all staff helps to promote ownership as well as a sense of value of, and for, the school's behaviour policy, which, it was suggested, are as important as its content (DfES, 1989; Lund, 1996). Dearden (1994) emphasised the importance of staff's involvement to agree aims, which should then be actively promoted and individually accepted and valued.

In my research, the lack of clarity in the school's behaviour policy affected who could and could not implement key aspects of it and, therefore, actively constrained both the TAs' actions and agency in managing behaviour. The British government currently expects all English schools to use rewards and sanctions as part of their behaviour policy (DfE, 2016). In practice, this is often in the form of a hierarchy which children progress through, either up or down. When looking at the policy for the school some of my participants worked in, although it would have been straightforward for a TA to have implemented many of the early sanctions the policy detailed it would have been much more challenging to issue sanctions further up the hierarchy without reference to the class teacher. These behaviours included commonly experienced aspects of low-level disruption such as 'moving constantly, continually not on task, interfering, hiding others' property', and were behaviours that TAs were very likely to have experienced when working with individuals or groups. Despite this, the school's behaviour policy stated that all sanctions at this stage required the class teacher's action, removing the possibility of the TA managing behaviour. This again reflects previous research suggesting TAs were marginalised and excluded. Their school actively – although I am sure unintentionally – worded their policies to preclude TAs taking any meaningful action to manage behaviour either positively or through sanctions.

The lack of access to the strategies detailed in the policy to manage behaviour left the TAs in my study vulnerable and unable to take action, or confused about what was and was not acceptable. One of the participants in my research discussed an occasion when she had dealt with misbehaviour according to her understanding of the behaviour policy yet 'the teacher had the ultimate say, even though she hadn't witnessed it, she hadn't been involved in it, ultimately she took control of it'. This led to the TAs feeling powerless and may lead on to them becoming deskilled or unwilling to take action. This allied with one of my participant's description of herself as 'very much an observer', where she felt unable to actively participate in managing behaviour. The lack of any opportunities for professional decision-making on a TA's part, when children simply progress up or down the hierarchy of rewards and sanctions automatically in a policy, may increase TAs' sense of disaffection and powerlessness. This form of inevitability in a school's behaviour policy removes the possibility of 'self-direction' for TAs (and probably teachers too), which Abrams (1999) considered as defining agency. The issues had been recognised by the Elton Committee (DfES, 1989) thirty years ago, where they cautioned the hierarchical system of rewards and sanctions in schools could lead to a reduction in professional competence and collective responsibility with problems encountered not dealt with, but referred on.

A lack of involvement for TAs when drawing up a school behaviour policy can be seen as another example of the exclusion and marginalisation (Graves, 2012) we have discussed (see Chapters 5, 8 and 9). This can lead to feelings of frustration and suggestions from my participants that the school should 'involve TAs' and show 'confidence in them'. This may have shown an implied belief from my TAs that they saw the school as lacking confidence in their management of behaviour and contradicted the importance of trusting relationships between staff noted in a wide range of research (Gerschel, 2005; Groom, 2006; HMI, 2002; Houssart, 2013; Ofsted, 2008; Philpott, 2014; Rose, 2010). This concept of trust can be seen in the broader climate of education where parallel concerns over an implied lack of trust were also levelled at teachers through the government's micro-management of schools' responses to behaviour (Armstrong, 2014; Goodman, 2006; Maguire, Ball and Braun, 2010; Payne, 2015; Radford, 2000).

Smylie and Evans (2006) used the term 'social capital' to define the nature and function of social relationships and the role these play in both group and individual behaviour. Within Smylie and Evans's (2006) research three main components of social capital were suggested to influence the degree of policy implementation: social trust, channels of communication and norms, expectations and sanctions. This is a relevant consideration given, as discussed, some of the issues TAs experienced in implementing the school's behaviour policy. Social trust from Smylie and Evans' (2006) perspective is associated with the reliability and integrity of the individual or group introducing the policy. In schools this is usually either the headteacher or the SLT. The second considered the flow of and access to information, in this case the behaviour policy, whilst the final component was defined as influencing 'individual behaviour by encouraging some actions and constraining others'. Smylie and Evans (2006) proposed that policy was central to either create or constrain situations that developed relationships and interactions capable of generating productive social capital.

Turnbull (2002) noted that teachers were often consumed with the daily pressures of the classroom and that, rather than teamwork, teachers' primary allegiance was to their classrooms rather than any other adults working within them. It was suggested that a reduction in the amount of time teachers could spend on forms of classroom work actually decreased their commitment and motivation to collaborate (Mulholland and O'Connor, 2016; Turnbull, 2002). We have noted in a number of chapters (Chapters 8, 9 and 10) the importance of time for planned and purposeful communication between teachers and TAs. Turnbull's (2002) research suggests that if specific time is not carved out for these channels of communication teachers will avoid them and focus their efforts on other – possibly more pressing or urgent – aspects of their work.

In addition, as has been considered (see Chapters 8, 9 and 11), TAs and their work can often be seen as separate and peripheral by schools (Graves, 2013; Mansaray, 2006). This runs contrary to the importance of being part of school culture and any whole-school approaches. In fact, it could also be suggested that TAs' opportunities to experience the full range of facets of school life and develop this sense of community are less than those of teachers, particularly if they did not have access to in-school training. We have considered the impact of training on the work TAs do as well as their professional identity (Chapter 10); however, in-school issues can also be a barrier to accessing any training available. Marr, Turner, Swann and Hancock (2002) reported that only one in ten of all TAs in their sample who were required to attend staff meetings were paid; as this research is now well over ten years old and school budgets have demonstrably shrunk in the intervening years it might be suggested that this figure in now actually lower for many TAs.

Others (Datnow, 2000; Datnow and Castellano, 2000; Hill, 2001) have shown that some of the prerequisites for improved policy take-up include specific and extended training as well as regular meetings with a high degree of participation in decision making. Datnow and Castellano (2000) found that the greater involvement individuals had in the policy, the more likely they were to take responsibility for it. This is important when thinking about TAs' ability and agency in implementing a behaviour policy and links to some of the points that have been raised earlier (Chapters 7 and 8). Groom and Rose (2005) also highlighted in their research, the necessity for schools to establish what they termed effective channels of communication through for example, regular meetings. It was also suggested that the degree of implementation of a policy was influenced by a range of factors including shared goals and responsibilities, collaboration and social trust (Coburn and Stein, 2006). A lack of access to these could result in what Sikes (1992, cited in Datnow and Castellano, 2000) reported as the formation of 'grumbling cliques' of old guard versus new guard which, he observed was a common by-product of policy implementation.

 Pause point

Time for TAs to talk together and with others in planned and purposeful ways has been highlighted as essential but difficult to manage in practice. Think about:

- What time is there in the school day where TAs are paid and teachers available to talk?

- What would be the advantages of these conversations?

- What stops them happening?

- What other ways might there be in your school, setting or experience to develop 'effective channels of communication'?

- What might these 'channels' look like if they are not face-to-face conversations?

Ofsted (2008) found that schools tended to recruit TAs to ensure the requirements of the workload agreement for teachers were met (including the need to plan cover for planning, preparation and assessment (PPA) time for teachers), rather than with a carefully considered view of how TAs' evolving role contributed to whole-school development. This recruitment to plug the gaps rather than doing so strategically reflects others' assertions that TAs' wider role expansion and drives to increase their numbers were simply for the benefit of the system rather than a strategic move by the British government (Bland and Sleightholme, 2012; Hammersley-Fletcher and Adnett, 2009; O'Brien and Garner, 2002; Wilkinson, 2005; Wilson and Bedford, 2008). Blatchford, Russell, Bassett, Brown and Martin (2007) proposed that TAs had essentially been relied on to fill the gap that had been formed by a range of government drives and by complex issues associated with behaviour, new curriculum initiatives and teachers' increasing workload. Without an understanding of TAs' role as part of a whole-school context, which it has been suggested the culture of schools 'actively seems to eschew', TAs depended on their own ideas about what they should to be doing (Devecchi and Rouse, 2010). This is particularly problematic if we reflect on the fact that many, if not all, of the expectations of TAs managing behaviour are implicit and unspoken. This may mean, then, that without feeling part of the whole-school culture or without clear understanding of their role broadly, and in managing behaviour specifically, TAs in many schools are, as my participants described, 'left to get on with it'.

What this might mean in school

In this chapter we have looked at whole-school factors and how these directly and indirect send messages to TAs about their place in school and role in managing behaviour. Research has repeatedly pointed to TAs not being central to the life of schools, yet at the same time they have been described as indispensable. The research we have considered here highlights the importance of TAs being what has been described as immersed in the school culture.

1. **Careful planning needs to take place to consider how to draw TAs into all facets of the life of the school. For example, being encouraged (and paid) to attend briefings and staff meetings.**

Research has also suggested that forming close working relationships can be a key factor in developing both consistency and coherence when managing behaviour, as well as producing staff groups that are 'tough and flexible'. Few could argue these are not positive traits. However, as we have discussed, there are a range of barriers to TAs and teachers developing these forms of relationships.

2. **TAs and teachers need time set aside to engage in professional and supportive discussions, specifically around behaviour.**

Although time for TAs and teachers to talk together has been repeatedly signalled as vital, the research considered in this chapter suggested that if it took teachers away from their usual time for preparation, marking and so on, they were less inclined and able to collaborate effectively. The time required for these collaborative discussions, therefore, needs to be in addition to – and not a part of – routine expectations. This is challenging considering the time pressures in school.

3. **TAs and teachers need time away from the normal classroom routines and pressures to have meaningful and collaborative discussions. This time needs to be planned in and safeguarded.**

We have considered the importance of communities of practice as potential sources of the sort of informal, on-the-job learning that we discussed in the previous chapters (Chapters 10 and 11). Although these can be very useful sites of learning, they may expose TAs to a wide range of strategies and ideas about managing behaviour that might be contradictory.

4. **TAs may benefit from time to discuss the range of strategies and techniques they see the teachers they work with use. Being exposed to a range of strategies and time to discuss their efficacy and/or how they relate to the behaviour policy could form the basis of a supportive CPD programme for TAs.**

In my research, TAs felt that, due to implicit messages from the policy and a lack of understanding of their place, school as an institution (rather than any specific individual) did not trust them to manage behaviour. Developing social capital and trust more widely can be supported through clear channels of communication, with norms and expectations in relation to managing behaviour set through collaborative discussions between teachers and TAs.

5. **Developing TAs' social capital is important. Thought needs to be given to how to enhance communication, make expectations clear and develop trust as a two-way relationship between TAs and school leaders.**

 ## Reflection activity

In this chapter, as with others, we have thought about the importance of channels of communication and we have noted the importance of TAs feeling part of the school community. Using the diagram shown in Figure 12.1, can you begin to reflect on all of the different formal and informal ways of communicating with TAs and whether these might enhance or diminish their feelings of being part of a whole-school community? For example, TAs might see the theme of that evening's staff meeting on the notice board but not be facilitated to attend. This may well diminish their feeling of actively engaging in a community.

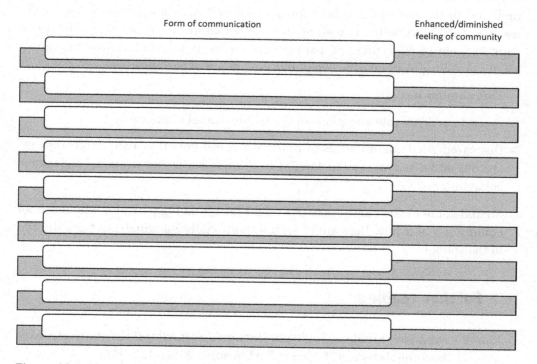

Figure 12.1 How communication might affect TAs' sense of inclusion in the school community

🗝 Summary

Social practices and whole-school approaches have been examined in this chapter. Both are an important consideration given, as discussed (in Chapters 9 and 11), TAs' relative lack of status, power and agency within the school system to manage behaviour. We have discussed how TAs might be exposed to different views about behaviour through wide-ranging membership of diverse communities of practice, which may lead to a greater range of perspectives on the behaviour policy and possibly improve the range of strategies they develop to manage behaviour in the classroom. We also looked at the opposite possibility – that TAs are only part of one, or maybe even no communities of practice and as a result do not gain any opportunities for informal learning about behaviour or skill and knowledge development.

It has been suggested that when professionals with different beliefs, experiences, roles and status came together to implement a policy for which they each have their own personal and unique readings, uniformity is actually the least likely outcome (Coburn and Stein, 2006; Jennings, 1996). This variability in teachers' implementation of the school's behaviour policy, as we have discussed (in Chapters 7 and 10), can make it even more challenging for TAs to manage behaviour. McLaughlin (1991) also classified implementer's responses to policies as 'idiosyncratic, frustratingly unpredictable, if not downright resistant' and reported that this 'variability was an anathema to policy makers' as consistent approaches were very unlikely to ever occur (McLaughlin, 1991). We have seen how, if TAs are immersed or actively included in the life of the school, purposeful dialogue can happen between the teachers they work with, as well as in their communities of practice, which can support them in managing and perhaps even actively benefitting from the multiplicity of strategies to manage behaviour they might experience.

This chapter has:

- Considered TAs' role and place in the whole-school community

- Discussed what communities of practice are and how they can both be advantageous and disadvantageous for TAs to develop skills and strategies to manage behaviour

- Shared some of the challenges TAs might face in being part of a whole-school community and how they are often unintentionally marginalised from the life of the school

📚 Further reading

 Bland, K. and Sleightholme, S. (2012). *Researching the Pupil Voice: What Makes a Good Teaching Assistant? Support for Learning*, 27(4), 172–176.

■ Rose, R. (2010). *Understanding Inclusion: Interpretations, Perspectives and Cultures. In Rose, R. (Ed.), Confronting Obstacles to Inclusion* (pp. 1–7). Oxon: Routledge.

■ Visser, J. (2003). *A Study of Children and Young People who Present Challenging Behaviour – Literature Review.* London: Ofsted.

References

Abrams, K. (1999). From Autonomy to Agency: Feminist Perspectives on Self-Direction. *William and Mary Law Review, 40*(3), 805–846.

Armstrong, D. (2014). Educator Perceptions of Children Who Present with Social, Emotional and Behavioural Difficulties: A Literature Review with Implications for Recent Educational Policy in England and Internationally. *International Journal of Inclusive Education, 18*(7), 731–745.

Bedford, D., Jackson, C. and Wilson, E. (2008). New Partnerships for Learning: Teachers' Perspectives on Their Developing Professional Relationships with Teaching Assistants in England. *Journal of In-Service Education, 34*(1), 7–25.

Bland, K. and Sleightholme, S. (2012). Researching the Pupil Voice: What Makes a Good Teaching Assistant? *Support for Learning, 27*(4), 172–176.

Blatchford, P., Russell, A., Bassett, P., Brown, P. and Martin, C. (2007). The Role and Effects of Teaching Assistants in English Primary Schools (Years 4 to 6) 2000–2003. Results from the Class Size and Pupil–Adult Ratios (CSPAR) KS2 Project. *British Educational Research Journal, 33*(1), 5–26.

Blatchford, P., Russell, A. and Webster, R. (2012). *Reassessing the Impact of Teaching Assistants.* Oxon: Routledge.

Coburn, C. and Stein, M. (2006). Communities of Practice Theory and the Role of Teacher Professional Community in Policy Implementation. In Honig, M. (Ed.), *New Directions in Education Policy Implementation: Confronting Complexity* (pp. 25–47). Albany: State University of New York Press.

Datnow, A. (2000). Power and Politics in the Adoption of School Reform Models. *Educational Evaluation and Policy Analysis, 22*(4), 357–374.

Datnow, A. and Castellano, M. (2000). Teachers' Responses to Success for All: How Beliefs, Experiences, and Adaptations Shape Implementation. *American Educational Research Journal, 37*(3), 775–799.

Dearden, J. (1994). Using Support Effectively at Primary Level. In Gray, P., Miller, A. and Noakes, J. (Eds.), *Challenging Behaviour in Schools* (pp. 42–55). London: Routledge.

Department for Education. (2013). *Behaviour and Discipline in Schools: Guidance for Governing Bodies.* London: DfE.

Department for Education. (2016). *Behaviour and Discipline in Schools: Advice for Headteachers and School Staff.* London: DfE.

Department of Education and Science. (1989). *Discipline in Schools. Report of the Committee of Enquiry. (Chairman: Lord Elton.).* London: DfES.

Devecchi, C. and Rouse, M. (2010). An Exploration of the Features of Effective Collaboration between Teachers and Teaching Assistants in Secondary Schools. *Support for Learning, 25*(2), 91–99.

Gerschel, L. (2005). The Special Educational Needs Coordinator's Role in Managing Teaching Assistants: The Greenwich Perspective. *Support for Learning, 20*(2), 69–76.

Goodman, J. (2006). School Discipline in Moral Disarray. *Journal of Moral Education*, *35*(2), 213–230.

Graves, S. (2012). Chameleon or Chimera? The Role of the Higher Level Teaching Assistant (HLTA) in a Remodelled Workforce in English Schools. *Educational Management Administration & Leadership*, *41*(1), 95–104.

Graves, S. (2013). New Roles, Old Stereotypes – Developing a School Workforce in English Schools. *School Leadership & Management*, *34*(3), 255–268.

Groom, B. (2006). Building Relationships for Learning: The Developing Role of the Teaching Assistant. *Support for Learning*, *21*(4), 199–203.

Groom, B. and Rose, R. (2005). Supporting the Inclusion of Pupils with Social, Emotional and Behavioural Difficulties in the Primary School: The Role of Teaching Assistants. *Journal of Research in Special Educational Needs*, *5*(1), 20–30.

Hammersley-Fletcher, L. and Adnett, N. (2009). Empowerment or Prescription? Workforce Remodelling at the National and School Level. *Educational Management Administration & Leadership*, *37*(2), 180–197.

Haroun, R. and O'Hanlon, C. (1997). Do Teachers and Students Agree in Their Perception of What School Discipline Is? *Educational Review*, *49*(3), 237–250.

Hill, H. (2001). Policy Is Not Enough: Language and the Interpretation of State Standards. *American Educational Research Journal*, *38*(2), 289–318.

HMI (2002). *Teaching Assistants in Primary Schools an Evaluation of the Quality and Impact of Their Work*. London: HMI.

Houssart, J. (2013). 'Give Me a Lesson and I'll Deliver It': Teaching Assistants' Experiences of Leading Primary Mathematics Lessons in England. *Cambridge Journal of Education*, *43*(1), 1–16.

Jennings, N. (1996). *Interpreting Policy in Real Classrooms: Case Studies of State Reform and Teacher Practice*. New York: Teachers College Press.

Kubiak, C., Fenton-O'Creevy, M., Appleby, K., Kempster, M., Reed, M., Solvason, C. and Thorpe, M. (2015). Brokering Boundary Encounters. In Wenher-Trayner, E., Fenton-O'Creevy, M., Hutchinson, S., Kubiak, C. and Wenger-Trayner, B. (Eds.), *Learning in Landscapes of Practice: Boundaries, Identity and Knowledgeability in Practice-based Learning* (pp. 81–96). Oxon: Routledge.

Lund, R. (1996). *A Whole-School Behaviour Policy: A Practical Guide*. London: Kogan Page Limited.

Mackenzie, S. (2011). "Yes, but...": Rhetoric, Reality and Resistance in Teaching Assistants' Experiences of Inclusive Education. *Support for Learning*, *26*, 64–71.

Maguire, M., Ball, S. and Braun, A. (2010). Behaviour, Classroom Anagement and Student 'Control': Enacting Policy in the English Secondary School. *International Studies in Sociology of Education*, *20*(2), 153–170.

Mansaray, A. (2006). Liminality and In/Exclusion: Exploring the Work of Teaching Assistants. *Pedagogy, Culture & Society*, *14*(2), 171–187.

Marr, A., Turner, J., Swann, W. and Hancock, R. (2002). *Classroom Assistants in the Pimary School: Employment and Deployment*. Milton Keynes: Open University.

McLaughlin, M. (1991). The Rand Change Agent Study: Ten Years Later. In Odden, A. (Ed.), *Educational Policy Implementation* (pp. 143–156). Albany: State University of New York Press.

Mulholland, M. and O'Connor, U. (2016). Collaborative Classroom Practice for Inclusion: Perspectives of Classroom Teachers and Learning Support/Resource Teachers. *International Journal of Inclusive Education*, *20*(10), 1070–1083.

Nias, J., Southworth, G. and Yeomans, R. (1989). *Staff Relationships in the Primary School*. London: Cassell Educational Limited.

O'Brien, T. and Garner, P. (2002). Tim and Philip's Story: Setting the Record Straight. In O'Brien, T. and Garner, P. (Eds.), *Untold Stories – Learning Support Assistants and Their Work* (pp. 1–10). Stoke on Trent: Trentham Books Ltd.

Ofsted. (2008). *The Deployment, Training and Development of the Wider School Workforce.* London: Ofsted.

Payne, R. (2015). Using Rewards and Sanctions in the Classroom: Pupils' Perceptions of Their Own Responses to Current Behaviour Management Strategies. *Educational Review, 67*(4), 483–504.

Philpott, C. (2014). *Theories of Professional Learning: A Critical Guide for Teacher Educators.* Northwich: Critical Publishing.

Radford, J. (2000). Values into Practice: Developing Whole School Behaviour Policies. *Support for Learning, 15*(2), 86–89.

Rose, R. (2010). Understanding Inclusion: Interpretations, Perspectives and Cultures. In Rose, R. (Ed.), *Confronting Obstacles to Inclusion* (pp. 1–7). Oxon: Routledge.

Rose, R. and Forlin, C. (2010). Impact of Training on Change in Practice for Education Assistants in a Group of International Private Schools in Hong Kong. *International Journal of Inclusive Education, 14*(3), 309–323.

Rose, R. and O'Neill, Á. (2009). Classroom Support for Inclusion in England and Ireland: An Evaluation of Contrasting Models. *Research in Comparative and International Education, 4*(3), 250–261.

Smylie, M. and Evans, A. (2006). Social Capital and the Problem of Implementation. In Honig, M. (Ed.), *New Directions in Education Policy Implementation: Confronting Complexity* (pp. 187–208). Albany: State University of New York Press.

Spillane, J., Reiser, B. and Reimer, T. (2002). Policy Implementation and Cognition: Reframing and Refocusing Implementation Research. *Review of Educational Research, 72*(3), 387–431.

Symes, W. and Humphrey, N. (2011). The Deployment, Training and Teacher Relationships of Teaching Assistants Supporting Pupils with Autistic Spectrum Disorders (ASD) in Mainstream Secondary Schools. *British Journal of Special Education, 38*(2), 57–64.

Tucker, S. (2009). Perceptions and Reflections on the Role of the Teaching Assistant in the Classroom Environment. *Pastoral Care in Education, 27*(4), 291–300.

Turnbull, B. (2002). Teacher Participation and Buy-in: Implications for School Reform Initiatives. *Learning Environments Research, 5*(3), 235–252.

Visser, J. (2003). *A Study of Children and Young People Who Present Challenging Behaviour – Literature Review.* London: Ofsted.

Watkins, C. and Wagner, P. (2000). *Improving School Behaviour.* London: Paul Chapman Publishing Ltd.

Wenger, E. (1991). *Communities of Practice: Learning, Meaning, and Identity.* Cambridge: Cambridge University Press.

Wilkinson, G. (2005). Workforce Remodelling and Formal Knowledge: The Erosion of Teachers' Professional Jurisdiction in English Schools. *School Leadership & Management, 25*(5), 421–439.

Wilson, E. and Bedford, D. (2008). "New Partnerships for Learning": Teachers and Teaching Assistants Working Together in Schools – The Way Forward. *Journal of Education for Teaching, 34*(2), 137–150.

13 Deployment and the TA

This chapter rounds off Part 3 of the book and will end our consideration of the in-school factors that affect how TAs manage behaviour. I have purposefully left our discussions of how TAs are deployed to work in schools until the end of this section. At times, to address the issues TAs experience in schools or the issues schools experience working with TAs, simple changes to deployment are seen as some sort of magic bullet. I am keen help you see (although I am sure you can already!) that the ways in which TAs work in school and the types of groups, staff and children they work with are actually governed by many of the factors we have already considered. For example, changing a TA's deployment from one-to-one to general class support will not make any significant impact unless underlying aspects such as a lack of training or professional development are considered; just as deploying a TA with one teacher rather than another will not address the systemic issues they have with status and power in schools. Supporting a TA in working their way to HLTA status will not on its own ameliorate issues of role creep and boundary crossing, and so on.

The preceding chapters have, I hope, begun to illustrate that although we may think about issues that affect TAs as discreet categories, they actually act together like a web, all interwoven and interconnected with each other. Although the way TAs are deployed in schools is a very important and a very visible factor, it is not necessarily the most, or least, important aspect when considering how they can be supported to manage behaviour.

This chapter will:

- Look at the ways TAs are often deployed in schools

- Consider how the range of deployments TAs might experience impacts on their relationships with teachers

- Discuss how TAs are challenged or supported in developing relationships with children through their deployment

- Share the strengths and limitations for TAs, teachers and children of a range of different forms of TA deployment

What does the research tell us?

 Pause point

Before we even begin the discussion, consider the ways in which TAs could be deployed. How many can you list? Try to get to ten! Think about:

- What advantages might each form of deployment provide for TAs, teachers and children?

- What disadvantages might each form of deployment provide for TAs, teachers and children?

- What other aspects will affect whether the form of deployment is broadly advantageous or disadvantageous?

- Which do you think is the most supportive and beneficial in terms of TAs' ability to manage behaviour?

- Which group does it have most advantages for and why?

The term 'deployment' in this chapter is used to refer to how and where TAs work in a school or setting. For example – this might be with one class and one teacher, across a year group or Key Stage, with a range of teachers, one-to-one with a specific child, or organised to fulfil a specific intervention or deliver a specific programme. TAs' deployment dictates which members of staff they work with and, therefore, who they learn from and the opportunities they are afforded to manage behaviour. Research (Sharples, Webster and Blatchford, 2015) has cautioned that particular care is required in TA deployment, which should be seen as part of an overall drive for whole-school improvement, as opposed to an isolated or reactive process, with decisions on TAs' deployment being where all other decisions about TAs flow from.

We begin this chapter with a review of the impact of role clarity and boundary crossing on the way TAs work. This has been a key part of the interwoven issues that affect TAs, both negatively and positively, throughout this book. The flexibility and fluidity in the roles TAs can, and do, fulfil in schools and their work as 'in-between' in schools (Howes, 2003) has been argued by many to be necessary. There have even been suggestions that schools would be unable to function if the adaptability in the expectations of TA roles was removed. It has been suggested that the requirement for flexibility, both in definitions of TAs' role and in their deployment, has enabled them to engage effectively with children who may have behaviour difficulties. This flexibility can be seen reflected in the wider definitions of behavioural difficulties and SEND, particularly those in use by the British government. Norwich and Eaton (2015) argued that the DfE/DoH (2015) reclassification of the language used around children with SEND did nothing to improve the ambiguity they saw as inherent in the previous terms. This was an issue they saw as problematic, particularly in multi-agency working, when the hazy definitions and language used meant that not all members of the team might necessarily be talking about the same thing.

This mirrors challenges for TAs in their own forms of multi-agency working – where they may regularly have to engage with parents, children, teachers, special educational needs and disabilities co-ordinators (SENDCos) and other professionals, as well as working with the ambiguities of understanding their place, or role in managing behaviour. It has been suggested that schools and staff have a powerful influence (Beaman and Wheldall, 2000) on children's behaviour, with healthy pupil development resulting from positive relationships with staff (Hajdukova, Hornby and Cushman, 2014). Nevertheless, research (Boxall, 2004; Gray, Miller and Noakes, 1994; Spratt, Shucksmith, Philip and Watson, 2006) suggested that developing this type of rapport with children was challenging due to the myriad of roles schools are required to fulfil. Parallels could be drawn here between the tensions schools face in building relationships with children due to their multifaceted roles and that of TAs and their similarly polyvalent roles.

Research has shown that the absence of a clear, whole-school definition of the TA role often results in a large amount of variation and inconsistent deployment (Webster, Blatchford, Bassett, Brown and Russell, 2011). UNISON (2013) described TAs' deployment as 'something of a lottery', suggesting that there was no generally agreed blueprint for effective TA deployment. Despite highlighting the widely reported deployment and management of teachers and TAs as 'teams' in their survey, UNISON (2013) did not comment of the success of this. Instead they noted the continued training deficit TAs experienced (as discussed in Chapter 10) with the need for good practice examples of TA deployment to support schools. Gerschel (2005), in her research, described the deployment of TAs as complex and ill-defined. This would suggest that at this stage, research is unable to provide schools with a model of TA deployment that works well, but there are examples of how TAs are not effectively deployed. Webster et al. (2011) highlighted the need for explicit questions about TA deployment, which he suggested should then be followed by unambiguous answers. Houssart and Croucher (2013) called for a more collaborative approach to the deployment of TAs than those that they argued had been advocated by the government and leading experts. This brings the discussion around again to ensuring that TAs are deployed in a planned and proactive way that reflects the aims and priorities of schools, rather than to fill gaps or react to situations – such as problems with behaviour. If schools unequivocally consider the way in which they organise TAs, this might well provide a specific rationale for their deployment in the broader whole-school context and could provide opportunities for positive TA–teacher relationships to develop.

The Education Endowment Foundation's guidance on 'Making the Best Use of Teaching Assistants' (Sharples et al., 2015), for example, has produced guidance on how to work with TAs in school but little of this focuses on the ways in which they could be deployed. One example is using TAs to deliver high-quality interventions, which does indeed suggest a specific deployment, but this would not be practicable for all TAs throughout the year in all classes. The guidance does, however, clearly state that 'The status quo isn't an option! The evidence is clear: poor TA deployment has a negative impact on attainment; effective TA deployment can have positive impacts'. Again, if we think about how TAs are used and the narratives of performativity and value for money (considered in Chapter 11) then this caution by the EEF seems to relate solely to TAs' quantifiable impact – their success in achieving an outcome when working with children that can be measured – their academic attainment. If we think about TAs' support for what has been termed children's 'soft skills', their non-academic achievements, things like support for behaviour, social skills and so on then this statement from the EEF does not have quite the same impact. We will now investigate the advantages and disadvantages of a range of TA deployment in schools.

Working in a range of classes with a range of teachers

We will initially consider what research suggests about TAs being deployed with a nomadic brief, that is, working with a number of classes, teachers and children across a day or week. HMI (2002) had previously noted that although schools tried to place TAs with specific classes, this often did not work in practice and led to 'fragmentation', which was seen as particularly damaging as it prevented teachers and TAs developing a close working partnership. This fragmented or inconsistent deployment might mean that TAs work with a number of teachers – and therefore, children – in different Key Stages and classes over a week or even a day. It was argued that deploying TAs to work with a range of classes made developing teamwork more complex and challenging for all involved (Houssart and Croucher, 2013). Within this fragmented model, TAs are also at risk of what had been termed 'internal exclusion' by regularly being deployed to work with withdrawal groups outside the classroom (Mackenzie, 2011). Quinn and Carl (2015) argued that a lot of the work TAs and teachers undertook in schools was in 'relative isolation from colleagues', particularly for TAs who are regularly expected to work with groups outside the classroom. Bowers (1997) had earlier warned that the practice of TAs working with individuals and groups with SEND had the potential to cause what he termed 'out-group denigration' leading to 'polarising group identities' – for both children and TAs. This was reinforced by Mackenzie's (2011) research where a TA had described her role as isolating due to the peripatetic nature of her deployment, stating that, as a result, she was unable to build relationships with staff. Whittaker and Kikabhai (2008) also signalled that TAs could end up in an 'educational cul-de-sac' where both they and the children they worked with were felt to be equally devalued and disengaged from the ordinary life of the school.

Ideas about TAs being separate and marginalised (as we have discussed in Chapters 5, 8 and 9) can also be seen to be a theme with the way they are deployed in schools. 'Isolation' might be experienced by TAs due to the lack of time available to spend with individual teachers, some of whom they might only see for one lesson a week. A lack of time for teachers and TAs to talk together and reflect on their approaches in the classroom (as discussed in Chapters 8 and 9) has been suggested by a wide range of research to constrain opportunities for professional learning (Eraut, 2004, 2007; Gerschel, 2005; Marr, Turner, Swann and Hancock, 2002; Philpott, 2014; Rose, 2000; Sharples et al., 2015; Thomas, 1992; Webster et al., 2011). On the other hand, the professional communities that could develop between teachers and TAs with stable deployment have been proposed to:

> counteract the effects of classroom isolation. They may also operate as structures that foster professional agency to the extent that they provide opportunities for educators to engage in sustained dialogue and interaction rather than didactic processes.
>
> (Quinn and Carl, 2015, p.747)

It can be seen from this that the impact of being deployed to work across a range of classes and with a number of teachers causes significant issues for TAs in developing relationships with teachers. As we have discussed (in Chapters 7, 8 and 9) the importance of developing positive relationships with teachers cannot be underestimated and the lack of knowledge of a teacher and the way they work, including their often unspoken expectations of TAs generally and of their role in managing behaviour specifically, is a significant barrier for TAs.

Visser (2003) had suggested that most teachers had neither the time nor training for pastoral work, and that the responsibility fell instead to TAs, which was supported by my research findings. My participating TAs highlighted 'direct pastoral support for pupils' as one of the most important aspects of their role. Despite this, my participants argued that the way in which they were deployed by the school, where they worked daily with a number of different teachers and classes, or groups of children, limited their ability to fulfil this pastoral role. My own participants suggested that stable deployment – where they worked with the same class or children – was necessary to support this form of work with children. They argued that less fragmentation and variation in the way they were deployed would enable them to get a much clearer understanding of the children they worked with and particularly, of their behaviour. Working consistently with the same group of children would mean that the TAs' knowledge of the child, or children's behaviour would not just be isolated in that moment or lesson, but they would be able to contextualise the behaviour in what had happened earlier in the day. This could then support TAs in developing an understanding of what was usual behaviour for specific children, by building relationships with them and spending time with them. One of my TAs stated that her lack of ability to form relationships with children, due to her deployment in the school, positioned her simply as an 'observer'. This she suggested, left her unable to 'intervene' and manage any behaviour. This was noted by other participants in my research as a 'lack of insight' into children's behaviours and difficulties in 'bonding' with them and 'being on their level'. TAs in my study additionally suggested that if they knew children well, they were able to 'go the extra mile' to support them, regardless of whether or not it was 'within your role written down on paper', a theme also noted by TAs in Watson, Bayliss and Pratchett's (2013) research.

 Pause point

Participants in my research suggested that when they worked with a range of teachers, classes and children, they became merely 'observers' of the behaviour that happened in the classroom. Think about:

■ How might this role as an 'observer' impact on TAs' agency and professional identity?

■ How might TAs simply observing affect the teacher and children?

■ How might TAs who are deployed in this way be supported to become active rather than passive in managing behaviour?

Working in one class with one teacher

It can be suggested from the research we have considered that TAs working across the school did not have many advantages. Rose (2000) noted that although it was unlikely that any single model of classroom support would be applicable to all staff in all schools and settings, it would be logical to deploy TAs with specific teachers to encourage relationships to be built and to enable them to develop flexible practices which benefited and supported them both, as well as the children. This was supported by findings (Balshaw and Farrell, 2002) that a degree of flexibility in teamwork developed as TAs and teachers became more comfortable working together. It would seem that deploying one TA with one teacher would allow these relationships to develop over time. This form of deployment could enable a joint understanding about each other's aims and purposes with clarity about joint approaches to managing behaviour (Balshaw and Farrell, 2002). The importance of clarity in role has been highlighted as a current stumbling block in the wide range of research we have considered and discussed (in Chapters 5, 8 and 9). Stable deployment and the formation of joint understandings and approaches between teachers and TAs could also be suggested to support TAs' agency in managing behaviour. Lehane's (2016) research echoed this, with TAs in her study acknowledging that communication and collaboration between the two groups were contingent on developing rapport and relationships between teachers and TAs. However, and rather worryingly, this was suggested to be reliant on the individual teacher's disposition rather than whole school practices or procedures.

One of my participating TAs was in the unusual position of understanding both what it was like to work as a TA with fragmented deployment and also as a teacher working with only one TA – which she had just experienced on school practice as part of her Initial Teacher Training. When discussing the benefits of this stable deployment she suggested that from a teacher's perspective it was '100 per cent better', for 'a million reasons'. In relation to behaviour, she reiterated my other participants' views about the importance of establishing a relationship with the child which it was felt stable deployment enabled. She suggested:

> I think it is easier for the teacher, I think it's easier for the TA, it is easier for the pupils because they get consistency, standards of behaviour are better because they get the same people and they know exactly what they're doing. I think you're more likely to crackdown on things quickly because you know how they [the children] normally behave.

Rose (2000) stated that TAs' deployment with a single teacher enhanced effective and collaborative procedures for classroom management. This supported Groom's (2006) suggestion that effective deployment was dependent on team management and support, as well as a positive partnership between TAs and teachers, a key aspect of which was clearly outlined roles and expectations. The wealth of understanding and knowledge TAs developed with stable deployment with the same children was cited by participants in Lehane's (2016) study of TAs' work. It also resonates with other earlier findings about the importance of continuity in TAs' work with children, particularly when managing behaviour (Collins and Simco, 2006; Stoll and Seashore Louis, 2007). It was suggested in Lehane's (2016) study that this consistent deployment not only supported TAs' work with children but also the development of their relationships with teachers who, a TA in their study asserted, they needed to learn 'how to handle the teachers as much as you know how to handle the kids'.

Despite the proposed benefits, particularly the opportunity to form a teacher–TA team and to develop relationships, the deployment of a TA with one teacher or class has been criticised. It was argued that actively flexible, rather than stable deployment of TAs had advantages, with Rose (2000) suggesting that TAs should have a roving brief in their classroom work. The teacher participants in Wilson and Bedford's (2008) study argued that schools were what they described, rather worryingly as, colluding in 'de-skilling and devaluing teachers' by deploying TAs to support children with SEND. This was because the TA developed expertise with that child which was, the participants suggested, superior to the teacher's. These perceptions may be due to the views of the teachers in the sample that were linked to fears that TAs' deployment would impact on their own career progression, as well as 'personal resistance to workforce reform' (Wilson and Bedford, 2008). This might also challenge teachers' views that they were, as my TAs proposed, the ones in charge in the classroom.

Nevertheless, Whittaker and Kikabhai (2008) also found that due to TAs' ability to form different sorts of relationships with children than teachers could, that

TAs might well have understood children's behaviour better than other members of staff – specifically the class teacher. Others (Quicke, 2003; Roffey-Barentsen and Watt, 2014; Stoll and Seashore Louis, 2007) concurred, stating that where TAs were deployed with a single class, they often had a deeper knowledge of the pupils than the class teacher, who at times still handed over responsibility for these children to the TA. This was supported by participants in my research, where one TA stated she felt that due to the autonomy she had been afforded in her work with children, she was required to make key judgements about them. It was acknowledged by my other participating TAs that 'it isn't really your job to judge' and that children's well-being and welfare are 'in your hands then'. The updated 2014 SEND Code of Practice highlighted teachers' accountability for children with SEND, but was silent on TAs' role (Blatchford, Russell and Webster, 2016). This was interpreted by some (Webster, 2014) as a 'coded warning' about TAs continuing to work with children with SEND, which historically and still in some schools, they largely have. Lewis's (1999) earlier research had also highlighted tensions – specifically for teachers – between inclusion and maintaining order. This could also be seen as a specific consideration for TAs whose work managing behaviour or deployed with identified children is often used to support inclusion (Blatchford et al., 2016; Butt and Lowe, 2011; Lehane, 2016; Mansaray, 2006; Webster, 2014; Webster and Blatchford, 2013). Giangreco (2013) furthered this and suggested that TAs had become 'almost exclusively *the way*' to support children, opposed to simply 'a *way*'.

Stable deployment where TAs work with specific children, despite being seen by participants in my study and in a range of research as advantageous, can actually be problematic. TAs' ability when deployed consistently in this way to develop a deep understanding of the children they work with and 'know what makes them tick', as my TAs described it, has been highlighted as an important factor which made TAs specifically suited for working with children with behaviour difficulties (Mackenzie, 2011). Nevertheless, some of the issues with this form of deployment were raised by the TAs in my study. The difficulties they faced were more commonly due to issues with teachers than with children under this form of deployment. This was illustrated by my participants where one TA described the challenges she faced: 'I'm not saying I'm brilliant but you just get to know those kids'. This understanding of children that TAs could develop was, my TAs noted, not always achieved by the class teacher; 'the teachers themselves can sometimes press the wrong buttons to be honest, and you can see the effect it has on the child but as a teaching assistant I would never be able to say'. This view also reflects the issues previously discussed, such as status and concerns my participants expressed about overstepping the mark and undermining the teacher. It could also be suggested to be a source of frustration for TAs. One of my TAs stated that when children worked with her in groups they were isolated from the rest of the class, which made them fearful about returning – something she found both frustrating and upsetting. Her concerns were also noted by another participant who argued:

they [the children] don't like it when you send them back [to the classroom] because they're not managed the way they understand. I think perhaps because I've not got however many others I can deal with it a bit better, and more on their level, in a way that they understand.

The DfES (1989) have long recognised that in the complex mix of events in the classroom, the most central of the multiple influences is that of relationships. The importance of relationships with children has also been highlighted by a wide range of research over many years, noting the impact that positive relationships with teachers – and the same could be suggested for TAs – has on children's behaviour (Collins and Simco, 2006; Hajdukova et al., 2014; Houssart and Croucher, 2013; Lehane, 2016; Stoll and Seashore Louis, 2007; Way, 2011; Whittaker and Kikabhai, 2008). Lewis (2001) found that relationship-based discipline was most commonly established in primary schools, and this was noted by the TAs in my research who suggested, when talking about managing behaviour, that 'it's a relationship thing'. TAs' responses about the importance of having a relationship with children when managing their behaviour could be associated with the less formal and more friendly relationships research suggested TAs are able to form with children compared to teachers (Armstrong, 2008; Bland and Sleightholme, 2012; Blatchford et al., 2004; Blatchford, Russell, Bassett, Brown and Martin, 2007; Fraser and Meadows, 2008; Rubie-Davies, Blatchford, Webster, Koutsoubou and Bassett, 2010; Whittaker and Kikabhai, 2008).

This discussion shows again how a range of factors either support or constrain TAs' work regardless of their deployment. It also links us back to the start of the chapter where it was highlighted that changes in deployment alone would not automatically change the efficacy of TAs' work supporting behaviour.

 Pause point

Participants in my study and wider research have noted the importance of relationships, not only those between the teacher and the TA but also those between the TA and child as a support for managing behaviour. Think about:

■ How might relationships between children, TAs and teachers be maximised in the way TAs are deployed in schools?

■ How can TAs' suggested 'deep knowledge' of the children they work with be utilised rather than being a site of tension?

■ TAs working on a one-to-one basis with children has not been discussed. What additional tensions might they experience?

What this might mean in school

We have looked at a range of deployment methods in this chapter, but also considered the need for TA deployment to be part of a whole-school plan, as opposed to being seen as an add-on, or in some way separate from the rest of the school priorities. TA deployment has been described by the research we have considered here as complex and difficult to define – like many other aspects of a TA's role! If TAs are expected to take an active part in managing behaviour, the way in which they are deployed can either help or hinder them in this. As the EEF guidance (Sharples et al., 2015) and much research shows, teachers can benefit from effective deployment of TAs as it can reduce their workload and stress, and improve classroom behaviour.

1. **TA deployment, specifically if they are expected to manage behaviour or are being deployed with children whose behaviour challenges, needs to be considered as a key aspect of whole-school planning.**

In the research considered there have been no clear best-practice examples of TA deployment to follow, although some guidance has been provided to increase the effectiveness of TAs in relation to supporting children's academic achievement. When thinking about effective deployment in a more holistic sense, there are no specific forms of deployment that research suggests are more beneficial than others. All forms of TA deployment have advantages and disadvantages, and these are mediated by the context and environment the TA works in and who they work with specifically.

2. **When deploying TAs there is no exemplar model to follow. Ensure careful evaluation to consider how successful the deployment strategies have been, so it is clear which groups are benefiting, including TAs, teachers and children.**

Relationships, between the teacher(s) and TA(s) and between the TA and children have been shown to be very important, particularly when managing behaviour. These relational aspects of managing behaviour have been highlighted as particularly important in primary schools. The research drawn on surrounding deployment seems to present something of a professional 'love triangle' where either the teacher or the TA is in some way excluded from the relationships that are made with children.

3. **If TAs are deployed with a number of teachers across a number of classes, they will not form collaborative or positive relationships as easily with either. Clarity in the teachers' expectations of the TA's role in managing behaviour is needed to bridge this gap.**

To remedy some of the issues caused by the lack of familiarity with the children and the teacher when TAs work in a range of classes, research shows that it is even more important that TAs are clear on what role they are expected to play. TAs in my research reported that without this understanding of what the teacher expected them to do, they become passive observers, which negatively affects their agency and professional identity and may well cause frustration for the teacher and the TA. Time will need to be specifically and regularly set aside for the teacher(s) and TA(s) to meet one-to-one to share their expectations of each other. This is most important when the teacher–TA team is new as there is no prior experience to draw on and when classes begin at the start of the year.

4. **Clear channels of communication between TAs and the teachers they work with need to be facilitated, especially when teams and/or children are new, for example, at the start of the academic year.**

When TAs are deployed to work with specific children or groups they may well, as the research we have considered and the TAs in my study argued, develop a better understanding of the children's behavioural needs and strategies to manage them than the class teacher. Not being able to share this information is a source of frustration for TAs as well as teachers. Some teachers may be challenged by TAs having this form of deep understanding of the children they work with, as this is often unattainable by teachers who do not work with the children individually or in groups as often as a TA might. Careful consideration will need to be given to how best TAs can share this knowledge with teachers. This is an aspect that would need managing carefully, as my TAs were concerned about undermining teachers and overstepping the mark in relation to managing behaviour, so both teachers and TAs will need careful support to do this effectively.

5. **Systems and support needs to be in place for TAs to effectively share knowledge of children and groups' behaviour and strategies to manage it with teachers, as well as vice versa.**

When TAs are asked to work with individuals or groups, this is sometimes outside of the classroom. Although there may be a range of reasons for this, many of them purposeful and positive, if TAs are always asked to work outside the classroom this will limit the relationship they can develop with the class teacher and their knowledge of the systems (including those for managing behaviour) that the teacher has in place. It is important that even when working on specific interventions with specific groups, the same TA or groups of TAs are not always expected to be working outside of the classroom community.

6. **If TAs are always expected to work outside of the teacher's classroom, their opportunities to learn about the teachers' strategies to manage behaviour and expectation of the TA to do so become very limited.**

Reflection activity

In this chapter we have compared and contrasted two of the key ways in which TAs can be deployed; either with a range of teachers or with just one. At the beginning of this chapter in one of the pause points (p. 171) you were invited to think about all of the different ways in which TAs work in schools and settings, or in your own experience. Using what we have discussed from the research findings and the impact on practice in schools can you begin to reflect on the table in Figure 13.1. When you have thought about it, or completed it, consider the changes that it might be possible to make in your school or setting, or in your own experience, to minimise some of the disadvantages of the different forms of deployment you have identified.

 Summary

In this chapter we have begun to consider how TAs are deployed and the number of ways, and the people, they might work with in schools. The importance of seeing TA deployment as interlinked with a range of other in-school factors has been highlighted. These might include: the levels of training possible, TAs' ability to exercise

Form of deployment	Advantages for TAs	Disadvantages for TAs	Advantages for teachers	Disadvantages for teachers	Advantages for children	Disadvantages for children

Figure 13.1 The advantages and disadvantages of a range of TA deployment on stakeholders

agency, an understanding of what their role does or might encompass and centrally, the relationships they are able to form as a result of their deployment, both with children and adults. As with Collins and Simco's (2006) findings, the TAs participating in my study felt that having an existing relationship with a child was necessary to manage their behaviour. Collins and Simco (2006) found that all the TAs in their study agreed on the importance of continuity in their work with children, stating that the deep knowledge they had of children was part of their 'unique contribution' to managing behaviour. We have considered the importance of developing relationships through the ways TAs are deployed; participants in my study stated that deployment could enable them to develop a closer relationship with the children – to understand 'what else is happening in their life' – as well as with the class teacher.

The importance of time to build relationships and to share information and skills professionally and collaboratively has been repeated again in this chapter. The chapter, and indeed this part of the book, has ended considering the importance of deployment in relation to TAs' ability to manage behaviour – but also the need to see it as one in a range of factors that is likely to need addressing, as opposed to the only factor.

This chapter has:

- reviewed a number of ways TAs might be deployed in schools

- reiterated the interconnectedness of the range of factors that influence TAs' ability to manage behaviour

- considered the strengths and limitations of TAs working with a number of teachers and a number of classes

- discussed working with just one teacher and class has evaluated and its advantages and disadvantages

- reflected onthe challenges in different forms of deployment of forming relationships with children and teachers

- reiterated the importance of TAs' deployment being part of, and stemming from whole school planning

 ## Further reading

- Balshaw, M and Farrell, P. (2002). *Teaching Assistants: Practical Strategies for Effective Classroom Support*. London: David Fulton Publishers.

- Blatchford, P., Russell, A. and Webster, R. (2016). *Maximising the Impact of Teaching Assistants: Guidance for School Leaders and Teachers* (2nd ed.). London: Routledge.

- Department of Health and Department of Education (2015). *Special Educational Needs and Disability Code of Practice: 0 to 25 Years Statutory Guidance for Organisations which Work with and Support Children and Young People Who Have Special Educational Needs or Disabilities.* DfE/DoH: London.

- Whittaker, J. and Kikabhai, N. (2008). How Schools Create Challenging Behaviours. In Richards, G. and Armstrong, F. (Eds.), *Key Issues for Teaching Assistants: Working in Diverse Classrooms.* London: Routledge.

References

Armstrong, F. (2008). Inclusive Education. In Richards, G. and Armstrong, F. (Eds.), *Key Issues for Teaching Assistants: Working in Diverse Classrooms* (pp. 7–18). London: Routledge.

Balshaw, M. and Farrell, P. (2002). *Teaching Assistants: Practical Strategies for Effective Classroom Support.* London: David Fulton Publishers.

Beaman, R. and Wheldall, K. (2000). Teachers' Use of Approval and Dissaproval in the Classroom. *Educational Psychology: An International Journal of Experimental Educational Psychology, 20*(4), 431–446.

Bland, K. and Sleightholme, S. (2012). Researching the Pupil Voice: What Makes a Good Teaching Assistant? *Support for Learning, 27*(4), 172–176.

Blatchford, P., Russell, A., Bassett, P., Brown, P. and Martin, C. (2004). *The Role and Effects of Teaching Assistants in English Primary Schools (Years 4 to 6) 2000–2003: Results from the Class Size and Pupil Adult Ratios (CSPAR) Project. Final Report. (Research Report 605).* London: DfES.

Blatchford, P., Russell, A., Bassett, P., Brown, P. and Martin, C. (2007). The Role and Effects of Teaching Assistants in English Primary Schools (Years 4 to 6) 2000–2003. Results from the Class Size and Pupil–Adult Ratios (CSPAR) KS2 Project. *British Educational Research Journal, 33*(1), 5–26.

Blatchford, P., Russell, A. and Webster, R. (2016). *Maximising the Impact of Teaching Assistants: Guidance for School Leaders and Teachers* (2nd ed.). London: Routledge.

Bowers, T. (1997). Supporting Special Needs in the Mainstream Classroom: Children's Perceptions of the Adult Role. *Child: Care, Health and Development, 23*(3), 217–232.

Boxall, M. (2004). The Nurture Group in the Primary School. In Wearmouth, J., Richmond, R., Glynn, T. and Berryman, M. (Ed.), *Understanding Pupil Behaviour in Schools: A Diversity of Approaches* (pp. 196–214). London: David Fulton Publishing.

Butt, R. and Lowe, K. (2011). Teaching Assistants and Class Teachers: Differing Perceptions, Role Confusion and the Benefits of Skills-based Training. *International Journal of Inclusive Education, 16*(2), 207–219.

Collins, J. and Simco, N. (2006). Teaching Assistants Reflect: The Way Forward? *Reflective Practice, 7*(2), 197–214.

Department for Education and Skills (1989). *Discipline in Schools. Report of the Committee of Enquiry. (Chairman: Lord Elton).* London: DfES.

Department of Health and Department of Education. (2015). *Special Educational Needs and Disability Code of Practice: 0 to 25 Years Statutory Guidance for Organisations Which Work with and Support Children and Young People Who Have Special Educational Needs or Disabilities.* Retrieved from www.gov.uk/government/uploads/system/uploads/attachment_data/file/398815/SEND_Code_of_Practice_January_2015.pdf

Eraut, M. (2004). Informal Learning in the Workplace. *Studies in Continuing Education*, *26*(2), 247–273.

Eraut, M. (2007). Learning from Other People in the Workplace. *Oxford Review of Education*, *33*(4), 403–422.

Fraser, C. and Meadows, S. (2008). Children's Views of Teaching Assistants in Primary Schools. *Education 3-13*, *36*(4), 351–363.

Gerschel, L. (2005). The Special Educational Needs Coordinator's Role in Managing Teaching Assistants: The Greenwich Perspective. *Support for Learning*, *20*(2), 69–76.

Giangreco, M. (2013). Teacher Assistant Supports in Inclusive Schools: Research, Practices and Alternatives. *Australasian Journal of Special Education*, *37*(02), 93–106.

Gray, P., Miller, A. and Noakes, J. (1994). Challenging Behaviour in Schools: An Introduction. In Gray, P., Miller, A. and Noakes, J. (Ed.), *Challenging Behaviour in Schools* (pp. 1–4). London: Routledge.

Groom, B. (2006). Building Relationships for Learning: The Developing Role of the Teaching Assistant. *Support for Learning*, *21*(4), 199–203.

Hajdukova, E., Hornby, G. and Cushman, P. (2014). Pupil–teacher Relationships: Perceptions of Boys with Social, Emotional and Behavioural Difficulties. *Pastoral Care in Education*, *32*(2), 145–156.

HMI. (2002). *Teaching Assistants in Primary Schools an Evaluation of the Quality and Impact of Their Work*. London: HMI.

Houssart, J. and Croucher, R. (2013). Intervention Programmes in Mathematics and Literacy: Teaching Assistants' Perceptions of Their Training and Support. *School Leadership and Management*, *33*(5), 427–439.

Howes, A. (2003). Teaching Reforms and the Impact of Paid Adult Support on Participation and Learning in Mainstream Schools. *Support for Learning*, *18*(4), 147–153.

Lehane, T. (2016). "Cooling the Mark Out": Experienced Teaching Assistants' Perceptions of Their Work in the Inclusion of Pupils with Special Educational Needs in Mainstream Secondary Schools. *Educational Review*, *68*(1), 4–23.

Lewis, R. (1999). Teachers' Support for Inclusive Forms of Classroom Management. *International Journal of Inclusive Education*, *3*(3), 269–285.

Lewis, R. (2001). Classroom discipline and student responsibility: the students' view. *Teaching and Teacher Education*, **17**(3), 307–319.

Mackenzie, S. (2011). "Yes, but…": Rhetoric, Reality and Resistance in Teaching Assistants' Experiences of Inclusive Education. *Support for Learning*, *26*, 64–71.

Mansaray, A. (2006). Liminality and In/exclusion: Exploring the Work of Teaching Assistants. *Pedagogy, Culture & Society*, *14*(2), 171–187.

Marr, A., Turner, J., Swann, W. and Hancock, R. (2002). *Classroom Assistants in the Pimary School: Employment and Deployment*. Milton Keynes: Open University.

Norwich, B. and Eaton, A. (2015). The New Special Educational Needs (SEN) Legislation in England and Implications for Services for Children and Young People with Social, Emotional and Behavioural Difficulties. *Emotional and Behavioural Difficulties*, *20*(2), 117–132.

Philpott, C. (2014). *Theories of Professional Learning: A Critical Guide for Teacher Educators*. Northwich: Critical Publishing.

Quicke, J. (2003). Teaching Assistants: Students or Servants? *FORUM*, *45*(2), 71–74.

Quinn, R. and Carl, N. (2015). Teacher Activist Organizations and the Development of Professional Agency. *Teachers and Teaching*, *21*(6), 745–758.

Roffey-Barentsen, J. and Watt, M. (2014). The Voices of Teaching Assistants (Are We Value for Money?). *Research in Education*, *92*(1), 18–31.

Rose, R. (2000). Using Classroom Support in A Primary School: A Single School Case Study. *British Journal of Special Education, 27*(4), 191–196.

Rubie-Davies, C., Blatchford, P., Webster, R., Koutsoubou, M. and Bassett, P. (2010). Enhancing Learning? A Comparison of Teacher and Teaching Assistant Interactions with Pupils. *School Effectiveness and School Improvement, 21*(4), 429–449.

Sharples, J., Webster, R. and Blatchford, P. (2015). *Making Best Use of Teaching Assistants: Guidance Report.* Education Endowment Foundation: London.

Spratt, J., Shucksmith, J., Philip, K. and Watson, C. (2006). "Part of Who We Are as a School Should Include Responsibility for Well-Being": Links between the School Environment, Mental Health and Behaviour. *Pastoral Care in Education, 24*(3), 14–21.

Stoll, L. and Seashore Louis, K. (2007). *Professional Learning Communities: Divergence, Depth and Dilemmas.* Maidenhead: McGraw-Hill Education.

Thomas, G. (1992). *Effective Classroom Teamwork: Support or Intrusion?* London: Routledge.

UNISON. (2013). *The Evident Value of Teaching Assistants: Report of a UNISON Survey.* Retrieved from www.unison.org.uk/content/uploads/2013/06/Briefings-and-CircularsEVIDENT-VALUE-OF-TEACHING-ASSISTANTS-Autosaved3.pdf

Visser, J. (2003). *A Study of Children and Young People Who Present Challenging Behaviour – Literature Review.* London: Ofsted.

Watson, D., Bayliss, P. and Pratchett, G. (2013). Pond Life that 'Know Their Place': Exploring Teaching and Learning Support Assistants' Experiences through Positioning Theory. *International Journal of Qualitative Studies in Education, 26*(1), 100–117.

Way, S. (2011). School Discipline and Disruptive Classroom Behaviour: The Moderating Effects of Student Perceptions. *The Sociological Quarterly, 52*(3), 346–375.

Webster, R. (2014). 2014 Code of Practice: How Research Evidence on the Role and Impact of Teaching Assistants Can Inform Professional Practice. *Educational Psychology in Practice, 30*(3), 232–237.

Webster, R. and Blatchford, P. (2013). *The Making A Statement Project Final Report. A Study of the Teaching and Support Experienced by Pupils with A Statement of Special Educational Needs in Mainstream Primary Schools.* London: Institute of Education.

Webster, R., Blatchford, P., Bassett, P., Brown, C. and Russell, A. (2011). The Wider Pedagogical Role of Teaching Assistants. *School Leadership & Management, 31*(1), 3–20.

Whittaker, J. and Kikabhai, N. (2008). How Schools Create Challenging Behaviours. In Richards, G. and Armstrong, F. (Eds.), *Key Issues for Teaching Assistants: Working in Diverse Classrooms* (pp. 120–130). London: Routledge.

Wilson, E. and Bedford, D. (2008). "New Partnerships for Learning": Teachers and Teaching Assistants Working Together in Schools – The Way Forward. *Journal of Education for Teaching, 34*(2), 137–150. doi:10.1080/02607470801979574.

Part 3
conclusion

In this section of the book we have looked carefully at what research tells us about TAs, the role they play in schools and how this affects and influences the opportunities for them to manage behaviour. We have considered a range of in-school factors as well as some governed by wider constraints such as access to training and elements of TAs' status.

The ongoing evolution of TAs' role, a change from, as Bach, Kessler and Heron (2006) suggested, ancillary roles to curriculum delivery, has impacted on the expectations of them in terms of managing behaviour, and subsequent government publications have formalised these expectations (DfES, 2006; DfE, 2012, 2016). Kerry (2005) stated that roles of TAs were not clearly delineated and that the definitions provided of what was expected of TAs were 'pragmatic and functional' rather than grounded in 'professional appropriateness or a philosophy of education'. Blatchford, Russell, Bassett, Brown and Martin (2004) also noted that boundary issues between TAs' pedagogical and other roles were a grey area, with a UNISON survey (2013) describing the complex mix of TA responsibilities which included contrasting roles and an overlap between pastoral, pedagogical and administrative duties. The chapters in this section have focused on the impact of the boundary-crossing activities TAs may well regularly engage in when managing behaviour and how the range of in-school factors affect this.

The importance of relationships within schools, and specifically collaborations between teachers and TAs, have been cited as essential, but there is very little evidence of this in practice, or exemplars of what this might look like (Wilson and Bedford, 2008). Mackenzie (2011) found in her study that rather than collaboration, relationships were defined by negativity, with respondents 'almost wholly negative about their relationships with teachers and fellow TAs'. We have looked in this section about what tensions can occur when teachers and TAs try to work collaboratively together and what that might account for these tensions. These have included the lack of training TAs are able to access or be part of, as well as the challenges that occur in informal on-the-job learning. This may make TAs reliant on the strategies they see teachers use without understanding the pedagogical principles behind them. We have also considered the time available for developing relationships and how teachers' expectations of TAs and the roles they fulfil might lead them into a range of different management styles when working with TAs, not all of which support the development of agency or a professional identity for TAs.

We considered how the maternal and caring categorisation of the TA role has resulted in difficulties with TAs' status, professional identity and the relationships they are able to form with teachers and children. Difficulties in being involved in the school community, for example in staff meetings and so on, can magnify issues with TAs' status and power in schools. Ability to access the school's behaviour policy through a lack of inclusion, training or buy-in can exacerbate TAs' issues when managing behaviour.

We finally focused on how TAs were deployed throughout the school as a key determinant in their ability to form purposeful relationships with both children and teachers. We used examples of two forms of deployment to show how they could either support the development of these relationships or constrain them.

 ## Reflection activity

Before we move on to the fourth and final part of the book it might be good to sit back and reflect on what you have learnt and what you feel your school or setting may already have in place to minimise some of the issues that have been discussed in these chapters.

■ Have you read anything that has surprised you?

■ Are there any aspects covered that you would like to find out more about?

■ Are there any of the references you are interested in following up?

■ Have you read anything that has echoed the experiences in your setting or that you have seen or read elsewhere?

■ Are there any changes you would make in your setting or to your own practice in light if anything you have read so far?

References

Bach, I., Kessler, S. and Heron, P. (2006) Changing Job Boundaries and Workforce Reform: The Case of Teaching Assistants. Industrial Relations Journal, 37(1), 2–21.

Blatchford, P., Russell, A., Bassett, P., Brown, P. and Martin, C. (2004). The Role and Effects of Teaching Assistants in English Primary Schools (Years 4 to 6) 2000–2003: Results from the Class Size and Pupil Adult Ratios (CSPAR) Project. Final Report. (Research Report 605). London: DfES.

Department for Education and Skills. (2006). Raising Standards and Tackling Workload Implementing the National Agreement. Note 17. (Effective Deployment of HLTAs to Help Raise Standards). London: DfES.

Department for Education. (2012). Pupil Behaviour in Schools in England. In Research Report DFE-RR218. London: DfE.

Department for Education. (2016). Behaviour and Discipline in Schools: Advice for Head-teachers and School Staff. London: DfE.

Kerry, T. (2005). Towards a Typology for Conceptualizing the Roles of Teaching Assistants. Educational Review, 57(3), 373–384.

Mackenzie, S. (2011). "Yes, but...": Rhetoric, Reality and Resistance in Teaching Assistants' Experiences of Inclusive Education. Support for Learning, 26, 64–71.

UNISON. (2013). The Evident Value of Teaching Assistants: Report of a UNISON Survey. Retrieved from www.unison.org.uk/content/uploads/2013/06/Briefings-and-Circular-sEVIDENT-VALUE-OF-TEACHING-ASSISTANTS-Autosaved3.pdf

Wilson, E. and Bedford, D. (2008). "New Partnerships for Learning": Teachers and Teaching Assistants Working Together in Schools – The Way Forward. Journal of Education for Teaching, 34(2), 137–150.

Part 4

14 Empowering TAs to work with children

We are now moving into the final section of the book and by now, you will be familiar with a range of new and possibly not so new information, research, reading and policy. The previous chapters have dealt with discreet aspects that can influence TAs and suggested key aspects that schools and settings may need to give specific thought and strategic planning time to. This final section and chapter will have a more practical, as opposed to theoretical, focus. I will share the key findings from my research and discuss what this means in practice, building on discussions in the previous chapters. Unlike the previous chapters which involved lots of reading with some pauses to think and reflect, this section is going to flip that on its head. Here I am going to ask you to do lots of thinking, interspersed with a little reading. If you are leading a school or setting, or are part of the SLT, you might find this helps you to support the TAs in your care and employment and support the teachers and children your TAs work with. If you are a class teacher this section will aim to give you some ideas about what you can do to help the TA(s) that you work with and how, in turn they might be able to help you. If you are a TA, this section will help you reflect on how you work within your school or setting and what you might be able to do to develop your agency in managing behaviour. If you fall into none of these categories, this chapter will, I hope, give you some food for thought and exemplify the interlinking and complex connections that mediate TAs' work with behaviour.

By the end of this section you should have a number of practical strategies or changes you wish to make. You can celebrate the successes your school or setting already has and all of the positive ways TAs support behaviour.

This is the final chapter of the book. Here the aim is to draw together all of the strands I have introduced and help you to weave them together to produce positive and constructive changes in your school, setting, teaching and/or collaborations, as well as to celebrate all the great practice that you are currently engaged in (from a research-informed perspective).

This chapter will develop the concept of TAs' 'place' as well as a range of ideas to support TAs developing or embedding their professional agency. It will link to the tensions described in previous Chapters (10, 11, 12 and 13) and will consider how to limit or avoid these constraints by thinking about how TAs are used in your school, setting or experience. I will discuss how consistency in a range of forms can enhance TAs' ability to find their 'place' in managing behaviour. This chapter will also provide a range of opportunities to think about what this might mean in your context and how changes could be implemented.

This chapter will:

- Provide an overview of the concept of agency

- Share the key findings from my own research

- Consider how the tensions highlighted throughout this book might be minimised

- Discuss how TAs' professional identity and agency can be supported

- Support you in thinking about TAs' work in your context

Throughout the chapters in this book, the importance and impact of agency has been returned to again and again. Before this chapter begins in earnest, I would like to provide a little more information on agency to support your understanding, and to frame some of the subsequent activities.

What does the research tell us?

What is agency and why is it important?

Although agency was not explicitly referred to by any of the participants in my study or even in wider research on TAs, it appears to be at the centre of the range of interwoven tensions and issues we have considered in this book. It seems that it is a pervasive theme but one that is not explicitly articulated. This may be due to the challenges in defining this slippery term. Difficulties in considering how agency affects TAs are compounded by the challenges of a clear definition of agency and little research or theory development specifically concerning teacher agency (Biesta, Priestley and Robinson, 2015; Priestley, Edwards, Priestley and Miller, 2012; Toom, Pyhältö and Rust, 2015; van der Heijden, Geldens, Beijaard and Popeijus, 2015). It was also argued (Davies, 1991) that any definitions of agency that did exist were underpinned by masculine and elite assumptions that did not acknowledge the everyday, interactive nature of agency. Davies (1991) also argued that agency was the exception rather than the rule for women. This is pertinent when we think about TAs who are largely female (DfE, 2014) and can see this reflects Graves's (2011) argument that the TA role was and remains powerfully gendered which, she suggested, limits TAs' choices and agency.

Despite the difficulties surrounding a clear definition, some distinct ideas about the nature of agency have emerged from the literature which link with the broader issues for TAs. Robinson (2012) suggested agency encompassed internalising choices and analysing and reflecting on past experiences and future trajectories. Other influences also stated to impact on agency included its temporal nature, the expectations and assumptions of both the agent themselves (TAs in this case) and others (for example teachers, children) as well as the external culture (such as the school or setting and policy) (Biesta et al., 2015; Emirbayer and Mische, 1998; Robinson, 2012). All of these aspects have been identified as possible sites of tensions for TAs in the research we have considered (Barkham, 2008; Bland and Sleightholme, 2012; Blatchford, Russell, Bassett, Brown and Martin, 2007; Cockroft and Atkinson, 2015; Dixon, 2003; Graves, 2011; Mansaray, 2006; O'Brien and Garner, 2002; Spillane, Reiser and Reimer, 2002; Stoll and Seashore Louis, 2007; Watson, Bayliss and Pratchett, 2013). Eteläpelto, Vähäsantanen and Hökkä (2015) considered professional agency to;

> exist when subjects' agency is directed at work-related phenomena, and when they influence, make choices, and take stances in ways that affect their work and/or their professional identities.

> (p.662)

From this perspective, it can be seen that the themes discussed in this book as generic tensions for TAs (including role clarity, training, power, whole school approaches, deployment and relationships) may well also constrain their ability to 'influence', 'make choices' and 'take stances'. As a result, this might make exercising professional agency challenging for the majority of TAs. Toom et al. (2015) proposed that teacher agency was associated with 'active efforts to make choices and intentional action in a way that makes a significant difference (p. 615)'. Although this may be a less comprehensive definition of agency than the other research suggests, it is a helpful one to think about. Toom et al.'s (2015) definition included many of the key issues for TAs that have emerged, and highlights, notably, that TAs' ability to make choices and act intentionally are constrained.

This overview, I hope, illustrates the importance of supporting TAs to actively engage in schools. Much research, as well as my own findings, suggest a passive nature to TAs interactions and of things being done *to*, rather than *with*, them. This chapter will focus on strategies to support and enable TAs to actively engage, and to facilitate their agency in a range of ways.

Your context

The next sections of this chapter will now move on to consider actions that could be taken. Throughout all of these suggestions it is absolutely crucial that you hold at the front of your mind your own context. What will work for you, your colleagues, children and budget, as well as a host of other, constraints? Think too about what aspects of the existing ways of working are successful, celebrate these and reflect on what is going well and how this could be sustained and/or developed even further.

In many respects, TAs managing behaviour can be likened to images of icebergs. It is suggested that only 10 per cent of the iceberg is usually above water, meaning that we only see a tiny amount of what is actually there. The 10 per cent in the case of TAs is what actions they take to manage behaviour, what is seen and done in the classroom, in the playground and so on. The bulk of the iceberg below the water line represents the factors that govern the actions that TAs take to intervene or support children's behaviour.

 Reflection activity

Before we go further, think about your own context or experiences and reflect on what you have read up to this point in the book. Using the image in Figure 14.1, can you:

■ Label the actions you might see TAs take to manage behaviour – what they *do* – on the above-water part of the iceberg?

■ Think about the constraints and opportunities they are exposed to – what *influences*, positively or negatively, the actions they take to manage behaviour? Can you annotate the below-water part of the iceberg with these?

Have a look at the notes you have made on the image. This might help you gain a clearer understanding of some of the influences on TAs in your setting or school. You might also like to continue to annotate it as we go through this chapter.

Figure 14.1 Influences on TAs and the actions they take to manage behaviour

This would also make a very interesting whole staff activity:

- Do you think there would be differences between TAs' and teachers' reponses to this activity?

- Why?

- What might that reveal that was useful?

- What could you do with the responses you collected from this form of activity?

 Pause point

We are about to consider what could be done to support TAs in school when managing behaviour. Pause now and look back through the 'What this might mean in school' sections at the end of each chapter:

- How many references to the need for teacher and TAs to talk together have there been?

- What does this tell us?

If you have had a think about the activity here, I am sure it will be clear that this time, for TAs to talk – to teachers, to each other, to the school community widely – are pivotal. Research suggests this does not occur purposefully on the whole and where time for discussion is taken from teachers' usual classroom preparation time, that collaboration is even less likely. The first key point to consider then is when, where and how to make this possible?

 ## Professional, purposeful discussions

Reflecting on your own context, or a context familiar to you, think about how time could be carved out for these discussions, how they could be supported (rather than sidelined) and how often, ideally, they might take place. This might be a range of different times and places; for example, you might decide at the start, or end of the year that it would be helpful to have more discussions to support developing relationships if TA and teacher teams are changing or TAs are working with new children. It may also be that at some points in the year TAs and teachers are both free to meet during some form of whole-school activity such as during assemblies. At other times of the year, this may not be practical or desirable.

Much research has pointed to the main barrier to achieving collaboration between TAs and teachers as being a lack of both time and resources (Bedford, Jackson and Wilson, 2008; Cockroft and Atkinson, 2015; Devecchi, Dettori, Doveston, Sedgwick and Jament, 2011; Devecchi and Rouse, 2010; Houssart, 2013; Mackenzie, 2011; Marks,

Schrader and Levine, 1999; Mulholland and O'Connor, 2016; Radford, Bosanquet, Webster and Blatchford, 2015; Thomas, 1992; Tucker, 2009). Neill (2002) noted how respondents in his study stated that finding the necessary opportunities to talk added to teachers' workload and was very time-consuming. Houssart and Croucher (2013) reported 'hierarchical views', where TAs in their study prioritised sensitivity to teacher workloads above their own desire to share practice. Despite TAs in Mistry, Burton and Brundrett (2004) study wanted more involvement, they also acknowledged that allocating time for this would effectively reduce the time they spent with the children.

Lots of the research we have considered suggested time constraints and TAs' reported concerns over teacher workload effectively reduced opportunities for communication and instead relied on TAs' goodwill for it to happen (Marr, Turner, Swann and Hancock, 2002; Neill, 2002; Roffey-Barentsen and Watt, 2014; Sharples, Webster and Blatchford, 2015; Webster, Blatchford and Russell, 2012). Gerschel's (2005) research showed that the lack of prior notice and the resulting necessity to interpret teaching in the lesson were frequent sources of complaints from TAs. These themes recurred in research with TAs stating they often went into lessons 'blind', as there was not the opportunity to discuss sessions before they started (Neill, 2002; Sharples et al., 2015). Rose (2000) believed that without time to talk, the requisite climate of 'trust, mutual respect, confidence and shared purpose' which was argued to be necessary for collaboration between teachers and TAs could not be created. Without clear communication in the TA–teacher relationship, or any sense of shared purpose (Rose, 2000), TAs may rely on their own understandings of their role in managing behaviour.

 Reflection activity

Begin to think about adding some detail to the suggested headings in the table in Figure 14.2 – if you feel other headings might be better, feel free to amend and adapt them. Think carefully about the advantages and disadvantages of the times and frequency of meetings – who does it help? Are there any groups it would be difficult or unhelpful for?

Try to think about as many possibilities as you can. Flexibility and a range of options may be more successful and useful than a rigid schedule in many cases. You might also be able to think of good systems of communications that could be used in addition to face-to-face meetings. It is essential however, to ensure none of the times or strategies you consider add to TA or teacher workload or require TAs to participate at unpaid times (such as before or after school).

I have made reference in previous chapters to the lack of specific research examining how TAs manage behaviour. In my own study, I looked at the wider tensions research suggested TAs were affected by, as discussed in Part 3 of this book. Using the data my participants gave me I compared and contrasted the specific issues they raised in relation to managing behaviour with the general tensions from research. The table in Figure 14.3 here shows the links between the two.

Possible times for discussions	Ideal frequency of meetings	Who should be involved	How this time could be protected	What could be done to support discussions

Figure 14.2 Possible times for TAs and teachers to hold professional discussions

General issues highlighted by research	Specific issues affecting behaviour management
Role clarity	Role creep and vague role definition
Training	Personal experience and being a mother used in lieu of training
Power	'Know your place', worries about undermining the teacher, lack of concerns over support from the SLT
Whole school approaches	Lack of communication, lack of consistency in teachers' approaches to managing behaviour
Deployment	Getting to know and forming relationships with children and teachers
Teacher/TA relationship	Relationship with teachers, finding strategies to help and support the teacher

Figure 14.3 Generic issues for TAs and behaviour management specific issues for TAs

This shows that the wider tensions mirror those that affect managing behaviour. However, there is one factor that was not highlighted widely in research, in fact it was only reported in one other study (Watson et al., 2013) – this is the concept of a TAs' 'place'. As noted, I was originally horrified when this term was used by my participants. It was a phrase I was sure they had not heard teachers use in reference to collaborating with them, yet when I analysed the interviews and focus groups this was one of the most common references – the need for TAs to 'know their place'. As we touched on previously, this term 'place' was about where they felt they fitted in the school 'jigsaw' and related to having a clear understanding of their role(s). My participants (and common sense) suggest that without understanding what you are supposed to be doing – it is very hard to know what actions to take!

We will move on now in this chapter to look at the role of consistency across a range of factors. The diagram in Figure 14.4 shows what my research suggested – that ideas about place, agency and consistency are all connected. My TAs, as well as the wider reading that has been drawn on throughout this book, saw consistency – or rather a lack of consistency – across a range of interconnected issues as a real barrier in their management of behaviour. TAs felt that they were often left reliant on their own experience to guide any actions they took to manage behaviour. This left TAs often feeling uncertain and anxious about how, when and where they could, or should, take steps to support children's behaviour or intervene in issues of misbehaviour.

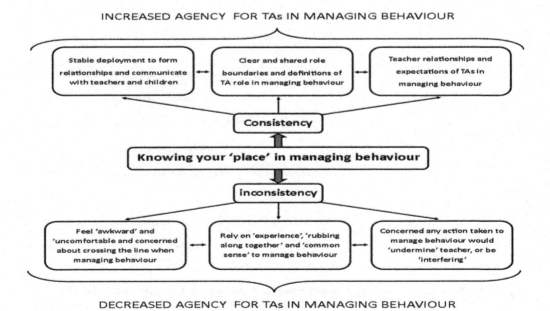

Figure 14.4 The impact of TAs' understanding of their 'place' on their agency

It could be suggested that to support TAs in developing an understanding of their role, consistency in some form is essential. Using the ideas in the diagram in Figure 14.4 we will think about the possibilities and challenges in each strategy. Across the top of the diagram are suggestions for supporting and developing place and agency, whilst the bottom shows some of the tensions and issues that affected my TAs when they were working with a range of inconsistencies.

Consistency through deployment

If we work across the diagram from left to right, the first form of consistency schools and settings could begin to consider offering is that of consistency through deployment. Consistency has the possibility to enhance relationships with teachers and children, both of which have been cited as necessary to manage behaviour.

First, we will think about TAs being deployed to work with either one teacher, or a very limited number of teachers. It has been suggested that, given the right conditions, this will help to support TAs and teachers in developing close, collaborative working relationships. The TAs in my research noted how in the absence of training or time to talk to the teachers they worked with they relied on experience of that teacher to judge what actions to take to manage behaviour. For the TAs in my study this was challenging as they worked with a number of teachers who all had different expectation of the TAs' role in managing behaviour, but these were never explicitly communicated. TAs over time picked up clues from the teacher and from any informal chats they had about how they could best help and support them. For some teachers this was TAs using low-level strategies to manage the behaviour of the children in the group they were working with, whilst they suggested other teachers were happy to work as a 'team' where the TA was much more active in supporting whole-class behaviour management. When working with other teachers they knew not to take any actions to manage behaviour at all.

The overriding issue that this form of deployment (one TA to between one and three teachers) may help to reduce is the lack of communication about expectations for managing behaviour. The absence of clarity meant TAs in my research were what they described as 'left to wonder' and work on 'assumptions' about what each teacher expected of them in terms of supporting behaviour. Their assumed and implicit role placed my TAs in what they described as an 'awkward' and 'uncomfortable' position in managing behaviour. Watson et al. (2013, p.108) found that when TAs worked with a number of teachers, they 'managed their different relationships accordingly … What was apparent in all cases was that TAs felt the need to be reassured that they were behaving in accordance with others' expectations of them'. This key point reflects my TAs' concerns about undermining teachers by managing behaviour, particularly in the teachers own classroom. This reassurance can in part, be provided through a comfortable working relationship with each other. The concept of reassurance was also drawn out of findings from Mistry et al. (2004), where their TAs highlighted the importance of constructive feedback from teachers to enable them to improve and develop their practice. Again, this idea about feedback would be much easier in a close and established professional working relationship.

The lack of clarity and understanding of roles can also be a two-way process. One of the TAs in my research recounted an incident where she was working with a teacher she was familiar with and, while he was busy with a child, she left the group she was working with to address an incident of misbehaviour in the classroom. At the end of the lesson, she recalled the teacher had rushed over to her to apologise that she had had to step in, despite the fact the TA had felt comfortable and confident dealing with the issue. This highlights that it may well be that many teachers are unsure of the actions they want TAs to take and are also relying on their experience of the TA.

Clearly experience is no substitute for professional, planned discussions. However, being in each other's company for longer periods of time can encourage these types of conversations to happen naturally. Respondents in Barkham's (2008) research described this as 'like a marriage', where the TA was telepathic and was, over time able to anticipate and fulfil their partner's needs. Although this is not necessarily recommended, as both members of the team get to know each other and feel confident each will gain a clearer understanding of the other, which could reduce TAs' concerns about their actions undermining the teacher or overstepping the mark. Barkham (2008) proposed in her research that what she described as personal friendships were used to mediate tensions that occurred. This also supported assertions that TAs knowingly relinquished their own position, status and as a result – agency – in order to benefit the teacher (Barkham, 2008; Watson et al., 2013). This was seen in the responses from my TAs, where rather than threatening the boundaries they worked across, resulting in the possibility of undermining teachers by crossing the line, they remained either as 'passive observers', or were 'subtle' and 'low key' in any action they took to manage behaviour.

Rather than axiomatically being a 'Good Thing', TA support was suggested to be perceived by some teachers to be more of a burden than a help, Thomas (1992) suggested. Marr et al. (2002) also cautioned that teachers and TAs working together easily was a continued assumption, which was described as 'more problematic and contentious than might appear at first sight' (Barkham, 2008; Blatchford et al., 2007). Others noted that the view of goodness in collaboration was actually overly optimistic and frequently minimised or even ignored the micro political dimensions of such work (Achinstein, 2001; Datnow, 2011; Hargreaves, 1994; Johnson, 2010). Other research (Devecchi, 2007; Devecchi et al., 2011) supported this suggesting that collaboration, although acknowledged as an important aspect of both the TA and HLTA role, was also one of the most challenging, with the TAs in Marks et al.'s (1999) study noting it as their prime concern. However, these challenges were not new with Cohen (1976, cited in Thomas, 1992) suggesting over forty years ago that classroom teams were trying to survive without effective preparation or support. This shows that placing TAs and teachers together without any planning or support is unlikely, on its own, to develop collaborative relationships. Nevertheless, with support and planning, being together and gaining an understanding of classroom routines and structures as well as how they are usually deployed will help TAs to understand their place within the systems in that classroom and with that teacher. This may support them, in time, in moving from passive to active in relation to managing behaviour.

Consistent deployment would reduce TAs' uncertainty over a range of key factors including role boundaries, teacher expectations of TAs managing behaviour – which are all key challenges. This was noted by TAs in my own research who suggested that they felt differently about taking action to manage behaviour outside the teachers' own classroom: 'things like kids messing about in the toilets I will go and sort out because it's out of the classroom, it is in no man's land'. This idea of TAs feeling more empowered to tackle behaviour in a 'no man's land' might be seen to allude to the subordinate role some TAs felt they fulfilled in the teacher's own space. As a participant in my research stated, 'it's their [the teacher's] class not mine', a view which confirmed Thomas's (2007) description of teachers as 'territorial' in their own spaces such as their classrooms. Consistent deployment with the same teacher, or a small number of teachers, may help TAs understand their role in the teachers' classroom and move towards considering it as a shared space rather than belonging solely to the teacher.

Another TA in my research shared concerns that her actions in managing behaviour were perceived as 'overriding' the teacher, making them feel 'inadequate' and 'bad' as a result. She contended that she did not want to damage teachers' self-perception and 'wouldn't want to put anybody in that position'. This was associated, she suggested, with an acknowledged obligation for TAs to 'remember who you are' and to 'know your place'. It was this understanding of 'knowing your place' that functioned to maintain positive relationships with teachers which could be seen to confirm Mackenzie's (2011) view of the 'connection' and 'strong commitment' TAs had to the teachers they worked with. TAs' reference in my research to a need for them to 'know their place' was unexpected yet key, and was a theme in only one other piece of research where it was proposed:

> knowing one's place communicates a shared understanding among educationalists of status and position and captures the everyday realities of TLSA's [TAs'] professional lives.
>
> (Watson et al., 2013, p.110)

Consistent deployment for TAs could help them to negotiate a shared understanding of their 'place' with teachers they work with.

 ## Reflection activity

As we have seen, developing relationships is not as easy as just pairing up TAs and teachers. It has been suggested that TAs' and teachers' views on working together

Figure 14.5 TAs and teachers working together

exist on a spectrum and fall somewhere between it being perceived as a chore and a team.

Using the arrow in Figure 14.5, annotate your ideas. Begin to think about:

- What might typify each end of the spectrum?

- How might TAs and teachers behave if they view working together as a chore?

- What might be seen at the other end of the scale?

- Is working as a team always possible or desirable (you might like to reflect back on the leadership exercises here in Chapter 9)?

- Would/will teachers and TAs have different views about what each end of the spectrum would look like?

Can you now begin to think about what actions could be taken as a whole school, by individual teachers and by individual TAs to begin to move from the chore towards the teamwork end of the scale:

- What support would need to be put in place to make those changes?

- Who could provide that support?

- Who would benefit from a movement towards teamwork?

- How would you know?

 ## Consistent roles

Moving across to the centre of the diagram in Figure 14.4, the next area I have suggested consistency could be developed in is that of TAs' roles. Consistency in this area means that TAs could be deployed peripatetically to work with a number of teachers and in a number of classes but would always be expected to fulfil the same types of roles. These roles could be working outside of the classroom as a one-to-one support for a named child, delivering specific interventions to groups or individuals across the school or acting in a broader capacity, for example as a learning mentor. It might also be working within the classroom in a specific pattern but with a range of teachers – a simple (but not necessarily recommended) example of this might be carrying out administrative tasks for the teacher.

We can see from the previous suggested strategy to develop consistency, that forming relationships may be more challenging in this type of deployment, as TAs are likely to be working with a range of teachers and pupils and consistency will not necessarily come from established relationships. We noted earlier that this can negatively affect the agency TAs have and as a result, how active they are able to be in managing behaviour in the teacher's own classroom. However, if TAs have a clearly defined role this could go a long way to reducing some of the tensions we have discussed (Chapters 8, 9, 10, 11 and 12), and we will consider more specifically now.

One of the tensions research suggests TAs experience is a lack of training – and then a lack of opportunity to implement any training they have received. If TAs were tasked with a specific role, it could be reasonable to assume some training would go hand-in-hand with this. As we discussed (in Chapter 10), this might be formal – with an external provider, possibly leading to a recognised qualification, or informal – on-the-job training or based on experience or specific personal qualities. TAs being trained or experienced to some degree for the specific role(s) they were undertaking would help to develop their professional agency. This specific role and (some form of) associated training may go some way to address concerns over the problems of 'mastery' as discussed by van der Heijden et al. (2015) previously (in Chapter 10), and positively, rather than negatively, affect both TAs' agency and an understanding of their 'professional self'. The concept of training and professionalisation of the role could well also have advantages in raising TAs' professional status in the school. Toom et al. (2015) suggested that:

> Becoming an active professional agent implies perceiving one's self as an active learner who is able to act intentionally, make decisions and reflect ... It also implies the motivation to implement and develop one's own expertise.
>
> (p.616)

Developing autonomy through having a specified role or roles within the school could support TAs in acting 'intentionally' rather than being reduced to the 'passive observers' my participants described themselves as, due to uncertainty over their role.

We have discussed (in Chapter 11) how status can limit what actions TAs feel they are able to take in managing behaviour, as well as how those actions will be received. We noted previously how research (Roffey-Barentsen and Watt, 2014) identified HLTAs as having the highest perceived status amongst the range of TAs due to the levels of agency and independence they had in the classroom, where in many schools they worked alone covering classes whilst teachers had PPA time. One of my participants noted;

> I think it's ultimately the teacher in the classroom, it's their responsibility to deal with behaviour. I would only do that if I was in the role of HLTA and the teacher wasn't there so the decision was mine ...

This reflects the idea that when working under the teacher's direction, TAs can be reticent to take action to manage behaviour as they are unsure of their 'place'. As we have discussed (in Chapters 8 and 9), the blurred definitions between teachers' and TAs' roles and TAs' 'boundary work' – where they cross between being a teacher and a TA – has been identified as a site of difficulty (Edwards, 2012; Fenton-O'Creevy, Dimitriadis and Scobie, 2015; Kubiac, Cameron, Conole, Fenton-O'Creevy, Mylrea, Rees and Shreeve, 2015; Mackenzie, 2011; Mansaray, 2006; Wenger-Trayner and Wenger-Trayner, 2015). Boundaries have been defined as places:

> where practices are alerted to changes which may affect actors' relative power, their resources and identities. Working relationally at organisational boundaries, therefore, involves the personal challenges of negotiating exper-tise in settings where one may not be able to manipulate practices; and where the practices that were being protected by the boundary may themselves be destabilised by your actions.
>
> (Edwards, 2011, p.35)

This suggests that actually moving between the TA and teacher roles, or role creep, may 'destabilise' the boundary between the two. This might have the effect of reiterating the diminishing professional status some teachers felt they had as a result of TAs increasingly pedagogical work, as well as the opposite, which was the increased professional status some TAs felt they had. Role creep and bound-ary-crossing issues are likely to be much more limited, although not resolved entirely, if both TAs and teachers are clearer about the specific role(s) the TA is fulfilling – such as a named intervention.

Much of the research we have considered, in many of the chapters (Chapters 8 and 9) highlight the importance of clear and consistent role definition for TAs (including, but not only, Blatchford, Russell and Webster, 2016; Devecchi and Rouse, 2010; Harris and Aprile, 2015; Kerry, 2005; Mansaray, 2006; Rose, 2000). Our discussions up to this point have shown how challenging that fixed definition might be to achieve when TAs are working with teachers in the classroom, indeed as we have noted it could actually be disadvantageous. However, by deploying TAs with specific roles they can fulfil both the 'roving brief' than has been advocated (Rose, 2000) to support children as well as having clearly defined roles to support their professional identity and reduce the associated issues of role creep.

My TAs noted concerns over defining their roles and that incremental changes often meant that their roles had changed significantly between the beginning and end of the academic year. Deployment by role may help TAs, teachers and the set-ting have a clearer understanding of the types of work they are expected to do. This form of deployment is also more likely to address calls from research (Sharples et al., 2015) to ensure that TAs are used in a strategic and planned way. For TAs, knowing what type of roles they were likely to be fulfilling, and with whom, at the start of the year may help them in feeling prepared and allow them to take more active ownership of the role and, as a result, reduce the comments my participants provided about being 'passive observers'. These forms of proactive deployment by role (not that deploying TAs with specific classes is necessarily *not* proactive deployment) may also support schools in addressing (rather pejorative) concerns about TAs being 'value-for-money' (Houssart and Croucher, 2013; Roffey-Barentsen and Watt, 2014; Sharples et al., 2015) as they may also show more explicitly how TAs were being used to add value.

It is worth mentioning here – although I hope this is clear from the rest of the book – that 'adding value' and being 'value-for-money' are not perspectives I argue should be used in relation to TAs and their work in schools. As we have discussed, TAs' work is often concerned with social, emotional and what have been referred to as 'soft-skill' work with children. This form of support is much more difficult to measure and quantify but just as (if not more so) important as academic development.

Reflection activity

As I have noted, discourses around value-for-money are prevalent in education at the moment. If TAs are used for academic support and one-to-one interventions, these often have specific end points or targets; when working to support children socially, emotionally and behaviourally the targets are often less specific and/or harder to define. It might be good to pause here and think about:

- If TAs were deployed to work on specific 'soft-skill' interventions, how could success be measured?

- How could this be articulated in a 'value-for-money' discourse?

Deploying TAs by task rather than assigning them to specific classes or teachers is yet another balancing act. What might be lost in terms of relationships might be gained in professionalism, status and training – although these are not automatic gains or losses. For the second reflection here, could you think about your own setting, or use your own experience to consider how relationships could be supported with this roving and peripatetic form of deployment? We noted (in Chapter 13) how Mackenzie's (2011) research had warned that TAs could easily become isolated – what could be done to limit this?

Can you annotate the 'see-saw' in Figure 14.6 to think about your context, with your staff and so on:

- How might it be possible to support and develop opportunities for increased professionalism, status and training for TAs whilst also maintaining and or developing existing relationships between TAs and teachers (and children) so they feel, and are, a key part of the whole school culture?

- How could it be ensured that TAs are not isolated in an 'educational cul-de-sac' where they feel 'devalued and disengaged from the ordinary life of the school' (Whittaker and Kikabhai, 2008)?

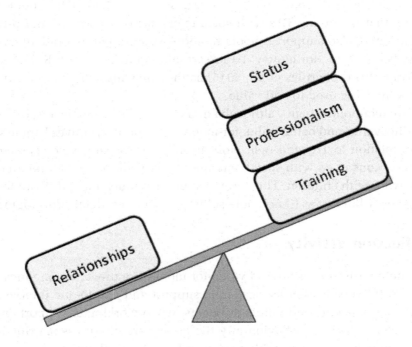

Figure 14.6 How the advantages of a peripatetic model of TA deployment could be maximised and the limitations minimised

Consistent inconsistencies

The final model we could consider is the rather illogical category of consistent inconsistencies. We have discussed regularly throughout this book the tensions that can be caused by inconsistencies for TAs and how this affects the actions they take and their agency in managing behaviour. The terms 'consistency' and 'inconsistency' were the most used terms when I transcribed the data from my participants. These inconsistencies can stem from a number of factors and many have been highlighted by research as tensions for TAs in their role(s) more widely and not just linked to managing behaviour (a recap of these was provided in the table at the start of this chapter). Schools and educational settings are necessarily flexible places, they need to be, and rigid consistency is never going to be an appropriate, reasonable or workable solution – at least not in the long term. When supporting behaviour, and working with children whose behaviour can challenge, flexibility is essential.

This perspective is something of a hybrid of the other two models and takes a pragmatic view of TAs working inconsistently, or flexibly, within a consistent framework. We discussed (in Chapter 7) Coburn's (2005) views of 'bounded autonomy' for staff in schools. This model could be seen as reflecting some of these tenets, but in a more positive framework. In this model, TAs could be deployed with 'bounded inconsistencies'. What I mean here is that they may be deployed to work in a range of situations that are themselves difficult to gain consistency in, but be consistently deployed in these situations. For example, they might work with a number of teachers whose expectations of the TA in their classroom are different; however, because the TA is consistently deployed with these teachers, they can manage these inconsistent expectations. They may also work to support some children one-to-one, or groups, or specific interventions, but again these should be consistent or routine so the TA and others develop a shared understanding of what will happen at these times and what the routines are.

The TAs in my research noted the importance of routines and how this made them feel more comfortable and confident taking steps to manage behaviour. They suggested that when classes or lessons followed routines it was helpful for them as it provided them with some 'ownership':

> to let us know what our role is and quite often we don't know what our role is, in some classrooms where you go 'I'm going to be doing that', it makes it a lot easier and you automatically feel more comfortable, because you know what your role is and what's expected of you.

If TAs worked in a small number of contexts but in a range of different ways, these routines could be embedded and support TAs' development of routines and relationships and their professional agency.

We have noted repeatedly throughout this book the importance of time to talk. Within this model, this would be essential to provide teachers and TAs from the start with an opportunity to explicitly discuss expectations and what they could each expect from the other. As TAs here would be working with a limited number of teachers and different contexts these conversations would be possible. In addition, because teachers in this model would be using TAs in fairly routine and predictable ways, these routines may have the possibility to become embedded quickly, unlike the other two models. This form of deployment would require careful and explicit planning at the start of each year or term and not be open to much change to allow TAs to develop an understanding of the routines of the teachers and roles they were deployed to fulfil. This model allows flexibility to pair TAs with teachers and roles where their own personal traits or experiences might be drawn on advantageously; however, without strategic planning this might look very similar to a reactive and unplanned model of deployment. There is also the risk with this model that TAs will be undertaking 'bit-parts' and not feeling ownership of any of the range of roles they might fulfil. As we have noted, this could impact negatively on their professional agency, and, as a result, their management of behaviour.

Within this model there is also an increased risk of isolation from the whole-school community as TAs would have a range of different roles, but possibly no clear 'place' within the system. This risk of marginalisation would need careful consideration and discussion with TAs. Perhaps one way to limit this would be to assign TAs mentors, or named members of staff they could approach to discuss issues with children or groups they worked with, as well as to share successes. Performance management may also be advantageous so TAs can see the value of their roles, not only for children and teachers they work with, but also for their own professional development. This could contribute to enabling TAs to see how the roles they are fulfilling are continuing to develop their skillset and how this in turn could contribute to developing their professional agency and autonomy, or 'trust' from the school. Ensuring TAs are invited to whole-school training, INSET and staff-meetings (and are paid to do so) may also mitigate feelings of professional isolation.

 ## Reflection activity

This final model of developing consistency for TAs and supporting them to develop agency has tried to take the flexibility from one of the models and marry it with the consistency of the other. This means that the advantages of each could be drawn on, but also that the disadvantages of each model may loom large instead. This form of working would need very specific strategic thinking to ensure the limitations were minimised and opportunities maximised; a good place to start would seem to be looking at the type of complementary roles TAs might fulfil in a school or setting.

Can you begin to consider:

- The range of roles TAs might undertake (you may have notes on this from activities earlier in the book that you can add to.

- Which roles could be grouped together that could maximise training and personal qualities of TAs?

- How many different teachers/children would this mean individual TAs were working with?

- What steps would the school/setting need to take to maximise the advantages of TAs working like this?

- What could the school/setting do to minimise the disadvantages of TAs working in this way?

This model of working, with consistent inconsistencies, needs careful consideration (as do all ways of working with TAs) to ensure a balance is struck between working inside and outside the classroom to ensure relationships can develop.

- Can you add some thoughts to the diagram in Figure 14.7 about what could be done to support professional autonomy and relationships?

- Would these strategies also work for teachers?

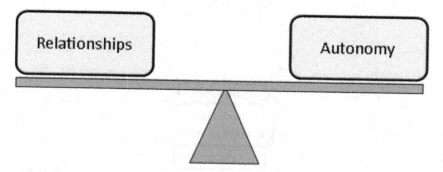

Figure 14.7 How the advantages of a 'consistent with inconsistencies' model of TA deployment could be maximised and the limitations minimised

 Summary

This last section of the book has covered a lot! We began this chapter considering some of the difficulties in defining what agency was. These difficulties were significant for teachers. It is reasonable to assume that the problems teachers have exercising agency are compounded for TAs due to the range of issues we have discussed throughout this book. including role clarity, training, power, whole-school approaches, deployment and teacher–TA relationships. A key facet of professional agency that the models which have been proposed in this chapter aim to address is the ability to 'take action'. This, my TAs reported, was a significant source of tension for them; they often felt awkward and unsure of what actions to take with their overriding concern being not to undermine the class teacher. This also reflects issues of power, status and relationships. My participants' passive approach to managing behaviour frustrated them deeply (and no doubt some of the teachers they worked with too). The lack of understanding of what they described as their 'place' meant that they often observed rather than acted.

If we consider the models of developing TAs' place discussed, I am not suggesting that I have provided an exhaustive list by any means. I have made some suggestions based on what the participants in my study told me, and supported by wider research. The diagram in Figure 14.8 shows some of the main tensions for the TAs in my study. I hope the models of working with TAs presented shows how some of these issues can be limited.

 Reflection activity

Figure 14.8 tries to show the interconnected and interwoven issues that need a holistic and planned strategy to mitigate them. You can see that addressing one facet alone will not necessarily resolve the additional constraints TAs experience. It might be

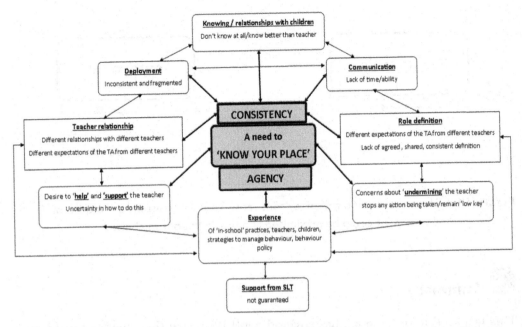

Figure 14.8 The web of interconnected issues around TAs developing a sense of 'place' in schools

worthwhile sharing this diagram with staff (TAs and teachers) to investigate whether all of the issues my participants highlighted are also relevant for them, or whether they would add any others. After this, you could label the arrows with possible strategies to mitigate these tensions that work for your staff in your context.

For the final (or possibly penultimate – depending on what you chose to do next) reflection I am going to ask you to draw together the key issues that have struck a chord for your setting or staff. Can you annotate the diagram in Figure 14.9 to support your ideas:

■ How do you currently help TAs to understand their 'place' in relation to managing behaviour in a positive and shared way?

■ What additional steps might you now want to take to help to develop this positive and shared understanding of TAs' place in managing behaviour?

■ Are there any aspects of current practice, policy or deployment in your school or setting that might make it difficult for TAs to understand their place, or that are negative or individualised?

■ What changes might you want to make to minimise this?

You might also find it helpful now to revisit some of the reflection activities at the start of the book to see if your thoughts have changed or what additional information you might like to add to them.

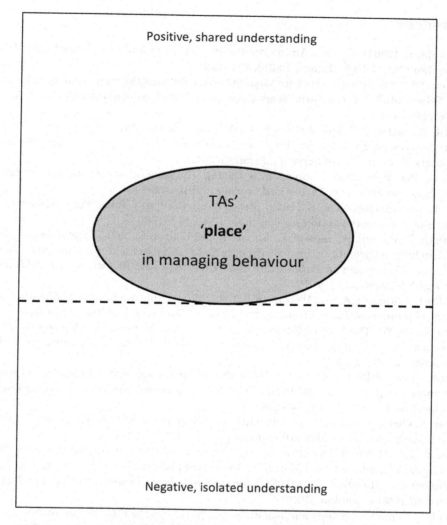

Figure 14.9 The key issues around TAs developing a sense of 'place'

 Further reading

- Biesta, G., Priestley, M. and Robinson, S. (2015). The Role of Beliefs in Teacher Agency. *Teachers and Teaching: Theory and Practice, 21*(6), 624–640.

- Stoll, L. and Seashore Louis, K. (2007). *Professional Learning Communities: Divergence, Depth and Dilemmas.* Maidenhead: McGraw-Hill Education.

- Watson, D., Bayliss, P. and Pratchett, G. (2013). Pond Life that 'Know Their Place': Exploring Teaching and Learning Support Assistants' Experiences through Positioning Theory. *International Journal of Qualitative Studies in Education, 26*(1), 100–117.

References

Achinstein, B. (2001). Conflict Amid Community: The Micropolitics of Teacher Collaboration. *Teachers College Record*, *104*(3), 421–455.

Barkham, J. (2008). Suitable Work for Women? Roles, Relationships and Changing Identities of 'Other Adults' in the Early Years Classroom. *British Educational Research Journal*, *34*(6), 839–853.

Bedford, D., Jackson, C. and Wilson, E. (2008). New Partnerships for Learning: Teachers' Perspectives on Their Developing Professional Relationships with Teaching Assistants in England. *Journal of In-Service Education*, *34*(1), 7–25.

Biesta, G., Priestley, M. and Robinson, S. (2015). The Role of Beliefs in Teacher Agency. *Teachers and Teaching: Theory and Practice*, *21*(6), 624–640.

Bland, K. and Sleightholme, S. (2012). Researching the Pupil Voice: What Makes a Good Teaching Assistant? *Support for Learning*, *27*(4), 172–176.

Blatchford, P., Russell, A., Bassett, P., Brown, P. and Martin, C. (2007). The Role and Effects of Teaching Assistants in English Primary Schools (Years 4 to 6) 2000–2003. Results from the Class Size and Pupil–Adult Ratios (CSPAR) KS2 Project. *British Educational Research Journal*, *33*(1), 5–26.

Blatchford, P., Russell, A. and Webster, R. (2016). *Maximising the Impact of Teaching Assistants: Guidance for School Leaders and Teachers* (2nd ed.). London: Routledge.

Coburn, C. (2005). The Role of Nonsystem Actors in the Relationship between Policy and Practice: The Case of Reading Instruction in California. *Educational Evaluation and Policy Analysis*, *27*(1), 23–52.

Cockroft, C. and Atkinson, C. (2015). Using the Wider Pedagogical Role Model to Establish Learning Support Assistants' Views about Facilitators and Barriers to Effective Practice. *Support for Learning*, *30*(2), 88–104.

Datnow, A. (2011). Collaboration and contrived collegiality: revisiting Hargreaves in the age of accountability. *Journal of Educational Change*, *12*(2), 147–158.

Davies, B. (1991). The Concept of Agency: A Feminist Poststructuralist Analysis. *Social Analysis: The International Journal of Social and Cultural Practice*, (30), 42–53.

Department for Education. (2014). *Statistical First Release School Workforce in England: November 2014*. London: DfE.

Devecchi, C. (2007). Teachers and teaching assistants working together: inclusion, collaboration, and support in one secondary school. *PhD diss.*, University of Cambridge.

Devecchi, C., Dettori, F., Doveston, M., Sedgwick, P. and Jament, J. (2011). Inclusive Classrooms in Italy and England: The Role of Support Teachers and Teaching Assistants. *European Journal of Special Needs Education*, *27*(2), 171–184.

Devecchi, C. and Rouse, M. (2010). An Exploration of the Features of Effective Collaboration between Teachers and Teaching Assistants in Secondary Schools. *Support for Learning*, *25*(2), 91–99.

Dixon, A. (2003). Teaching Assistants: Whose Definition? *Forum*, *45*(1), 26–29.

Edwards, A. (2011). Building Common Knowledge at the Boundaries between Professional Practices: Relational Agency and Relational Expertise in Systems of Distributed Expertise. *International Journal of Educational Research*, *50*(1), 33–39.

Edwards, A. (2012). The Role of Common Knowledge in Achieving Collaboration across Practices. *Learning, Culture and Social Interaction*, *1*(1), 22–32.

Emirbayer, M. and Mische, A. (1998). What Is Agency? *American Journal of Sociology*, *103*(4), 962–1023.

Eteläpelto, A., Vähäsantanen, K. and Hökkä, P. (2015). How Do Novice Teachers in Finland Perceive Their Professional Agency? *Teachers and Teaching, 21*(6), 660–680.

Fenton-O'Creevy, M., Dimitriadis, Y. and Scobie, G. (2015). Failure and Resilience at Boundaries: The Emotional Process of Identity Work. In Wenher-Trayner, E., Fenton-O'Creevy, M., Hutchinson, S., Kubiak, C. and Wenger-Trayner, B. (Eds.), *Learning in Landscapes of Practice: Boundaries, Identity and Knowledgeability in Practice-basedLlearning* (pp. 33–42). Oxon: Routledge.

Graves, S. (2011). Performance or Enactment? the Role of the Higher Level Teaching Assistant in a Remodelled School Workforce in England. *Management in Education, 25*(1), 15–20.

Gerschel, L. (2005). The special educational needs coordinator's role in managing teaching assistants: the Greenwich perspective. *Support for Learning, 20*(2), 69–76.

Hargreaves, A. (1994). *Changing Teachers, Changing Times; Teachers' Work and Culture in the Postmodern Age.* London: Cassell Educational Limited.

Harris, L. and Aprile, K. (2015). 'I Can Sort of Slot into Many Different Roles': Examining Teacher Aide Roles and Their Implications for Practice. *School Leadership & Management, 35*(2), 140–162.

Houssart, J. (2013). 'Give Me a Lesson and I'll Deliver It': Teaching Assistants' Experiences of Leading Primary Mathematics Lessons in England. *Cambridge Journal of Education, 43*(1), 1–16.

Houssart, J. and Croucher, R. (2013). Intervention programmes in mathematics and literacy: Teaching assistants' perceptions of their training and support. *School Leadership and Management,* **33**(5), 427–439.

Johnson, B. (2010). Teacher Collaboration: Good for Some, Not so Good for Others. *Educational Studies, 29*(4), 337–350.

Kerry, T. (2005). Towards a Typology for Conceptualizing the Roles of Teaching Assistants. *Educational Review, 57*(3), 373–384.

Kubiak, C., Cameron, S., Conole, G., Fenton-O'Creevy, M., Mylrea, P., Rees, E. and Shreeve, A. (2015). Membership and Identification. In Wenger-Trayner, E., Fenton-O'Creevy, M., Hutchinson, S., Kubiak, C. and Wenger-Trayner, B. (Eds.), *Learning in Landscapes of Practice: Boundaries, Identity and Knowledgeability in Pactice-based Learning* (pp. 64–80). Oxon: Routledge.

Mackenzie, S. (2011). "Yes, but…": Rhetoric, Reality and Resistance in Teaching Assistants' Experiences of Inclusive Education. *Support for Learning, 26,* 64–71.

Mansaray, A. (2006). Liminality and In/exclusion: Exploring the Work of Teaching Assistants. *Pedagogy, Culture & Society, 14*(2), 171–187.

Marks, S., Schrader, C. and Levine, M. (1999). Paraeducator Experiences in Inclusive Settings: Helping, Hovering, or Holding Their Own? *Exceptional Children, 65*(3), 315–328.

Marr, A., Turner, J., Swann, W. and Hancock, R. (2002). *Classroom Assistants in the Pimary School: Employment and Deployment.* Milton Keynes: Open University.

Mistry, M., Burton, N. and Brundrett, M. (2004). Managing LSAs: An Evaluation of the Use of Learning Support Assistants in an Urban Primary School. *School Leadership & Management, 24*(2), 125–137.

Mulholland, M. and O'Connor, U. (2016). Collaborative Classroom Practice for Inclusion: Perspectives of Classroom Teachers and Learning Support/resource Teachers. *International Journal of Inclusive Education, 20*(10), 1070–1083.

Neill, S. (2002). *Teaching Assistants: A Survey Analyed for the NUT.* London: University of Warwick/ National Union of Teachers.

O'Brien, T. and Garner, P. (2002). Tim and Philip's Story: Setting the Record Straight. In O'Brien, T. and Garner, P. (Eds.), *Untold Stories – Learning Support Assistants and Their Work* (pp. 1–10). Stoke on Trent: Trentham Books Ltd.

Priestley, M., Edwards, R., Priestley, A. and Miller, K. (2012). Teacher Agency in Curriculum Making: Agents of Change and Spaces for Manoeuvre. *Curriculum Inquiry, 42*(2), 191–214.

Radford, J., Bosanquet, P., Webster, R. and Blatchford, P. (2015). Scaffolding Learning for Independence: Clarifying Teacher and Teaching Assistant Roles for Children with Special Educational Needs. *Learning and Instruction, 36*, 1–10.

Robinson, S. (2012). Constructing Teacher Agency in Response to the Constraints of Education Policy: Adoption and Adaptation. *Curriculum Journal, 23*(2), 231–245.

Roffey-Barentsen, J. and Watt, M. (2014). The Voices of Teaching Assistants (Are We Value for Money?). *Research in Education, 92*(1), 18–31.

Rose, R. (2000). Using Classroom Support in a Primary School: A Single School Case Study. *British Journal of Special Education, 27*(4), 191–196.

Sharples, J., Webster, R. and Blatchford, P. (2015). *Making Best Use of Teaching Assistants: Guidance Report.* London: Education Endowment Foundation.

Spillane, J., Reiser, B. and Reimer, T. (2002). Policy Implementation and Cognition: Reframing and Refocusing Implementation Research. *Review of Educational Research, 72*(3), 387–431.

Stoll, L. and Seashore Louis, K. (2007). *Professional Learning Communities: Divergence, Depth and Dilemmas.* Maidenhead: McGraw-Hill Education.

Thomas, G. (1992). *Effective Classroom Teamwork: Support or Intrusion?* London: Routledge.

Thomas, G. (2007). *Education and Theory: Strangers in Paradigms.* Maidenhead: Open University Press/McGraw-Hill Education.

Toom, A., Pyhältö, K. and Rust, F. (2015). Teachers' Professional Agency in Contradictory Times. *Teachers and Teaching, 21*(6), 615–623.

Tucker, S. (2009). Perceptions and Reflections on the Role of the Teaching Assistant in the Classroom Environment. *Pastoral Care in Education, 27*(4), 291–300.

van der Heijden, H., Geldens, J., Beijaard, D. and Popeijus, H. (2015). Characteristics of Teachers as Change Agents. *Teachers and Teaching, 21*(6), 681–699.

Watson, D., Bayliss, P. and Pratchett, G. (2013). Pond Life that 'Know Their Place': Exploring Teaching and Learning Support Assistants' Experiences through Positioning Theory. *International Journal of Qualitative Studies in Education, 26*(1), 100–117.

Webster, R., Blatchford, P. and Russell, A. (2012). Challenging and Changing How Schools Use Teaching Assistants: Findings from the Effective Deployment of Teaching Assistants Project. *School Leadership & Management, 33*(1), 78–96.

Wenger-Trayner, E. and Wenger-Trayner, B. (2015). Learning in a Landscape of Practice. In Wenger-Trayner, E., Fenton-O-Creevy, M., Hutchinson, S., Kubiak, C. and Wenger-Trayner, B. (Eds.), *Learning in Landscapes of Practice: Boundaries, Identity and Knowledgeability in Practice-based Learning* (pp. 13–30). Oxon: Routledge.

Whittaker, J. and Kikabhai, N. (2008). How schools create challenging behaviours. In: Richards, G. and Armstrong, F. (eds.) *Key Issues for Teaching Assistants: Working in Diverse Classrooms* (pp. 120–130). London: Routledge.

Part 4
conclusion

This final section of the book highlighted the importance of TA agency and suggested three different models schools and settings might use that could support the development of professional agency. This list, as I noted earlier, is not exhaustive and there may well be a better model of working for TAs in your setting.

This chapter also looked at how to support TAs and other staff to understand TAs' 'place' or where they fit in the complex social, academic and micro-political environment of schools. This concept of 'place' was the key finding from my research, that TAs want to know what their roles are in schools and how to fulfil them without 'overstepping the mark' or 'undermining' the other staff they are working with. The diagram (see Figure 14.9), drawn from the research with my own participants, also hopefully reinforces the complex and interrelated difficulties the TAs in my research experienced in understanding their 'place' and, as a result, managing behaviour.

 ## Reflection activity

The final activity I invite you to do is to reflect on what you have read in this book and consider what specific strengths there already are in your school or setting in the ways in which TAs manage behaviour and any areas where you feel there could be improvements, for the TAs, teachers and children.

What currently works well			What improvement we could make		
For children	For teachers	For TAs	For children	For teachers	For TAs

Figure 14.10 The strengths and areas for improvement in the way you work with TAs

Index

Locators in *italics* refer to figures. The acronym TA stands for teaching assistants.

abuse 43

'adding value' 207

adverse childhood experiences (ACEs) 43

agency 193–195, *200*, *212*, 217; *see also* relational agency

annual reviews 102

attention deficit hyperactivity disorder (ADHD) 43

behaviour: 'continuum of tolerance' 19; current trends 18–19; in English primary schools 17–22; perspectives on 25–31; research 18–20, 25–29; school context 21, 29–30, *31*; structure of this book 1–3

behaviour management: agency *200*; approaches to 35–36, 46–48; deployment of TAs 176–177, 179–180, 201–203; disruptive behaviours 28, 65, 131; government context 20; iceberg analogy 196, *196*; medical and biopsychosocial models 43–44; perceptions of TAs 108, 119; psychological models 36–39, *40*; school budgets 19; school context 44–46; sociological models 39–43; status of TAs 148–149, 152; TAs supporting children's behaviour 64–71, *70*; training 128–129; whole-school planning 161–162

behaviour policy 75–84; 3 'c's 162; consistency in implementation 79–81;

expectations *21*; influence on TAs and teachers 77–79; research 75–81; responsibility for 164–165; rewards and sanctions 78, 82, 162–163; school context 30, 77, 81–83; social capital 163–164; status of TAs 144; TA training 132–133; zero tolerance 29, 30, 37

Behavioural, Social and Emotional Difficulties 20; *see also* special educational needs and disabilities (SEND)

behaviourism: as approach 36–39; behaviour policy 78–79; contrasting perspectives *40*, *42*, *43*, *44*; school context 45, 46

biopsychosocial models, behaviour management 43–44, *44*

'boundary work' 206

bounded autonomy 208–209

bounded inconsistencies 209

British government *see* government

budgets 19

caring/nurturing role of TAs 66, 108–109, 134–135, 176

child-deficit model 36–39

children's views on TAs 108–109

classroom context: children's views of TA 108–109; teachers' views of TA 109–112;

working in a range of classes 175–177; working in one class 177–180; *see also* behaviour management; teacher-TA relationship
cognitive-behavioural model 39, *40*
cohesion, behaviour policy 162
collaboration: behaviour policy 162, 163; deployment of TAs 174–175; planning and support for 202–203; school context 159–161, 166, 188–189; social capital 163–164, 167; special educational needs and disabilities 173–174; teacher-TA 109–112, 113–114, 146–147; time and resource constraints 197–198, *199*
communication, school community 166, *167*, 182
'communities of practice' perspective 130–131, 160–161, 166
consistency in behaviour policy implementation 79–81, 162, 200
consistency of deployment 201–204
consistency of role 204–207
'consistent with inconsistencies' model 208–210, *211*
containment, role of TAs 65
'continuum of tolerance' 19
curricular differentiation 65

Deployment and Impact of Support Staff (DISS) 12–13, 143
deployment of TAs 172–184, *183*, 201–203, 206–207, *208*
disabilities *see* special educational needs and disabilities (SEND)
discipline: behaviour perspectives 27–29; behaviourism 36–39; ideological differences 36; school context 30; status of TAs 148–149, 152; TAs supporting children's behaviour 64–69; zero tolerance 29, 30, 37; *see also* behaviour management
disruptive behaviours 28, 65, 131
diverse range of behavioural needs 45

Education Bill (2011) 27–28

Education Endowment Foundation (EEF) 12, 174–175
Elton Report 26, 37–38, 79–80
empowering TAs 193–194
episodic interventions 76
evidence-based decision making 13
experience, years as a TA 131–132, 161

'factotum' 55
feedback: professional learning 129; reassurance 201–202
feminisation of TAs 10, 66

gender: agency 194; feminisation of TAs 10, 66; status of TAs 145
Gibb, Nick 126
Gove, Michael 28
government: behaviour management 20; behaviour perspectives in recent history 25–29; changing role of TAs 52–60; standards for TAs 126–127; workloads 165
guidance: from research 13; standards for TAs 126–127

Hadow Report 18, 25
head teachers: leadership styles *113*; recruitment of TAs 124; TA training 124–125, 133; whole-school community 159–160
Higher Level TA (HLTA) positions: creation of 54; role clarity 96; status of 143, 148, 205; teaching tasks as part of role 89; training 126, 127, 129
historical context: behaviour 25–28; changing role of TAs 52–60; professionalism of TAs 52

identity of TAs 99–100, 151, 159; *see also* perceptions of TAs; *under* teaching assistants (TAs)
ideological differences, behaviour management 36
informal learning 128–129
internal regulation (self-management) 39, 45

interpersonal learning 128

isolation of TAs 175, 176, 209–210

job descriptions 96, 101–102

'knowing your place' 150, *153*, 200, *212–213*, 217

leadership: recruitment of TAs 124; styles *113*; TA training 124–125, 133; whole-school community 159–160

management of behaviour *see* behaviour management

maternal figure, perception of TAs as 108–109, 145; *see also* caring/nurturing role of TAs

medical models, behaviour management 43–44

Morris, Estelle 26, 53

multi-agency working 174

National Literacy Strategy 53

National Numeracy Strategy 53

neglect 43

nurture caring/nurturing role of TAs

Ofsted inspections: behaviour 19; behaviour perspectives 28; caring/nurturing role 66; 'Reading for Purpose and Pleasure' 54; TA training 123–124

oral tradition of the school 77

papa-professional 107

parent helpers 109, 124

Parentline Plus 19

pastoral support 176; *see also* caring/nurturing role

pay bands 96

perceptions of TAs 107; behaviour management 108, 119; 'knowing your place' 150, *153*, 200, *212–213*, 217; papa-professional 107; power and status 147–148; pupils 108–109; school context 112–114; teachers 109–112

'place' of a TA 150, *153*, 200, *212–213*, 217

planning *see* whole-school planning

planning, preparation and assessment (PPA) 54, 96

policy *see* behaviour policy; government

power/status: agency 194–195; behaviour policy implementation 80–81; empowering TAs 193–194; inability to criticise teacher 179–180; 'knowing your place' 150, *153*, 200, *212–213*; meaning of 142; TA status in schools 142–154

primary schools, behaviour in 17–22; *see also* school context

proactive behaviour policies 77–78

professional agency 193–195

professional discussions 113–114, 134, 135, 197–198, *199*, 202

professional learning *see* training

Professional Standards for Teaching Assistants 126

professionalism of TAs: caring/nurturing role 66; changing role of 52; identity 99–100; perceptions of TAs 107; teacher-TA relationship 109–112; training 124–125, 205

psychological models, behaviour management 36–39, *40*, *42*, 43, *44*

pupils: relationship with TA 66; views on TAs 108–109

'Raising Standards and Tackling Workload: A National Agreement' 54

reactive behaviour policies 77–78

'Reading for Purpose and Pleasure' 54

recruitment of TAs 53, 109, 124

relational agency 130

relationships *see* pupil-TA relationships; teacher-TA relationship

research: behaviour 18–20; behaviour perspectives 25–29; behaviour policy 75–81; TA training 123–133; TAs supporting children's behaviour 64–68; TA roles 10–12, 13

restorative approaches 40–41, *42*

rewards: behaviour policy 78, 82, 162–163; behaviourism 38; sociological models 40; whole-school planning 45
role clarity 95–103, 111, 118–119, 125
role creep 98–99, 206
routines 209

salary bands 96
sanctions: behaviour policy 78, 82, 162–163; behaviourism 38; sociological models 40; whole-school planning 45
school budgets 19
school context: behaviour 21, 29–30, 31; behaviour management 44–46; behaviour policy 30, 77, 81–83; changing role of TAs 55, 58–59, 188; collaboration 159–161, 166, 188–189; deployment of TAs 181–182; perceptions of TAs 112–114; role clarity 101–102; status of TAs 143–144, 150–152; TA training 130–131, 134–135; TAs supporting children's behaviour 68–69; TAs in 12–14; see also whole-school planning
school policy see behaviour policy
School Teacher's Review Body 53
self-management 39, 45
senior leaderships team (SLT) 124–125; see also leadership
skills audit 135; see also training
social capital 163–164, 167
social, emotional and behavioural difficulties (SEBD) 12; see also special educational needs and disabilities (SEND)
Social, Emotional and Mental Health Needs 20; see also special educational needs and disabilities (SEND)
sociological models, behaviour management 39–43, 42, 43
soft skills: of children 11–12, 13, 207; of TAs 66, 69
solution focused (SF) approaches 42–43, 43
special educational needs and disabilities co-ordinators (SENDCos) 174

special educational needs and disabilities (SEND): changing role of TAs 52–53; deployment of TAs 173–174; responsibility for 179; role of TAs 10–11, 65; terminology 20
standards for TAs 126–127; see also training
status of TAs see power/status
Steer Report 27

tacit knowledge 129, 159
Teacher Support Network 19
teacher-TA relationship: chore vs. team approach 203–204, 204; 'communities of practice' perspective 130–131; deployment of TAs 174–175, 181–182; feedback 201–202; perceptions of TAs 109–112; power and status 146–148; professional discussions 113–114, 197–198, 199, 202; time and resource constraints 197–198, 199; working in a range of classes 175–177, 181–182; working in one class 177–180; workloads 111, 165
Teacher Wellbeing Index 19
teachers: distinction from TA role 98–99, 102; influence of behaviour policy 77–79; ratio of teachers to TAs 10; views on TAs 109–112; workloads 19, 21
teaching assistants (TAs): changing role of 51–60, 88–89; defining the role 55–58, 97; distinction from teacher 98–99, 102; influence of behaviour policy 77–79; perceptions of role 107–115; recent trends 3; role clarity 95–103, 111, 118–119, 125; school context 12–14; structure of this book 1–3; supporting children's behaviour 64–71, 70; teaching tasks as part of role 53, 54, 88–89; as term 4, 55; who are TAs and what do they do? 9–15
time constraints, professional discussions 197–198, 199
token economy 40; see also rewards
training: behaviour management approaches 46; behaviour policy

implementation 82; informal learning 128–129; options for TAs 123–133, 205; and professionalism of TAs 124–125, 205; whole-school planning 161

trust, behaviour policies 83, *83*

'value-for-money' 89, 207

whole-school planning 158–168; behaviour management approaches 45–46; deployment of TAs 181–182; research base 158–166; school context 166–167; TA role 13; workloads 21

working conditions 53

workloads: behaviour 19; teacher-TA relationship 111, 165; whole-school planning 21

years of experience 131–132, 161

zero tolerance 29, 30, 37